FATHER OF THE IDITAROD

THE JOE REDINGTON STORY

BY LEW FREEDMAN

EPICENTER PRESS

FAIRBANKS ✦ SEATTLE

Epicenter Press, Inc. is a regional press founded in Alaska whose interests include but are not limited to the arts, history, environment, and diverse cultures and lifestyles of the North Pacific and high latitudes. We seek both the traditional and innovative in publishing nonfiction tradebooks, contemporary art and photography giftbooks, and destination travel guides emphasizing Alaska, Washington, Oregon, and California.

Editor: Tricia Brown
Mapmaker: Russell Nelson
Proofreader: Sherrill Carlson
Cover and text design, typesetting: Elizabeth Watson

ISBN 0-945397-74-7

To order single, trade paperback copies of *Father of the Iditarod*, mail $16.95 (Washington residents add $1.46 sales tax) plus $5 for first-class mailing to: Epicenter Press, Box 82368, Kenmore, WA 98028.

Booksellers: Retail discounts are available from our distributor, Graphic Arts Center Publishing, Box 10306, Portland, OR 97210. Phone 800-452-3032.

Printed in Canada

First printing July 1999

10 9 8 7 6 5 4 3 2 1

Front cover: The view from the runners of an Iditarod sled as Redington heads into a storm along the Bering Sea. Photo courtesy Joe Redington, Sr. Collection. Inset: Joe Redington, Sr. and one of his best-known leaders, Feets. Photo by Bill Devine.
Back cover, top: Redington worked at a fish-processing plant in Unalakleet, Alaska, from 1969 to 1975, but dogs were still his top priority. Photo courtesy Joe Redington, Sr. Collection.
Below: Even past his eightieth birthday, Redington continued to run dogs. Here he trains in the shadow of North America's highest peak, Mount McKinley. Photo by Jeff Schultz/Alaska Stock.

ACKNOWLEDGMENTS

*I dedicate this book to my wonderful wife Vi.
And a special thank you to my family and all my dear
friends who I've known through the years.*

—Joe Redington, Sr.

■

*The author wishes to thank all of the people who
provided information and generously gave of their time
to help prepare this book. A special thanks goes to Jeff Schultz.
And an extra special bow goes to Jo Derry Wood
for her cooperation and assistance, her work and research.
Without her help, this manuscript would not
have become a reality.*

—Lew Freedman

When I was a boy back in Oklahoma, no one ever dreamed that someday I'd be mushing dogs in Alaska. Even then, I always had dogs. Not sled dogs, but pet dogs. I was raised with always having as many as three, four, or five dogs. Then when I started reading Jack London's books, I knew someday that I was going to mush dogs in Alaska. Now I'm eighty-two years old and looking back at fifty years of mushing. I can hardly believe it myself.

When I first came to Alaska, I didn't know anything about anything, really. I was very fortunate to meet an old-timer who was the last sled-dog mail carrier here in Knik. He always seemed to talk to me about dog mushing, and he gave me a lot of the history of the Iditarod Trail. I fell in love with the Iditarod immediately, and I felt that it was a trail that should continue to be used.

Vi and I and the kids homesteaded at Flat Horn Lake and also here in Knik. We did a lot of work on the Iditarod Trail. And finally, with the race, the trail became a reality. The trail was added to the National Historic Trail system. It's a well-known trail now where before it was completely dead.

I've been a big-game guide, a Bush pilot, and I did a little bit of mining. I even bought some mining claims. But I loved dog mushing and commercial fishing a lot better. We would commercial fish in the summertime, and I was able to mush dogs in the wintertime.

Working for the military in rescue and recovery work, the dogs and I helped salvage millions of dollars' worth of airplanes and also did a lot of rescue work. My work took me all over Alaska, and I was able to buy dogs from a lot of the villages. In 1948 we started our kennels, and we soon started adding good dogs from some of the top mushers.

But then dog mushing started to die out. It was down to where there were very few races. Finally, when I went into the villages and saw the dogs disappearing and the snowmachines appearing, I felt that something needed to be done. So I started the Iditarod race. And it's been very successful. It will continue to be successful because it's one of the greatest sports, I think, in the world.

There are still a lot of opportunities, especially for young people, to get involved in some of the things that I did. Maybe not in commercial fishing anymore, but dog mushing has really expanded, and mushers all over the world now are making good money just mushing dogs.

If a young person wants to become a dog musher or is interested in raising good dogs, there are plenty of dog opportunities. But you've got to start small and build yourself up like we did. We started with just a few dogs in the kennel, and by 1990 we had five hundred and twenty-seven dogs. We leased out as many as ten teams a year to other mushers—Knik Kennels is the one really responsible for the Iditarod becoming international.

I would say, get with it and you can be successful at anything in Alaska. There are still many, many opportunities. Alaska has been real good to me. I love it. And I think that dog mushing has been the greatest thing in the world.

Well, I hope that everyone enjoys this book. I've enjoyed living it.

—J. R., Sr.
Knik, Alaska
May 1999

TABLE OF CONTENTS

ACKNOWLEDGMENTS 3
A MESSAGE FROM JOE REDINGTON, SR.   4

MAP: HOMESTEADING IN THE MATANUSKA-SUSTINA VALLEY 35–36
MAP: IDITAROD TRAIL SLED DOG RACE—1999 CHECKPOINTS 118–119

EPILOGUE 317
INDEX 318

1	GONE MUSHING	11
2	ON THE MOVE	19
3	ALASKA, FOR REAL	28
4	HOMESTEADING THE VALLEY	33
5	EXPERIMENTS IN DOG MUSHING	45
6	LIVING OFF THE LAND	55
7	RESCUE AND RECOVERY	64
8	WHEN SPRINTERS WERE KINGS	79
9	SEEDS OF A GREAT RACE	89
10	BIG DOLLARS AND COMMON SENSE	101
11	THE FIRST IDITAROD	116
12	NO RACE FOR SISSIES	134
13	THE INFECTIOUS IDITAROD BUG	146
14	CRASHES AND SCRATCHES	153
15	SEARCH FOR FINANCIAL STABILITY	170
16	TRAINING THE UP-AND-COMERS	181
17	TO THE TOP OF MOUNT MCKINLEY	193
18	PROTECTING AN HISTORIC TRAIL	209
19	PRESIDENTIAL TREATMENT	216
20	TRAIL WOES, HIGH HOPES	222
21	SIDELINED, NOT STOPPED	231
22	A WOMAN TAKES THE TITLE	239
23	INTERNATIONAL FLAVOR	247
24	NEAR MISSES	253
25	STAYING THE COURSE	263
26	TOURISTS ON THE TRAIL	274
27	OLYMPIC TRIALS	280
28	STILL RACING AT EIGHTY	287
29	DOING BATTLE	293
30	FATHER OF THE IDITAROD	302
31	BACK ON THE RUNNERS	310

JEFF SCHULTZ/ALASKA STOCK

Traveling in a convoy during the early days of the Iditarod Trail Sled Dog Race, Joe Redington, Sr. snapped this picture from the rear. "The trail ran out," he says. "You can see, it ain't very well marked."

1

GONE MUSHING

*—There hasn't been a year in fifty-one winters
I haven't been on the Iditarod Trail.—*

A good friend and neighbor, Joyce Garrison helped Joe
rebuild his strength and get back on the runners after his surgery.

It was a day a man could inhale. A bright Alaska sun, cloudless sky, temperature in the thirties. The crisp air heralded the impending arrival of winter. A fine day for walking.

Joe Redington, Sr., his face weathered with age, but his spirit undampened by hardship, stepped beyond the arctic entryway of the low-slung wood home he shares with his wife Vi on a homestead established in tiny Knik a half-century ago. More than a hundred huskies, tethered to dog houses made from black, fifty-five gallon drums by metal chains,

Friends and family pitched in to look after the kennel and exercise the dogs while Joe was off his feet. He looked forward to the day when he could resume his normal chores.

interrupted rests or sips from water bowls and rose immediately. The thought rippled through the vast open yard like electrical current: *We're going mushing.* And the symphony of howls that followed mixed anticipation and excitement.

The sight and sound elicited pleasure from Redington. Sled dogs who want to run do that for him. After all these years they still bring forth his trademark lopsided grin. It is an all-knowing slash of a smile, both unconscious and expressive, accompanied by a mischievous twinkling in the eyes.

Redington's is one of the most recognizable faces in Alaska and likely most of the people who think of the man who gave them the Iditarod Trail Sled Dog Race picture the off-kilter grin and the I-have-a-proposition-for-you gleam in the eye.

This time Redington turned away from the sleek, athletic animals he loves so much, and began striding down his long, dirt driveway, taking short, brisk steps on his own. It was October 1998, and Redington had a most vigorous step for a man of eighty-one. Especially for a man of eighty-one recovering from cancer. Especially for a man of eighty-one recovering from a cancer that was supposed to kill him months before.

Less than a year earlier, doctors told Redington the tumor on his esophagus was too large to remove surgically and there was nothing to be done. For just a moment, he believed them. Then he went back to being the Joe Redington everyone knew. That was a Joe Redington who feared nothing, tackled all challenges head-on, and through relentless determination always found a way to prevail.

Naysayers told him he was nuts when he chucked his life in Pennsylvania and set out for Alaska so long ago. Did it anyway. They told him it couldn't be done when he said he was going to put on a dogsled race from Anchorage to Nome, more than a thousand miles across the frozen tundra. Got it done anyway. Then they told him it was all over, that his health couldn't be fixed. And he fooled everybody again.

Here he was the next autumn. Healed up. Getting stronger by the day. That's what this walking was all about—to make him fit. Part of the daily exercise routine. A small man, but possessed of a wiry strength, Redington always had remarkable stamina. That cancer will wipe you out, though. It took time to rebuild. The stamina was coming back now.

Several months before, Joyce Garrison, Redington's friend, neighbor, nurse and exercise partner, could barely stifle concern. Hauling himself to his feet from the favorite chair in the living room where he reposed was a breath-sapping ordeal and difficult to watch.

"He was as weak as a puppy," said Garrison.

Weak as a puppy. A perfect analogy for a dog man like Redington.

Now Redington walked four miles daily, at a pace of twenty minutes per mile, sometimes faster. The dogs could still out-run him, but men half his age strained to keep up.

Sure was a fine day for walking. The gaze settled across the street from the house, where the placid water of Knik Arm glittered. And in the distance, beyond the community of Wasilla, the snow-covered summits of the Talkeetna Mountains were bathed in a sunshine that gave them a robust glow. Plenty to inhale.

Mostly, though, Redington looked down, watched where he placed

Nothing makes Joe Redington happier than stepping on the runners of a dogsled. In this 1997

photo, he runs his team along the foot of the Alaska Range as Mount McKinley towers overhead.

his feet with each step on the uneven terrain on a downhill path. Before he reached Knik-Goose Bay Road, the paved street where cars now whiz past, but which Redington remembers when it was muddy enough to swallow wagon wheels, he darted left into the trees. Birch, alders and spruce trees line the eight-foot-wide path that becomes a full-fledged dog-mushing trail once the snow falls. This trail is tucked between homes that have sprouted in the once-sparsely populated area Redington knew in his early days in Alaska. Frost lingered in spots because the canopy of trees deflected much of the sunlight, but it was mostly muddy underfoot.

Usually, Redington walked with Joyce Garrison, a retired registered nurse who mushes dogs and was looking forward to entering the Iditarod race. A former home health care specialist, Garrison's ministrations and Redington's aspirations to return to full strength meshed neatly.

Typically, the walks were completed in solitude.

"We hardly ever see anyone on the trail," said Redington.

But sometimes another dog-team driver, with team hitched to the type of four-wheeler all-terrain vehicle mushers use when their sleds are shelved for the season, comes speeding around a bend, the dogs breathing hard, the musher yelling "Trail!" Pedestrians are forced to the side, into ankle-deep brush.

You never knew what else might come your way, either, and Redington packed a pistol on his hip. A superb shot with a rifle all his life, Redington had only recently obtained a handgun permit and begun practice at a local shooting range. His aim remained true so if a bear or moose came charging out of the trees, he would be ready. Or even a runaway dog in ill temper. Since there are twenty-one dog lots in a square mile where Redington lives, that was a very real possibility.

When Redington wished to make a right turn off the trail he alerted me by saying, "We 'gee' here." It was the same command he would call out to a dog team.

The famed Iditarod Trail, founded as a mail route, used as a rustic highway to gold fields, and reinvigorated by the establishment of the world's best-known dogsled race, skirts the edge of this local training trail. Redington's route looped through the woods, emerged in a clearing, blended with a gravel road, and collided with the profit-making dreams of an entrepreneur who was building the Iditarod Trail Subdivision, where streets are named for checkpoints in the race. Some day property owners will live on Rohn Street, McGrath Way, or Nikolai Avenue, approaching their homes by turning off Malemute Run.

Redington, fearful that some governmental body might outlaw dog mushing where he lives, protected himself by purchasing five acres of land in the midst of this burgeoning suburbia-in-the-woods. The Iditarod Trail runs on the south side of his property.

"I think I've got about five hundred feet of trail," he said. Meaning that even if rezoning assaults the neighborhood where he and Vi live, Redington has the fall-back position of being able to just pull a dog team off this land directly onto the trail. He erected a cozy cabin on the property and sometimes uses it for a training base. At this point in his recuperation he was using it for an exercise base, where a combination treadmill-hand cycling contraption kept him active whipping his weakened body into shape.

Three miles into the walk, Redington reached the cabin. Time out for peppermint tea and vanilla cookies. In a city, the oblong little building might be described as a studio apartment. An alpine-style roof gives it a ski chalet appearance outside, but inside it is surprisingly well developed. There is a stove, table, chairs, refrigerator, microwave and rollaway bed. For a person like Redington, who has spent a considerable portion of his life in sleeping bags under the stars, or in tents, these accommodations approximated a four-star hotel.

For a half-hour intermission, before resuming his walk, Redington sat in a straight-backed chair at the Formica-topped table, sipping tea, munching cookies, talking of how anxious he was for a good blizzard to strike. He sounded a great deal like a kid urging Christmas to hurry up and get here: "I want to get out. I'm usually the first one on the Iditarod Trail, the first one to cross Fish Creek."

Winter was Redington's favorite season. The snow and ice were his friends. You can't wade a wide river in summer, but you can mush across the frozen highway in winter.

"I love winter," he said. "You can travel and use the dogs. I just like to ride along. Being out there is what it's about."

For decades, it had been Redington's habit to hook his dogs up for a first run as soon as a freeze stopped the flow of Fish Creek, three miles north, and snow cooperated. The cancer slowed him the winter before, but between 1948 and 1998, Redington probably traveled two hundred thousand miles by dog team across Alaska. Two hundred thousand miles. Much of the mushing traversed the trail he revived, preserved and popularized.

"Due to all this trouble I've had, I did less mushing than any time since I've been in Alaska," said Redington of his hard winter of 1997-98. "But there hasn't been a year in fifty-one winters I haven't been on the Iditarod Trail."

As soon as that darned snow flew and the year spilled over into 1999, he would make it fifty-two.

ON THE MOVE

—During his elementary school years,
Redington discovered a window to a new, different
world through the printed page—

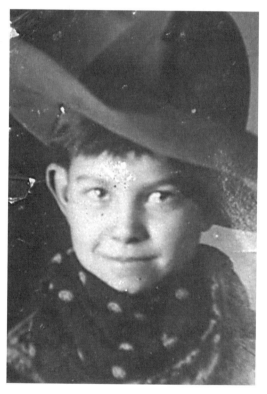

Because the Redingtons often were on the move, few photos of Joe exist
from his boyhood. In this rare image, he's dressed in a favorite cowboy outfit.

■

The vague feelings of attraction to a place he had never seen stirred in
Joe Redington as a youngster. The mysterious territory of Alaska was
thousands of miles away from Oklahoma and the other Lower 48 states,

and he never met anyone who had been there, but during his elementary school years, Redington discovered a window to a new, different world through the printed page.

By no one's accounting, least of all his own, was Redington a scholar. He and his family led a peripatetic existence and he was fortunate to experience any coherency in his schooling. Nonetheless, he became an avid reader and his subject matter of choice was either Jack London fiction or nonfiction tales of Alaskan adventure.

"I never was much for school," said Redington, "but when I was in school I'd stay in at recess and read. I read lots of books. Anything I could get on Alaska. You couldn't find much on Alaska in those days, but what I read I liked."

The stories that left him wide-eyed were not only *The Call of the Wild*, but real-life tales of the trail. There were the stories about the All-Alaska Sweepstakes races in Nome, which ended just about the time Redington was born. There was the famed Serum Run of 1925, when mushers delivered life-saving diphtheria medicine to Nome by dog team. And Redington loved reading about the exploits of Leonhard Seppala.

Norwegian-born Seppala came to Nome in 1900. He lived in Alaska for forty-seven years and once estimated that he mushed a quarter of a million miles on a dogsled—the only man Redington believes may have mushed more miles in Alaska than he has. Seppala clearly was the state's most enduringly prominent dog driver of the first half of the twentieth century. As a youth, Redington envied Seppala's lifestyle. Seven decades after he first heard about Leonhard Seppala and the Serum Run, Redington has a framed photograph of a handsome, wavy-haired Seppala hanging on his living room wall.

"A dog team, that's what I wanted," remembered Redington.

But the way his family lived, it was barely possible to care for a single dog as a pet.

Most of the first two decades of Redington's life there was nothing much to hold him to a place. Not for long, anyway. His was a drifting lifestyle, defined by a mother who abandoned the family when he was a child and driven by a father who roamed incessantly in search of reliable work.

Joe Redington was born February 1, 1917 on the Chisholm Trail.

Joe was eight years old when Leonhard Seppala and other Alaskans ran a dog-team relay across Alaska with diphtheria antitoxin. The famed 1925 serum run from Nenana to Nome saved the lives of dozens in the remote village, and each musher was awarded with a medal thanking them for their courage. The stories thrilled Joe, and he grew up reading about the exploits of Seppala and other Alaska mushers such as Iron Man Johnson and Scotty Allan.

BILL DEVINE

He was born in a tent on the banks of the Cimmaron River, north of Kingfisher, Oklahoma. For years the accuracy of the date and circumstance of his birth was anecdotal. He relied on the telling by his dad, James Wesley Redington, as proof. To this day, Redington has no birth certificate. Since his time in the service during World War II, he has used Army records to prove his date of birth. That record, however, came on his say-so.

"During 1940, the Army wasn't too choosy," said Redington. "In fact, I think they would have taken you if you were green."

Some years later, Redington said he learned he was recorded in a 1920 Kingfisher census, one which indicated he was three years old then. Between the time he was born and the time the census was taken, the Redingtons moved into the community, to an old bottling company, across the railroad tracks from town. He believes his brother Ray, four years younger, was born in that building.

Much later in life, as a dog musher who tested all limits and dared the elements of winter, Redington became expert at judging the strength and thickness of river ice. However, as a youngster he had a near-fatal accident in circumstances that approximate the conditions of a dog team plunging through thin ice.

Riding along on a two-wheeled scooter on Kingfisher Creek, at the age of six or seven, Redington was fooled into believing the ice was strong enough to hold his weight because the wintry weather seemed so cold. The conditions were deceptive, though, the ice collapsed, and Redington and his scooter fell in.

"A guy just happened to see it from a nearby power plant and he ran down and dived in and got me out," he said. "They told me I was unconscious for another day or so, but I never knew it. I do remember the guy who saved me coming over to see me a couple of days later."

When Redington's father asked how he could ever repay him, the man said his watch had been ruined when he jumped in the water, so James Redington bought him a new one.

Redington was very young when his mother, Mary Elizabeth, left him, his younger brother Ray, and his father behind and disappeared. That unsettling development provoked the Redingtons' exit from Oklahoma, mostly because Redington's dad thought the family might disintegrate if they stayed.

After he grew up, Redington said his father told him "the righteous women" in town felt it was inappropriate for a single man to raise two children and they put increasing pressure on him to put them up for adoption.

"And he fought them," said Redington. "He said, 'They weren't going to get those boys'."

The best way the older Redington knew how to fight for his family was to pack up the boys and all their belongings in a car and flee the area. Thus began a years-long odyssey in which the Redingtons spent warm-weather seasons following wheat harvests from Texas to Nebraska to the Canadian border. Winters, they settled temporarily.

At times, Redington's father worked for railroads. He drove horses and delivered freight. Eventually, he did remarry, but Redington does not believe his father chose wisely on that occasion, either. This wife, named Evelyn Montgomery, said Redington, was an outlaw who came from a family of outlaws in Oklahoma. One brother was in jail for robbing a bank. Once, when he was around eleven, Redington recalled being a member of a family group who visited a different brother in jail for another offense. When that brother was paroled, he came to live with Joe, Ray, their dad and stepmother. Later, that man and his son robbed a bank and killed the cashier. They were caught and sentenced to life in prison.

Joe and Ray, however, never got into any kind of serious trouble. Their father was an honest man and raised them with principles. Redington is pretty sure he finished first grade in Kingfisher, but after that he was an itinerant student. He did some time in classrooms in Spearman, Texas, Fairberry, Nebraska, and Aurora, South Dakota.

And the poverty-stricken family did some time in makeshift shelters, wherever they could find a roof and four walls. Redington was twelve when the trio moved into an abandoned brewery in Hannibal, Missouri. It seemed to be a life of close calls, for one reason or another.

For fun, Redington and an acquaintance plunged into the Mississippi River for a swim. They came ashore about two miles downstream, only to realize they had no easy way to return to their starting point. So they climbed the riverbank and started crossing a railroad bridge. Sure enough, a train was headed right for them.

"There was nothing to do but to hang down underneath the bridge and let the train run over us," said Redington.

The other boy was so scared, said Redington, that when they reached home he immediately confessed what they had done to his father and his father beat him for the misadventure. Redington's dad merely told him not to do it again.

Another time, the Redingtons wintered in a Geary, Oklahoma, granary that had holes and cracks in the walls. That was a frigid winter, with temperatures falling to fourteen degrees below zero, and snowstorms pounding them and piling up huge drifts, some that seemed thirty feet high to a young Joe.

"We were burning corncobs to stay warm," said Redington, "and when there weren't enough corncobs in the pig pen, my dad would go down to this little school house and borrow coal from their coal bin at night. He'd carry back fifty to sixty pounds of coal, and that's how we made it through that cold snap."

A trick the Redingtons applied that amounted to creative caulking of the holes was throwing water against the side of the granary. Almost instantly it would freeze and cover the holes.

"That warmed it up quite a bit in there," he said.

Such an early life left Redington perfectly suited for the rigors of the Alaska Bush.

Redington also demonstrated his future Iditarod Trail resourcefulness by making his father a sleeping bag out of an old air mattress.

"You'd get into it and it wouldn't breathe, so you'd just sweat," he said. "It was a miserable thing."

But better too warm than too cold at that point.

Once Redington's mother left, he never saw her again; his father never gave him any information about her.

"My dad never talked about my mother," said Redington.

Much later in life, however, Redington's mother tracked down Ray and Vi and wrote a few letters, but that was as much of a relationship as they ever had. Joe never saw the letters. Vi said she and Ray kind of kept the correspondence to themselves because they knew Joe didn't care.

"I wasn't interested," he said. "She left me when I was six."

Still later, when Joe became famous for his connection to the Iditarod and received worldwide publicity, he received surprising, out-of-the-blue contacts by phone and mail from a man claiming to be his half-brother. Initially, Redington's response was, "I don't think so." However, this man had newspaper clippings showing that even before Redington's mother had abandoned him and Ray, she had deserted a family of four children on an Enid, Oklahoma, street corner. And the man informed Redington that his mother married a third time and had a daughter. Redington had some contact with these relatives as they aged, but no close friendships evolved.

During the Redingtons' winter stopovers, when they were always newcomers, it wasn't always easy to find acceptance. Redington recalls the winter of 1930 in Jersey City, New Jersey. This was a fresh experience for many reasons. Previously, the family spent most of its time in small towns. The school alone in Jersey City had twenty-three hundred students. The Redingtons lived in an Irish neighborhood, and there was an Irish connection in their past.

Redington can trace his American genealogy back to the early 1600s. The first Redington appeared in the New World in approximately 1639. A female member of the family was an accuser during the Salem witch trials in Massachusetts. One ancestor, Daniel Redington, from Topsfield, another Massachusetts north shore community, fought in the Revolutionary War. And still other Redingtons fought for the northern side during the Civil War.

Joe said that a couple of generations back on his father's side, the Redingtons lived in Dublin, but in the 1970s, when his name was noticed through the Iditarod, a man named A.C. Redington in London sent him the family tree. It informed him of all these early doings by Redingtons who emigrated from England.

It was fine being in a New Jersey Irish neighborhood and being considered Irish, but it wasn't so great having to cut through an Italian neighborhood to get home from school.

"They used to beat the hell out of me every day," said Redington, who eventually took a less-convenient route home to avoid conflict.

Redington grew to detest school and never attended class after the sixth grade. He obtained work papers freeing him from the obligation. The lack of schooling, however, was no barometer of his intelligence. When he joined the Army in 1940, Redington's IQ was measured at 127. And as anyone who has ever requested an autograph can attest, he developed a beautiful penmanship under his father's influence.

Harder times and economic chaos were on the horizon for the nation soon after the Redingtons first visited Jersey City. The Great Depression of the 1930s loomed, but in reality, their lifestyle, quality of living, and opportunities for work already mirrored what others would soon experience. In fact, while Redington said that John Steinbeck got it exactly right in his descriptions of the hardships Okies endured in *The Grapes of Wrath*, he remembers that period in his life with a certain fondness.

"We never missed any meals, and though we didn't have any money, we had no worries," said Redington. "We had no rent to pay. From 1926 on, Dad took us from place to place."

From the late 1920s into the mid-1930s, the Redingtons were constantly on the move. They picked cotton in Oklahoma for a dollar per hundred pounds and splurged on suppers of cherry pie on Saturdays for twenty-five cents. They saw bankers riding the rails, met farmers who sold their land, bought a car and set out for California, falsely believing that golden opportunities awaited. In March of 1934, the Redingtons scratched together $12 to purchase an automobile in Jersey City, a car that would enable them to more easily follow the trail of the harvest as migrant workers. They worked the wheat harvest in Minnesota, then in South Dakota and North Dakota.

"You would pull up on either side of the threshing machines with the wagon and it would take two men on each wagon, pitching wheat as fast as they could pitch," said Redington.

Wheat farmers, it turned out, fed the help much better than cotton farmers. In Oregon, the Redingtons picked prune plums. In Washington, it was wheat again. Joe worked on a combine that had thirty-six horses pulling it. He tied closed the sacks of grain. They picked peaches in Marysville, California, then shucked beans in Modesto before picking walnuts in Central California and finding work on a turkey farm.

The Okies who fled the dust bowl disaster of their home state for the supposed paradise of California funneled into huge, crowded camps by the hundreds. Often, said Redington, he saw the migrants victimized simply for being who they were. The Redingtons were luckier because they had New Jersey license plates on their car and were mistaken for northerners.

"We were 'guests' of the state," said Redington, who saw other Oklahomans suffer brutal treatment from the police during raids. "What the police didn't know was that we were as Okie as the next guy."

Decades later, Redington remembered clearly the signs posted at the borders of California and Arizona warning Okies to turn back, that they weren't welcome.

Eventually, in Mexico, the Redingtons sold the car—for $12.50, a fifty-cent profit—and began riding the rails back to Oklahoma as unauthorized passengers in boxcars. Only Joe got sick and the border patrol helped them get to a hospital in Bisbee, Arizona. Redington was covered with coal dust and contracted both the measles and pneumonia.

"I was in bad shape," he said. His father and brother lived in the police station while he was ill. When Joe was healthy again, the Redingtons out-smarted the "bulls" guarding the trains and with great difficulty and relying on expert timing and ingenuity, rode the rails to El Paso, Texas, Tucumcari, New Mexico, Amarillo, Texas, and finally, back to Oklahoma.

Not that much awaited them. The stories in those Alaska books that Joe read as a youngster kept reverberating in his head, so in 1934, he took his first run at moving north.

He and a friend named Cliff Lear embarked on a wild journey using a cashed-in Lear insurance policy for funds. The first mistake was stopping in Las Vegas.

"We tried to get rich and lost most of our money," said Redington. Then they swung through Mexico and California and at last reached Seattle, since Gold Rush days, the gateway to Alaska. But by that time they were virtually broke, and despite being young and energetic could convince no one to hire them. It cost just $34 for the boat to Skagway, but they couldn't raise the money. Chastened, they turned around and headed back to the East Coast.

The young men were as low on fuel as they were on money, but Lear was a whiz at siphoning gas from other cars' tanks. They invested some of their remaining cash in a one-inch rubber hose and as they traveled Lear's lungs kept them gassed up.

"He could actually sneak up after a guy had pulled up at a traffic light, open the can, give her a suck, and drain five gallons of gas out before the light changed," said Redington. "He had some honor, though. He would always put the guy's gas cap back on."

Redington never told his father about that part of the trip.

It would be nearly another decade and a half before Redington turned his attention back to Alaska.

3

ALASKA, FOR REAL

—I decided that wasn't what I wanted . . .
I decided overnight to go to Alaska.—

Joe discovered a talent for photography while he was in the service.

■

Go to Alaska.

Do it now. Or you'll never get there.

That was the voice in Joe Redington's head, growing from a whisper to a shout in the spring of 1948. Pretty soon the voice got so loud others heard it. Even if it didn't seem to make much sense. Redington was married and had two sons. And he was just building a new house in Kintnersville, Pennsylvania, in Bucks County, now a bedroom community for Philadelphia, but then more of a rural, farming area.

The new house meant putting down roots that would bind.

"I decided that wasn't what I wanted," said Redington. "I decided overnight to go to Alaska."

The move seemed now-or-never abrupt, but it was the culmination of the fantasy Redington had formed as a boy and tried to make reality on his aborted mission with Cliff Lear in 1934. It was an acknowledgment that time was passing since he was now in his early thirties. This was the last-chance grab for the life Jack London had made so real for him.

Those stories of gold rush days, of tough men mushing dogs through the wild in sub-zero temperatures, all appealed to a boy's sense of adventure, and they carried the same appeal now. Alaska seemed like the kind of place where a man could make his own way if he had the gumption, where nobody cared who you were or what you did before.

Redington had to make everyone see that Alaska, not Pennsylvania, was where the future lay.

In 1931, when Joe, Ray, and their dad came to Kintnersville for one of their winter layovers, it was just another place. There was no reason to suspect that here Redington would meet someone who would become the most important person in his life.

One of the kids in the small Pennsylvania community was an outgoing girl, seven years old at the time, a girl named Violet Elizabeth Hoffman.

Redington's life in Alaska is a northern journey of wilderness living. It's about a love of the huskies that defined the opening of inaccessible country, and it's about a bold vision culminating in the creation of the state's most popular sporting event. It is all of that. But it is equally a love story of his life and partnership with Vi.

Far from love at first sight, though, this true love traversed a path at least as crooked as the Yukon River.

Although James Redington continued the family journeys around the nation chasing work, the Redingtons ultimately made Kintnersville a quasi-permanent base. Vi became a playmate of Ray, logical since she and Ray were closer in age and Joe is seven years older than she is.

By the time she was sixteen, Vi was Ray's steady girlfriend. Not that Joe minded. He had his own love interest, a woman he'd met in Oklahoma. Pretty soon he got married, to Cathy Sullivan, his first wife. And pretty soon Vi, nineteen in 1943, married Ray.

"My folks just threw a fit," she recalled years later.

Not that short-notice marriages were uncommon then. World War II was raging and in those uncertain times often the last thing young men did before going off to war was try to lasso their sweethearts.

Joe, who had developed some skill as a mechanic, joined the Army in 1940 and landed in the paratroopers as a motor pool sergeant after being bumped around from anti-aircraft to Officer Candidate's School to the stables.

"They were the meanest horses I'd ever seen," said Redington. "They'd bite, kick and tromp on you, anything they could do.

Once, he had to deal with a runaway—just practice for later days when runaway dog teams would leave him stranded in the Bush, or dump him off a sled in a fit of pique.

Despite the birth of a son, Joee, in 1943, Redington was not getting along well with Cathy. Often, in fact, Vi helped take care of the boy. Many of the men he served with were sent overseas and killed, but for a time Redington was stationed close to home. Once, before he was sent overseas, Joe traveled to Easton, Pennsylvania, to visit the baby.

In the motor pool, Redington monitored as many as a hundred jeeps at once, but eventually he was shipped to the Pacific Theater. His old friend Cliff Lear—from the poorly planned attempt to reach Alaska—was sent there as well, but caught malaria and died on Guadalcanal.

Redington served on Okinawa, and while there learned the ins and outs of photography, a hobby that paid many dividends in future years. Color photography was almost unknown amongst civilian non-professional photographers then, but the knowledge Redington picked up in the Army helped him take high quality color slides and document his early years in Alaska at a time when the average family's snapshots were all in black-and-white.

Just before Redington mustered out of the service in 1945, after five years and four months on active duty, he got involved in a moneymaking photo scam in the South Pacific. He and another guy convinced a captain to allow them to take pictures of the military cemeteries and different companies. Redington and his pal said they were going to give black and white photos to the men. The officer must have thought he was providing them with nifty souvenirs. They got the souvenirs, but Redington and his pal also trafficked in other photos.

Redington also took pictures of the grave of Ernie Pyle, the famed war correspondent who had been killed at the front while writing about the tribulations of everyday grunts. However, behind the scenes, Redington and his partner came into possession of a picture of a Japanese Geisha girl, which revealed just enough to be enticing to thousands of men who had lived without sex for months at a time.

The first day they were in business working on "souvenirs" they sold a hundred dollars' worth of pictures. The next day they had about three hundred uniformed servicemen in line anxious to buy. Business tripled the third day and by then General Douglas MacArthur, the supreme commander in the Pacific, got wind of the doings. He personally ordered the business shut down. Redington said he was forced to leave bags full of yen behind when he departed.

"I had pictures of all kinds of airplanes," said Redington. "One that was a good seller was a P-47, used for bombing. It was so big that once in a while it would not be able to take off, but it would go off the airstrip and over the side of a cliff. It had a picture of a girl with big breasts and it was called 'too big' and 'too heavy.' I think my first wife destroyed the pictures of the Geisha girl."

Joe and Cathy did divorce, and Vi took young Joee in to live with her and her mother for a time, keeping Joe apprised of his condition. Once, she mailed Joe a gold pen and chocolate-chip cookies to complement his canned rations. He threw the box away with the pen in it because he thought it contained only cookies. Vi and Joee formed a bond.

"He's always seemed like mine," said Vi of Joee, who grew up to be a world championship sprint musher in Alaska. "I forget that he's not."

However, when Joe learned Cathy was pregnant again with son Raymie, who was born in November 1944, they remarried. For a time, when Joe and Ray were still at war, Cathy, Raymie and Joee all lived with Vi.

After Redington was released from the Army he returned to Pennsylvania and became a civilian mechanic specializing in fixing Nash automobiles in the town of Easton. His pay was forty dollars a week. Only when the boss made him work on upholstering rather than letting him do the work he was suited for, he quit.

Then Joe became a jeep salesman. He excelled at selling. The farmers in the area who couldn't get tractors bought the jeeps and adapted them for hauling.

"The only thing I found that I couldn't pull was a manure spreader in a barnyard," said Redington.

The man who owned the dealership was really a psychiatrist by trade, one who worked at a nearby mental institution. More than once, Redington had the thought that the guy should be residing on the other side of the gates permanently. Redington was selling so many jeeps the owner wanted to change the way he paid him. Redington didn't like the man, didn't like the plan, and instead of agreeing, the snap decision to make a new life in Alaska was made.

On a Friday, he collected his wages. On Monday, when he didn't show up for work, Redington figured, the man would know he was gone.

In less than twenty-four hours, Joe and his son Joee, plus Ray and Vi, and their fifteen-month-old son Tommy, were on the highway—in a caravan of two jeeps. Raymie and Cathy, pregnant with Joe's daughter Shelia, temporarily headed in the other direction, to her mother's in Alabama, to give birth. Joe helped Cathy to Alabama, then rejoined Ray and Vi in Chicago. Cathy came north later. James Redington, Joe's father, took care of various affairs and followed within a few months. Even Vi's parents later moved to Alaska.

Alaska. For real this time. This time fiction and fact blended for Joe Redington.

4
HOMESTEADING THE VALLEY

—Yes, you can homestead in Knik.
The Redingtons were home.—

Part of the extended family gathered for this 1953 photo
inside the tent at Flat Horn Lake. Clockwise from top are Joe and Vi,
her father, Milton Hoffman, Joee, Raymie, a friend named
Darlene Nesja, and Vi's mother, Cora Hoffman.

■

Fifteen minutes after the gang of Redingtons crossed the Canadian border
into Alaska on the way to Tok, Vi Redington owned an Alaskan husky.

The jeeps were parked at the Border Trading Post for a break and a
lady with a litter of puppies let them run loose. Vi couldn't resist petting
them all and the lady asked if she wanted one.

The adoption was consummated and the first Redington Alaskan dog
was named Dodger.

Dodger joined the motley group of seven dogs already in the family.

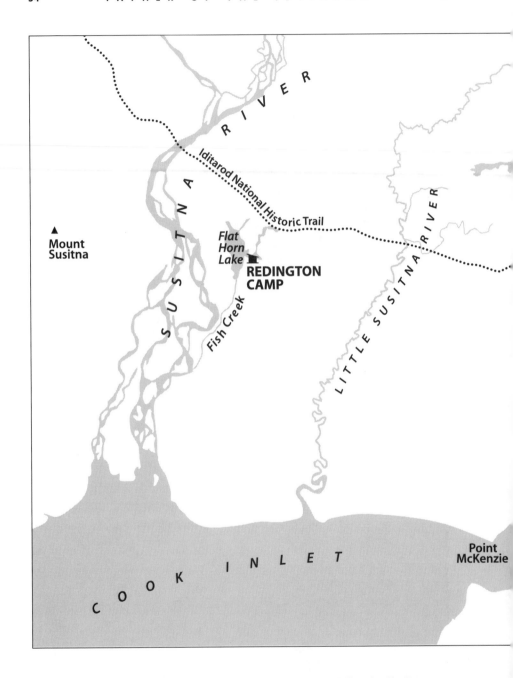

The Redingtons split their time between properties in Knik and at Flat Horn
Lake, further west. At either location, Joe found himself drawn to the historic
route of the Iditarod Trail, which passed nearby. From Flat Horn, the family

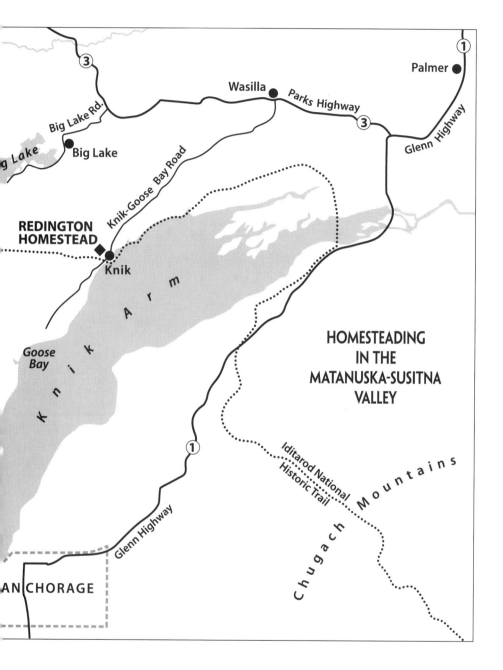

could get to Cook Inlet via Fish Creek and the Susitna River. For many years, the Redingtons sustained themselves on fish, seals, moose, and income from commercial fishing.

The Redington family and Vi's parents, Cora and Milton Hoffman, lived in a tent for their first year at the Flat Horn Lake property. From 1953 to 1968, the homestead at Flat Horn was the Redingtons' primary residence.

These were dogs Joe imagined might be suitable for mushing, including an English sheep dog. He had no clue.

During World War II, prompted by the fear of Japanese invasion, American troops hurriedly built the Alaska-Canada Highway. It became the best way for civilians to travel north without flying or taking passage on a boat. In 1948, and for many years after, the road was quite rugged, though. It was always advisable to carry spare tires since the gravel and dirt road was pockmarked with potholes and services were far apart, or nonexistent. Weather also affected the quality of the ride.

"It was either mud or dust," said Vi.

Their research was sketchy and the Redingtons knew little about the vast differences in climate between sections of Alaska. Their thinking was simplistic. Alaska? Snow. Cold. You can mush dogs. Not in Haines, the small community in Southeast Alaska where they first stopped. In very rainy Haines, umbrellas were more common than dogsleds.

Someone told the Redingtons that if they wanted to homestead, the place to go was the Matanuska-Susitna Valley, about fifty miles north of Anchorage. Many hundred miles more of driving brought the tandem travelers to Palmer, the colony settled by farmers in 1935. There they learned the town of Knik was just opening up for government-regulated homesteading.

On June 5, 1948, the Redingtons pulled into Wasilla. Now a community of more than five thousand people (many of whom commute to jobs in Anchorage) and home to the Iditarod Trail Sled Dog Race headquarters, Wasilla then was barely a whistle stop on the Alaska Railroad. A half century ago, Wasilla had four businesses: the Teeland family store, a bar, a roadhouse, and a gas station.

In her own way, May Carter, the United States Territorial Commissioner for the region, as well as postmistress, presided over all doings with common sense advice and wise authority. Yes, she told the Redingtons, you can homestead in Knik. The rules permitted claims of up to one-hundred-and-sixty acres. You just might not be able to get there at the moment, she warned. The narrow, dirt road was likely a sea of mud and it might be that no one had made the trip down it yet that season. Undeterred, the Redingtons charged ahead.

"It was all forest, thick forest," said Vi Redington. "It was a wagon trail and there was one homesteader."

The population was about to grow. The Redingtons were home.

Joe Redington arrived in Alaska with eighteen dollars in his pocket and he plunked down thirteen of those greenbacks to cover the filing fee for a hundred and one acres. That was all he could afford then, though he did later increase the claim to a hundred and forty acres. He also later split his claim by receiving twenty acres of land at Flat Horn Lake, about thirty miles away. Ray and Vi claimed a hundred and sixty acres. When James Redington came later in the summer he claimed three lots, but because he was not a veteran he was obligated to clear the land. He eventually turned one lot back and kept one thirty-acre lot and one fourteen-acre lot. It was easier for veterans. They were only required to build a cabin and live on the land for seven months before they gained control of it. Much of the same land remains in the hands of the Redingtons today.

The federal government didn't ask for much from men and women who wanted to settle the land in rural Alaska. The paperwork costs were minimal and other than that you pretty much only had to move in and begin improving it.

"They only had to live on the place and build on it," said Carter.

The people who came north had a glint in their eye and hope in their hearts. To settle in the Mat-Su area they all came through Carter, who moved to Wasilla in 1940. There were between fifty and seventy-five residents then, she recalled many years later. Knik, while a thriving town in the early part of the twentieth century, was almost abandoned.

"Knik was pretty dead," said Carter. "Everything from Knik had moved to Wasilla and Anchorage."

But Knik showed signs of being re-invigorated after World War II. Joe and Ray Redington were typical of the settlers, men who fought for their country and wanted a fresh start in their civilian lives. Carter said she was on vacation in Montana early in 1948 when she saw a newspaper article announcing the government would allow homesteading in her area. That alerted her that she would be busy.

"It was then that the GIs came up," she said. "They fell in love with the country. Some of them had been stationed in Alaska. They came back with their families."

Carter and her late husband, Thomas, better known as Pat, were often the first to greet the newcomers, the *cheechakos*. The Carters never could guess with accuracy, though, who would become stick-it-out sourdoughs.

"I saw them all," she said. "They would fool you."

The settlers came by car up the dusty highway. And they came by train, across the vast open spaces and through forested land. One couple just off the train caught the Carters' eye. The man was dressed in a business suit, the woman in a dress. They had two children with them and no winter footgear.

"What do we have here?" Carter remembers her husband saying, thinking how unlikely it would be for this group to make it through a winter.

The family stayed with them a couple of nights, found a cabin, and became Alaskans.

So did the Redingtons.

By 1949, Joe had already established Knik Kennels, but he hadn't yet acquired a proper dog truck. This one, parked in front of Teeland's store in Wasilla, was one of his first. "A lot different from today!" he says.

The Redington homestead is thirteen miles from Wasilla. Today the street known as Knik-Goose Bay Road is a mini-highway, with a speed limit of fifty-five mph. Fifty years ago, it was really an unpaved path. It was so skinny that two cars could not pass in opposite directions. In the winter, the road was coated with snow and best traveled by dog team. Joe Redington would mush into town for supplies, bringing the dogs right to Teeland's door. He tied up just as if he were a cowboy in the old west throwing the horse reins around a hitching post.

In spring, breakup turned the road into a quagmire and Joe hiked to Wasilla, an old Army pack board on his back to carry the groceries home. That first winter there were so many geese and ducks, he also carried a shotgun, on the lookout for dinner. He may have thought it was common, but the population of waterfowl was unusual, perhaps because all water holes farther north froze. He even trapped some geese, something he was sure was illegal.

Vi may have posed with this black bear, but she makes it clear that she wasn't responsible for its death. "I wouldn't shoot a bear!" she says. "I ate it, but it was already too late then."

The remarkable surplus of geese and ducks was a one-time thing, but Redington was a crack shot and a superb hunter. Some years later, at Flat Horn Lake, Redington connected on the most fruitful and unbelievable shot of his life.

Patiently awaiting a good opportunity, he rested his shotgun on a tree stump. A flock of two hundred geese landed and Redington took aim. He waited for some geese to form a line opposite him, squeezed the trigger and killed seven geese with a single shot. That put a bird in every pot in the house.

"Proving up" is what the government asked in return when it gave away land, almost for free. Putting up homes was the first thing on the agenda for the Redington families. The house that Joe built was a two-story log cabin. He put in an eight-by-twelve kitchen on the bottom floor and a twelve-by-twelve bedroom upstairs, although he said the "stories" were a rather low six feet apart. Didn't matter much to Joe. He was only five-foot-six. He also ran a pipe from a nearby spring to a barrel in the cabin and had running water. Though he replaced the shelter within a year or so with something more solid, the cabin his father built across the street stood until 1997 when a tree fell on it and collapsed the roof.

There were about 130,000 people spread across 570,000 square miles of Alaska at the time, compared to a present-day population of 621,000, but only a handful resided in "sunny" Knik. Knik was initially a trading center, but took on more importance as part of the Iditarod Trail. By 1909, the mail trail from Nome to Seward was formed and gold was transported on the trail by dog sled through Knik to Anchorage, where it was loaded on ships.

By 1915, there were more than five hundred people in the thriving community termed "Sunny Knik, the California of Alaska" because it reputedly received more sunshine than surrounding areas. However, soon after, when the Alaska Railroad was built and bypassed the community, it gradually died out. Only now, with modern subdivisions being built on side roads, is the community once again reaching toward the five hundred-population mark again.

In the 1990s, only two buildings remain from "old" Knik. About a mile from the Redington homestead off Knik-Goose Bay Road stands a dilapidated log cabin dated to 1906. The other old-time building is the Knik Museum and Dog Mushers Hall of Fame building. A red, wooden building constructed in 1910, the structure was originally the Fulton and Hirshey Pool Hall. Some other cabins lasted a long time. Redington remembers one built in 1912 out of spruce logs that fifty years later still had a reliable, waterproof birch bark roof on it.

In the summer of 1948, cabin building began right away for the Redington families. But they also had to eat. On his second day at the homestead, Joe shot a black bear. Sweet meat it was, too.

"There was so much wildlife," said Joe. "You'd cut a birch tree down and there would be a moose eating the other side of it."

And some of the other homesteaders who lived within a few miles rolled out the welcome wagon Alaska-style. No, they didn't bake the Redingtons a cake. Bush dwellers were far too practical. Fred Hurd, Heine Snider, and Jay Levan brought over a hundred-pound sack of potatoes and some canned goods because they knew that almost everyone moving in was poor and living close to the margin. The potatoes were an excellent complement to the bear meat. Vi said her first bear tasted more like pork than anything else.

Joe Redington read about dog mushers and adventurers when he was young and now that he was in Alaska, he wanted to mush. Right away he began accumulating huskies. By his first winter in the territory, the man who one day would promote the world's most famous dogsled race, and race to Nome himself, and teach novices how to mush more than a thousand miles across barren tundra for fun, owned twenty-five dogs. Vi and Ray had another seven.

"We had a small team," said Vi, who said she was not originally in favor of the move to Alaska. "I didn't really want to come in the beginning. I was never used to anything like it. But I loved the trip up here. I loved the lifestyle of building it up yourself. And I liked mushing as soon as I knew what it was."

Joe acquired dogs from some of the old-timers in the area, Jim Kennedy and Bill Betts. They weren't using their dogs and readily let them go.

It wasn't long after the first heavy snowfall that Redington had his first meaningful mushing experience with someone who did use dogs. He accompanied neighbor Lee Ellexson, on an eighteen-mile trip to his trap line on the Iditarod Trail.

Ellexson, then about seventy years old, and his wife Grace, were true Alaskan pioneers. When she came to the state about 1904, Lee was already there. He homesteaded at Knik Lake, just down the street from where the Redingtons settled, around 1912. Joe Redington believes Lee Ellexson got an additional three hundred acres for the bargain price of ten dollars when a neighbor left for Seattle.

The older man had been a mail carrier on the Iditarod Trail and maintained a trapline at an old lodge on the Little Susitna River. The dogs which hauled the mail, hauled wood, and helped fetch water, were hard-working and hardy, thick-coated dogs, often malemutes of wolf-sized proportions. Or larger. The seven dogs Ellexson used for transportation were gigantic.

"I think his lead dog weighed a hundred and thirty-five pounds," said Redington.

Ellexson's was the only full dog team in Knik in 1948, according to Redington, and the man had mushed thousands of miles. The overnight trip to the even more remote cabin, the dogs padding along, all captivated Joe.

So did the stories about the Iditarod Trail. Before coming to Alaska, Redington had never heard of the Iditarod Trail. It was only by accident, or fate, that he plunked down his roots just a few hundred feet away.

The construction of the Iditarod Trail was authorized by the Alaska Railroad Commission in the early 1900s, a time when gold seemed to be discovered everywhere in the territory any time someone stuck a shovel in the earth. The motive was to make it easier to bring gold out of the town of Iditarod, though it was actively used as a mail trail. Iditarod is more than six hundred miles from Seward. Iditarod, now a ghost town that springs to life briefly each March as a checkpoint in the Iditarod Trail Sled Dog Race, saw its heyday between 1909 and 1912 when more than a thousand miners lived there. The trail was finished in 1910. In all, a thousand miles in length, there was a roadhouse located every twenty miles, or one day's walk for a man.

For thirty-one years, between 1901 and 1932, until the airplane was established in Alaska, the Northern Commercial Company held an Alaskan mail contract for the region. Much of the delivery was done along a trail that evolved into the Iditarod Trail.

"I fell in love with the Iditarod Trail," said Redington. It would be a lifelong love affair, which, unfortunately, could not be said for the marital relationships between the Redington couples.

Both the marriage between Joe and Cathy and the marriage between Vi and Ray went sour in the first few years in Alaska. Joe and Cathy divorced for the second time and Cathy moved to Wasilla, taking their daughter, Shelia. Cathy stayed in Alaska and later remarried. Vi and Ray also split up. Vi felt Ray was a changed man after he returned from World War II service. She said he was often moody, sometimes verbally abusive to her. He would wave a pistol around casually, making her feel uncomfortable.

"He was a different guy when he came home," she said. "He was so mean. He never did beat me, but he was mean otherwise. He was not himself. He'd been through too much. I tried to get him help through the military."

She tried to get Ray committed to a mental hospital. She tried to get the courts to intervene, but it didn't work.

"Joe protected me from Ray," said Vi. "Ray got mean to everyone who was best to him."

After the court fiasco, Ray and Vi broke up. Her little boy Timmy, born in 1949, stayed with her and grew up with Raymie and Joee. Her other son, Tommy, was taken out of state with Ray and she did not see him again for nearly two decades. Joe and Ray, who died in 1997 in Washington State, were never close again.

"Finally, Joe and I got together," said Vi. "We'd grown up together, anyway."

The wedding of Joe and Vi Redington was performed by May Carter on February 18, 1953, as one of her many official functions. It cost three dollars for a marriage license and ten dollars for the ceremony, she said. Joe said he and Vi got married on credit because they were broke.

"We didn't have a dime," he said.

Carter doesn't remember that, but it was a common enough practice for her to extend such credit to people she knew in the area.

"They were always good for it," she said. The Redingtons were. They ultimately paid their debt to her.

Years after the somewhat painful dissolution of marriages and melding of families, Joe can joke about the circumstances and how he ended up with the right woman in his life.

"I think I had a choice of Cathy or the dogs," he said. "I took the dogs."

5
EXPERIMENTS IN DOG MUSHING

*—Joe stepped back in time to an era
when Alaskans traveled by dog sled.—*

**Joe fell in love with mushing and with the history of the Iditarod Trail soon after
landing in the Matanuska-Susitna Valley. This is the trail as it looked in 1953.**

After World War II, Americans became obsessed with the automobile. Progress was measured by how many new interstate highway miles were constructed. Joe Redington went the other way. He stepped back in time to an era when Alaskans traveled by dog team.

Redington's initiation on the Iditarod Trail occurred on his trip with Lee Ellexson, but the journey merely stoked an insatiable desire to learn. Ellexson's life as the last mail carrier on that segment of the trail fascinated Redington. The older man mushed endlessly on the trail, traveling for six months at a time. He custom-made a sled with waterproofing to keep the mail dry when he crossed streams and creeks in spring when the ice was out. The last trip of the year could be dangerously adventurous.

Ellexson's job ended in the 1920s, more than twenty years earlier, but to Redington, who hung on every word, it was fresh stuff.

"It got me thinking, 'This is where I want to be'," he said.

Not long after Ellexson took Redington mushing, he had an accident. Ellexson was alone, chopping wood at his trapping cabin, when he snagged the ax on a clothesline. Caught in the recoil, the blade slashed him in the head. He fell to the snow, bleeding profusely from the wound. But his trusty dog team rescued him by hauling him home. After that his wife didn't want him traveling solo in the wild and about that time, said Redington, Ellexson became enamored with his newfangled television and pretty much gave up mushing altogether.

Soon enough, Redington had new mushing pals. Stanley Collins moved into the Knik area and he had dogs. So did Clem Tellman. In 1949, for the first time, Redington listened to the North American championships on the radio from Fairbanks.

There hadn't been any serious dog racing in Alaska with major publicity since the All-Alaska Sweepstakes in Nome between 1908 and 1917. The annual race of four hundred and eight miles to Candle and back made legendary figures out of mushers like Leonhard Seppala, Scotty Allan, and Iron Man Johnson.

Now thirty years later, a new style of racing was coming into prominence. In Anchorage, the Fur Rendezvous World Championship dog race was created. In Fairbanks, the North American popped up. In these events mushers and dogs did not race long distances, but rather raced heats of twenty to thirty miles over three days.

The Fur Rondy remains a popular winter carnival. Conceived as a cabin-fever reliever, the gathering brought men and women from all over into the big city to party. The dog race became the showcase of the festival. The first competition, won by Jake Butler, was held in 1946. The next two titles were captured by Earl Norris, who as much as anyone since Seppala worked to perpetuate and develop the breed of Siberian huskies in Alaska. In 1949, Butler once again triumphed. It was not long before

In 1953, Vi entered a female Siberian in an American Kennel Club dog show in Anchorage. "We had registered Siberians and registered Malemutes then," Vi remembers. "She got first place, female, in her category."

Redington became friends with both men and within a few years Redingtons of all ages were racing dogs in the Fur Rondy.

Joe first contemplated entering dogs in the Fur Rendezvous in 1951. Since his original Knik cabin was hardly a four-star accommodation, in 1949 Redington built another. His dogs were of valuable assistance hauling logs from a sawmill. They were able workers, but he knew nothing about training dogs to run fast. He and his friend Stanley Collins merged their animals into a fifteen-dog team and experimented with a method they were sure guaranteed a high-speed performance.

They rigged up a system where an electric coil ran through the team. The plan was for Redington to stand on the sled runners, shout "Geronimo!" and then shock the dogs. When it came time to race, they believed the dogs would be trained to leap off the starting line at the mere act of yelling the old Indian warrior's name. This was using Pavlov's theory of conditioned response.

On the first day this scheme was unveiled, Collins was in the sled basket, while Redington stood upright in the rear. The shock device was triggered . . . and the dogs went berserk. Each dog thought that the dog next to him bit him. So each retaliated by biting back.

"We had one hell of a dog fight," said Redington. "They bit each other. Stanley got bit. Everything was a bloody mess."

A school bus driver came along and asked what was going on. He thought the men were hunting and told them if they were going to kill a moose they shouldn't do it in the middle of the road.

Many lessons were learned that day. Redington learned a bit about humane treatment of sled dogs. He learned that he was a damned fool for trying such a wacko maneuver and that perhaps he needed to develop his dogs more before entering them in the world championships. He also learned that Sharon Fleckenstein, the bus driver, was one heck of a knowledgeable, Alaskan character.

"He was my best source of information," said Redington. "Anything you wanted to know about, he had done it. He bought me my first sled at Teeland's. My others had been handmade."

Fleckenstein, a miner from the Willow Creek district farther north, first came to Knik in 1914. A stocky, thickly muscled man who exuded toughness and could certainly act tough, Fleckenstein was the son of the former U.S. Marshal of the territory. He inherited his dad's Colt .41 revolver and kept a shotgun or rifle mounted over the front door of his home. One way or the other, Fleckenstein got across the stern message that you didn't mess with him.

Once, Fleckenstein enlisted Redington's help in an attempt to reclaim a gold mine someone had moved in on. Gold was worth thirty-four dollars an ounce then, roughly one-tenth as much as it is in the 1990s. His original investment, with two other men, was swallowed up by a large company. For years, the company put watchmen on the property, but it hadn't performed the appropriate assessment work and simultaneously became increasingly lax about security. Fleckenstein monitored the situation and when the deadline loomed for doing the work approached, he went to May Carter and let her know he intended to get his mine back.

In the meantime, Fleckenstein sent Redington to watch over the

In 1954, Timmy Redington, flanked by his parents, stands as tall a king salmon is long.

mine for a couple of weeks from a rock-lined cabin. The first day, three men drove up in a pickup truck and challenged him.

"I'm here to take care of this property," Redington told them.

They told him to get the hell out. He figured they were others trying to grab the claim. They went away and nothing happened until a day before the deadline. That night, as Redington lighted his lantern in the open cabin doorway, a shot sang out. The bullet traveled through the open door and imbedded itself in the floor. Not before noisily ricocheting off some of the rocks, though. Redington doused the lantern, hunkered down, and about midnight slipped out of the cabin to seek out Fleckenstein. He told him he needed backup.

Fleckenstein formulated the plan for the next day. He woke up May Carter and told her he was ready to make his claim. Fleckenstein went to the cabin. Sure enough, around noon the following day, the same truck rolled up carrying the men. Fleckenstein stood in the dirt drive, showing his weapons. The truck never even stopped.

By coincidence, the mine was called "The Old Joe Mine." It was not named for Joe Redington.

Three of the Redington boys play near the army tent that housed the family at Flat Horn Lake in the 1950s. Joee and Keith ride in the wagon as Timmy watches at left.

"I wasn't so old then," said Redington.

Another time, Fleckenstein introduced an innovative way for horses to travel in deep snow. He put wooden snowshoes on their feet. Apparently impressed with the results, Fleckenstein then attempted to make snowshoes for sled dogs. He took a willow branch, bent it into a circle, and stretched moose hide across. Then he sewed booties on and mounted the snowshoes on five dogs, mushing them five miles. The dogs did not take to it.

"I never saw such a thing again," said Redington.

Joee Redington was very young during the Redingtons' first years in Knik, but he said he will never forget the muddy road connecting the homestead to Wasilla. Once he saw a horse going along carrying a case of milk. The case fell off and cans were strewn along the road. This road would not handle two lanes of traffic. Not even in winter when the vehicles were dogsleds.

"The rule of the trail was that the one with the most dogs had the right of way," said Joee. "The trails were fairly narrow."

Most trails were. The Iditarod Trail had fallen into disuse and was overgrown. Only a small percentage of the trail in the Knik area was free of brush. When it snowed heavily the trail might be completely wiped out.

In his fifty-plus years in Alaska, Joe Redington has seen more snow than a polar bear. He has mushed through blinding blizzards and rarely been fazed. It takes a lot to impress him, but the Christmas, 1953 storm that dumped feet of snow on the Redingtons as they attempted to mush between their secondary homestead at Flat Horn Lake and Knik set off a chain of events that produced hysterical, unwanted statewide attention. The trip became known as the famous "Lost Redington" expedition, though Joe insisted he was never lost at all.

At the time the Redingtons were establishing a new homestead, they were the first residents of Flat Horn Lake on Joe's subsidiary land claim of twenty acres, where they lived in a large wall tent. For the holiday, they loaded up two twelve-dog teams, Joe driving one, Vi the other, and began mushing on the Iditarod Trail to Knik with four-year-old Tim. From Knik, they were scheduled to go on to Anchorage and visit Vi's parents, Milton and Cora.

When the Redingtons left Flat Horn, they wrote a note with the date and left it pinned to the tent, a common Bush lifestyle informational practice. The goal was to mush twelve miles, spend the night in a trail camp, and go from there. Only that night it snowed. And snowed. And snowed. It snowed three feet. Their parked sleds were buried. Tree branches were weighted down with so much snow they bent low and blocked the trail.

So Joe strapped on snowshoes and became the lead dog of his team. He cleared branches by hand, climbed on the sled runners, and mushed ahead a little, got off and repeated the process. He mushed a mile, then backtracked to Vi and Timmy and they followed him with the second dog team.

Inch by inch they advanced until nightfall. Night came early, though, around the Winter Solstice. They came upon a small cabin on the Little Susitna River that was once operated as a halfway house lodge between

In the early 1960s, unpaved Knik-Goose Bay Road was a muddy mess every spring.
More a trail than a road, during break-up the surface was too soft for vehicles, but still
passable for dog teams.

Knik and Susitna Station. There they stopped. The cabin had been
vandalized. It was missing the front door, but it was the best shelter
around. Joe made a fire.

"I made a stove pipe out of five-gallon Blazo cans and hung a tarp
over the door," said Joe. "I shot a moose. We hadn't eaten for two days.
We roasted it and ate the kidney. I fed a hind quarter to the dogs."

Each morning Joe set out to make headway on the trail, but the snow
was so deep the dogs kept sinking. Where were Sharon Fleckenstein's
snowshoes now? The Redingtons abandoned one of the sleds, and they all
bundled into the other. Christmas passed and Vi's parents worried. They
sent a friend by small plane to Flat Horn Lake to see what was going on.
The pilot read the note indicating the family's date of departure and flew
down the trail. When he saw the abandoned sled, he grew alarmed. He
flew back to Anchorage and reported what he saw to the Civil Air Patrol.

The authorities put out the word on radio and television that the
Redingtons were missing.

"That night we heard on the radio they'd found our sled and that we were lost," said Joe. "We knew exactly where we were. We just couldn't do much about it. It was just a question of breaking trail."

In the morning, Redington resumed slow-progress movement down the trail. While he was gone, however, a plane flew overhead and spotted Vi. A note was dropped saying, "If you're the Redingtons, walk in a circle." Vi followed instructions, which led the pilot to believe the worst about Joe. A single K ration was dropped out of the plane. Weighing less than a pound, it contained a small box of raisins and a food bar.

The next radio report indicated Joe might be dead. Only he was right there with Vi listening. Sure enough, it snowed again, preventing an immediate return flight. When the snowfall ceased, the Redingtons packed the snow flat for a makeshift landing area. A plane landed and those aboard were overjoyed to see a healthy Joe.

Only they brought no food. Redington requested food for the family and food for the dogs. The message he wrote was delivered to Elmendorf Air Force Base. The response was gratifying, if a bit excessive. A C-47 transport plane loaded with supplies flew in and the food was dropped by the ton into the wild. Boxes of rations descended by the hundreds.

"It just rained down stuff," said Vi. So much food was dropped the Redingtons had to retreat to the cabin so they wouldn't get conked on the head. These were thirty-pound boxes containing breakfasts, lunches and dinners, lima beans, hash, ham, and beef stew. There were so many some got stuck in trees. There were so many they could not all be retrieved. Collins and Tellman arrived by dog team, carrying still more food.

Then a helicopter flew in. Rescuers prepared to pluck them out of the trees and whisk them to Anchorage, where television crews anxiously awaited the telling of the story of their "ordeal."

Joe's response? "Hell, no."

The well-wishers argued that the rescue was expensive and that they'd have to take someone back with them to justify the cost.

"So we said, 'Take Timmy,' " said Joe. The Redingtons promised that the little boy would be well behaved. But as soon as they handed him over he burst into tears. He wouldn't stop crying. Not because he touchingly feared being separated from them, as it turned out. It seemed he wanted the box of raisins he'd been eating.

As an adult, Tim has trouble remembering the incident in detail, except for the helicopter.

"It was kind of spooky," he said of being taken away. Joe and Vi mushed back to Flat Horn Lake, ducking the media. They thought. The entire episode was later written up in a man's magazine as a great survival adventure.

"I don't know where they got the pictures," said Vi, "but it looked like we were on the moon."

In reality, the Redingtons never strayed from the Iditarod Trail. The journey produced a humorous footnote. Off and on for years while mushing along the trail the Redingtons came upon boxes of rations, some of which were torn to bits by curious bears, but many of which proved perfectly edible.

"Whenever we'd go by, we'd pick up some more," said Vi. "We'd cache some of them." They collected the food, ate it, and stockpiled the cans near the lake. There were so many empties that someone reported them to the Army, assuming they must have stolen the food.

Some forty-five years after the crazy sled-dog trip, Vi Redington said it wouldn't surprise her if some of the rations were out there yet.

6

LIVING OFF THE LAND

—Forty or more years ago, if you lived in rural Alaska, fending for yourself was the way that it was done.—

Joe displays a rack from a successful moose hunt at Flat Horn. Hundreds
of pounds of moose meat would sustain the family for many months.

Vi Redington posed for the photograph against an Alaska mountain backdrop. Grinning under a cowboy hat, thick blonde hair sticking out the sides, she wore a red flannel shirt and wielded a rifle. "Annie Oakley," she said of the picture of herself from the mid-1950s at the Redington Flat Horn Lake homestead.

Humorous or not, it is the most appropriate of photos of the younger Vi in the sense that it defined a time when the Redingtons lived completely self-sufficiently in the Alaskan wild. Substitute sled dogs for horses and much of the time the Redingtons spent at Flat Horn between 1953 and 1968, when they moved back to Knik, can be compared to the way settlers lived who staked out nineteenth-century Montana, Utah, or Texas.

The subsistence lifestyle was demanding but rewarding for hard workers like the
Redingtons. In this 1956 photo, Joe strips off a seal's fat, which Vi used for cooking.

As the second half of the twentieth century began, Wasilla, never
mind Knik, remained a waystation at most. You could stand in front of
Teeland's store all day and not see two cars pass by. And that's where the
congested Parks Highway is located today. Still, the Redingtons sought an
even more remote Bush outpost.

For months at a time at Flat Horn Lake, they lived a pure subsistence
lifestyle, though Joe took on a variety of jobs to supplement family income
that took him out of the area, too. Once, nearly all Americans fed themselves without grocery stores. Those who make a living off the harsh terrain are under severe pressure in modern-day Alaska, but forty or more
years ago, if you lived in rural Alaska, fending for yourself was the way
that it was done.

And the Redingtons did carve out a home there by themselves.
Joe felled all the trees with an ax to clear the patch of two acres
they developed.

Vi has another picture that she posed for: It shows her next to two dead black bears, their tongues hanging out. They resemble cartoon bears with X's over their eyes. But she was no hunter. Joe did the shooting. Vi picked berries and tended a splendid, half-acre garden of potatoes, peas, carrots, broccoli, turnips, zucchini squash, beans, cabbage, and Brussels sprouts, a garden that clearly produced bountifully in the sandy, loamy soil.

The short, but intense growing season of Southcentral Alaska attracts entries of humongously sized vegetables at the Alaska State Fair each August. Big-as-beachball cabbages are the norm. The Redingtons grew such cabbages back then, but they ate them, they didn't enter them in contests.

"It's the best farming land in Alaska," said Joe. "The soil is so good there you could grow everything." Indeed, Joe chose well when staking out his twenty acres at Flat Horn, even though they really basically used only a tenth of their allotted space. The land produced superior crops. Game, particularly moose, was plentiful. And fishing the nearby Susitna River yielded salmon by the thousand. That was a ready supply of food for the dogs that by then numbered more than a hundred and before long approached two hundred. The Redingtons hunted seal there and sometimes even beluga whales. Son Joee became an expert seal skinner.

Redington's long-time friend Joe Delia of Skwentna is another who made his way with a rural subsistence existence. He visited Flat Horn and saw the Redingtons' holdings up close.

"It's an excellent place to homestead," Delia said. "You could get in from the Susitna by boat. He had a lot of things available to him."

One of those things was the Iditarod Trail. The Redingtons may have moved thirty miles from Knik, but they were still right by the trail.

"We were back and forth all the time, in the summertime by boat and in the winter by dog team," said Joe. "Sometimes three or four times a week. My dad stayed in Knik."

The Redingtons were the first to homestead at Flat Horn Lake, but a short time later Stanley Collins and his wife Doris joined them, and a handful of others followed. The first winter only the Collinses moved over and Joe provided the moving van. If you want to call it that. Joe towed the couple's boat from Knik because it lacked a motor. Going by water was a lot longer than going overland. The route followed was Knik Arm to Cook Inlet to the Susitna River to Fish Creek to Flat Horn Lake. A fifty-mile trip.

While preferring a comparatively solitary existence, the Redingtons were not attempting to become hermits. Once settled in they could even get mail. Sometimes. A plane would fly over perhaps once a week and bombs-away, mail would drop from the sky. That was one way to stay in touch with the outside world. Then Redington single-handedly improved communication by hooking up three miles of telephone wire. Pretty soon six families who settled at Flat Horn had phone service.

This was not fancy living. For a long time, the Redingtons lived surrounded by birch and spruce trees in a sixteen-by-thirty-two-foot army tent with a front door implanted. There were barrel stoves at each end to provide warmth, and a smokestack peeked out of the top of the canvas.

Joe was indefatigable in those days. He slept no more than four hours a night—good training for the Iditarod race later—and although he was a slight man, never weighing more than a hundred and fifty pounds in his life, he always pulled more than his weight. Redington called Vi "one of them good-looking blondes," but he himself had hazel eyes, a full head of black hair and rakish good looks, too.

Redington maintained that four-hour-a-night sleep pace—verified by Vi—for years, although when he was hauling fish from the mouth of the Susitna River to Anchorage, he worked virtually around the clock, maybe napping for a single hour out of twenty-four.

"I never found anybody that could go like I could," he said. "I used to be pretty tough. That was a long time before the Iditarod."

Those who homesteaded at Flat Horn Lake had dog teams, and the trail was so narrow a rule was quickly instituted that the musher with the biggest team had the right of way. Stopping was difficult and usually led to harness tangles in the deep snow by the side of the trail, so Redington came up with a simple plan to avoid such circumstances and work the rule to his advantage.

"Pretty quick we started using eighteen dogs all the time so I always had the biggest team," said Redington. By then he had plenty of dogs to choose from. Once Joe Redington threw himself into dog mushing, he became known as the guy with the biggest dog lot. The pool of huskies kept expanding until it reached an all-time peak of five hundred and twenty-seven in 1990. At Flat Horn Lake, though, the crowd was big enough, eventually pushing two hundred.

Redington never thought he would own that many dogs, but as Joee, Raymie, and Tim aged, they all got their own teams, joining Joe and Vi as mushers.

"I had a team, and each kid had a team," said Vi. "Pretty soon you've got a lot of dogs." So many that at times they were hard to care for and considering that the family had to provide all of the nutrition by hunting or fishing, sometimes hard to feed. In 1954, the Redingtons caught twenty-five thousand hooligan in the Susitna River. They were spread on

Joe's solution for clearing this logjam required some of the TNT that he sometimes used in airplane recovery work. "We took a whole box of TNT, about fifty pounds, and put a fuse on it," he says. "The motor on the boat was a perfect motor—never gave me any trouble. I lit the fuse, and the damn motor wouldn't start! Vi and I each grabbed an oar and we started rowing." Vi adds: "It was just like slow motion, like you were in a dream or something." No one was hurt, and after the sky rained chunks of wood, the logjam was clear.

A bearskin rug keeps Timmy and Keith entertained at Flat Horn.

four-foot-wide drying racks, hanging by chicken wire all over the yard. Row after row, rack after rack, of the small, oily fish.

"They were so easy to get. I'd dip them and they'd hang them," said Redington of the rest of the clan. "I'd get hundreds at a time. You could barely lift the net to get them in the boat. There were millions of them." The scene was reminiscent of the summer of 1949 when the Redingtons caught fifteen hundred salmon and had them drying in the open air at Knik.

The Redingtons have a picture of young Raymie from around 1953 standing on a metal gas can at Flat Horn Lake, a king salmon handing by a chain from a tripod of tree branches. The fish is about the same size as he is. Sometimes the boys collected seagull eggs. The eggs were three times the size of eggs laid by a hen. Gathered from a nearby island, the eggs were dark in coloring, brown-speckled or green with brown splotches. They picked them up by the hundreds. The taste was richer than chicken eggs, though critics in the kitchen claimed they were a bit rubbery even after frying. Vi found that they were best used for baking.

"She made real good chocolate cakes," said Joe.

Using their own eight-foot boats in the lake, the Redington boys set tiny nets to catch whitefish in imitation of the grownups. By the time the boys were in their early teens, though, they had their own commercial fishing licenses and caught silver, chum, and pink salmon.

Overall, it was definitely rustic living, in an isolated setting, but it was heaven for rambunctious young boys.

"I think if kids today lived like that they might turn out better," said Tim Redington, who as an adult lives in rural Kenny Lake in Southcentral Alaska.

The boys fashioned spears out of tree branches and learned how to make snares to catch game. Almost every year a different baby seal drifted into the lake and stayed for the summer, providing an unlikely playmate. Sort of an early *Free Willy*. One summer a baby eagle showed up at the homestead. They fed it a salmon a day, but after fishing season they had to shoo it away because the ready supply of food dwindled in winter.

The kids learned survival skills from an early age and how to become self-sufficient in the woods.

"I can't see how you can possibly starve to death in the wild," said Tim. "It's common sense." Of course, a city slicker might see things differently, and Tim agreed he might not fare so well in a large urban area after a lifetime in Alaska.

"If they dropped me off in New York tomorrow at seven A.M., by ten I'd be dead," he said. "But if you dropped me off on the far side of the Brooks Range, I'd be all right."

Living in a tent, fishing, hunting, mushing dogs will do that for you. As youths, the young Redingtons didn't even know New York City existed. Raymie said all the Redington boys were taught what to do to get by, and they all had to work hard. He used the old, flavorful word *skookum* as a synonym for savvy to describe the way they could handle themselves in a rural environment.

Joe assigned plenty of chores. The youngsters had to cut the wood and feed the dogs. Sometimes the cycle of feedings meant getting up in the middle of the night.

"The rule with my dad was that he brought the food in, and we did the cooking," said Joee.

Vi uses an ulu, or Eskimo women's knife, to cut salmon on this fall 1968 fishing trip. Income from commercial fishing counted for much of the year's cash income. The family also put up fish for their own use as well as for dog food.

There was no schoolhouse in the area, and the book learning the Redington boys got came from Vi as teacher. She obtained home instructional materials from a company in Baltimore and sometimes the boys got their education while sitting on a log outdoors. Reading, writing, arithmetic, history, and geography, they at least got smatterings of those subjects, even if fishing, hunting, and mushing seemed like a more enjoyable curriculum. The school schedule was anything but uniform: "Whenever I could hog-tie one of them," said Vi. "They'd rather be out doing something else."

Yet for all the fun they had and all the skills they acquired, Tim said he now regrets his limited formal education.

"We didn't get education enough," he said bluntly. "If I had a better education, I'd run for governor."

Although Tim, for one, thought a hundred dogs or more was too many, he participated in the same mushing activities as Raymie and Joee.

At first the trio played at mushing. Then they worked training puppies and racing their own teams. Dog mushing was woven into the fabric of daily existence. After listening to the big-time sprint races on the radio, the boys hooked up their own small teams and staged their own races. Anointed race marshal, Vi stood at the finish line with a stopwatch to time them.

Similar to the way boys of the era in the Lower 48 states might hear baseball games on the radio and mimic Ted Williams or Stan Musial with a batting stance, the Redington boys chose role models among the dog mushers. It made sense. One might be Dr. Roland Lombard, another might be Gareth Wright, and the third might choose to be George Attla. In the late 1950s and early 1960s, those were the heroes of the sprint-mushing world.

Some older Alaska Natives hunted seal and beluga whales in the area and became friends with Joe. Jake Butler, the world champion sprint musher, was one of these and he showed the boys how to build boats and sleds. They cut a birch tree, quartered it, and stretched moose hide across the wood.

"In two days we had a sled," said Joee. Later in life Joee, Raymie, and Tim put all that knowledge to good use. All of them became serious dog racers.

7

RESCUE AND RECOVERY

—Why did the military want Redington?
Because he had dogs.—

During the mid-1950s, Joe and his dogs worked for the military
on salvage operations. In this one, an Anchorage physician was flying his
family to the Lower 48 when he hit a mountaintop in the Nelchina area.
No one was injured. Here Joe is disassembling the airplane.

■

Twisted metal. Men mixed in with the wreckage. Bodies buried under
the snow that wouldn't stop falling. The scene was both horrific and
confusing. Joe Redington's assignment was to find the bodies, some under
twelve feet of fresh snow, and haul them out.

"One person didn't have a scratch on him," remembered Redington.
"He probably died of shock."

That time a Neptune military plane crashed. On another occasion, a civilian DC-3 plowed into Mount Susitna, the mountain commonly called Sleeping Lady, near Anchorage, killing all aboard. Still another time, a fighter plane hit the same mountain at about four thousand feet. In the 1950s, when the Air Force at Elmendorf Air Force base needed help with planes that crashed in remote, hard-to-reach areas, the call went out for Redington.

These were not search-and-rescue missions, but rather salvage operations. Sometimes the assignment was to bring bodies home for proper burial. Other times it was to somehow get the plane and as many pieces of it possible out of a mountain range and back to base. This was one of Redington's main part-time jobs while living at Flat Horn Lake. Why did the military want Redington? Because he had dogs. Virtually all these missions involved mushing into wild territory by dogsled, covering undulating terrain far from the nearest road, and sometimes even loading broken parts on the back of a sled and dragging them to more accessible ground.

This unusual job came Redington's way by accident. In 1950, Redington was making one of his usual runs between Knik and Wasilla. A jeep was coming the opposite way and was obviously driven by a man unfamiliar with the road because he didn't slow down to allow Redington to pass. The driver, an Air Force lieutenant, ran the jeep off the road and when Redington mushed over to help him, the man told him about a plane that had made an emergency landing down the street at Goose Lake. The plane was in good shape, but couldn't fly. He asked if there was any way to get to the remote location. Redington immediately replied, "Dog team."

Soon enough Redington was put on contract and for two years, 1954 and 1955, actually put most of his life on hold at Flat Horn Lake and took up residence at Elmendorf.

"I did everything," said Redington. "I picked up bomb sights."

Not so many years earlier, Redington was a novice musher. Now he was one of the most reliable. Typically, Redington and his dogs were flown to a crash sight. They spilled out of the plane, he hooked up the dogs, and they went to work. Other times they could not be let out within five miles of the scene and Redington mushed the remaining distance to begin work.

After he took the plane apart, Joe and his dogs made many
trips to transport the sections to the nearest road eighteen

miles away."It took sixteen days, and they were able to put it

back in service. I hauled it and never put a dent in it," he says.

"Rough-locking" the sled runners, or wrapping them with chain, gave added braking power for hauling the airplane wings downhill.

At least once, Redington hauled the wings of a plane out of isolated territory. A doctor and his family crashed into the top of a mountain in a single-engine plane. Redington cut down trees, lashed them together with a rope, laid mattresses on them, then placed the wings on top and supervised as the dogs pulled the land raft. One crash involved three separate eighteen-mile trips to the highway, hauling the fuselage, the engine, and wings.

Once in a while, Redington would be chauffeured home to Flat Horn after a job. A huge, half-gray, half-red, red-white-and-blue striped Air Force H-21 helicopter with propellers in front and back landed Joe and the dogs at the front door. If his neighbors didn't know better, they might think a UFO was landing.

As a rule, the jobs went off smoothly, but after one of Redington's first assignments it was a wonder that the Air Force wanted to have anything to do with sled dogs ever again. In 1951, Redington was summoned to

Elmendorf and informed there was a downed jet about eighteen miles west of Kashwitna, fairly close to Willow. Redington arrived in Anchorage with seven dogs, primarily malemutes, large dogs weighing sixty to seventy pounds. He always used big, strong dogs for big jobs. For a time, Redington owned a malemute named Chinook that weighed a hundred and twenty pounds.

It was too late in the evening to set out from the base and also too late for him to get any food for the dogs from the commissary. He tied them up in a hanger, wandered over to the cafeteria and investigated what was available in the way of human food. Someone asked him if the dogs would eat powdered eggs. "They'll eat anything," he said. Those could have been famous last words.

Redington returned to the dogs bearing a meal that might not be termed mouth-watering, but would do in terms of nutrition. He fed the dogs and left them in the hanger.

"Each dog may have had three dozen eggs, for all I know," said Redington.

Sometime in the middle of the night the dogs got free of their collars. And while they trotted around the hanger exploring, to quench their thirst, several lapped up puddles of anti-freeze that had spilled on the floor. It did not agree with them. And it most certainly did not mix well with the eggs in their bellies. The result was diarrhea and a stunning, disgusting mess. If the dogs had been housebroken there was no evidence in support of it.

"When we opened the door the next morning the smell about knocked us over," said Redington. Still, there was a mission to run. So Redington loaded the dogs into a cargo plane with plans to reconnoiter the area of the crashed plane and begin work. The flight to Willow, the landing area closest to the site, was a short one, but the plane bucked heavy crosswinds. Passengers were heaved from side to side. That did little to settle the dogs' queasy stomachs, and sure enough they began throwing up, all over everything. The smell of the dogs' vomit made two crewmen sick. Then the winds got so rough the plane couldn't land on the first pass and even Redington started to get ill.

Finally, on a second pass, the plane landed in Willow, and the crew chief angrily told Redington to get going and take the dogs. Redington

Joe was self-sufficient and all-Alaskan within a few years of his arrival. He even trapped, tanned, and sewed the fur hat he's wearing in this 1950s photo.

and the dogs caught a train, riding in a boxcar, to Kashwitna. Then they mushed fourteen miles to the downed plane. During the course of his trip, Redington took note that he passed the cabin of famous outdoors writer Russell Annabel. But that was the only part of the journey he wished to remember.

The crashed plane was resting in a swamp. Redington was on site for seventeen days. Part of the work involved jacking the plane up to help it dry out. It was repaired and later flown out.

Upon landing back in Anchorage, the plane was greeted by one incredibly irate crew chief.

"He came up to me and said, 'I'll kill you if you ever put another dog in one of my airplanes'," said Redington. "It took them a week to clean the airplane. They had to take out the flooring."

The rage was real, but the threat couldn't be backed up. The military repeatedly summoned Redington for help. "We produced," he said.

Redington was already doing anything it took to boost the profile of huskies. One Redington dog made its debut in the movies in a Walt Disney feature called *Nikki, Wild Dog of the North*. Released in 1961, the film starred Jean Coutu and Emil Genest. Based on a novel by James Oliver Curwood titled *Nomad of the North*, it was the story of a wolf-dog that is separated from his trapper master and then becomes embroiled in several adventures.

The dog scout was Bill Bacon of Anchorage, who has his own production company today. Bacon said he was working on another Disney film when *Nikki* was being planned. Only originally, the dog was supposed to be named Mickey. Bacon later heard about the day Walt Disney himself arrived on location and intervened in the script handling: "We've got a big problem here," Disney said. "We've got only one Mickey and he's a mouse."

Bacon owned a huge dog named Smokey, and Bacon brought him along when he was working on another film. Then a group of important-looking men showed up. When Smokey put his head in the lap of one of the men, he said, "This is the dog I want in the film." After the executives left, Bacon asked who the man was. "That," he was told, by disbelieving co-workers, "was Walt Disney." Bacon had never seen him. He didn't have television in Alaska, and he didn't go to the movies then.

Bacon's assignment was to round up dogs—as many as he could—that looked like Smokey at different ages. He was in Anchorage discussing his task when someone told him he really should check out this guy in Knik named Joe Redington, who had tons of dogs.

Bacon brought pictures of his dogs with him when he and Redington met for the first time.

"Yeah, I've got dogs that look like that," said Redington.

The dog that most resembled Smokey was an unlikely movie star—a little dog that the Redingtons called Polar. As a young pup separated from its mother, the dog had gotten chilled and was on the verge of death. "That puppy nearly died," said Vi. Tim Redington ended up bringing the dog into the house and nursing it until Polar was strong enough to romp in the yard again.

Bacon chose Polar to become a prominent on-field understudy of sorts to Smokey, which was considerably more exposure than many of the other

Among the various jobs that Joe held down was big-game guide and Bush pilot. This flight took him to Crater Lake atop Mount Katmai in the Valley of Ten Thousand Smokes.

dogs Bacon purchased during the 1958-1960 filming period near Banff in Alberta, Canada. It might as well have been an open casting call. He ended up gathering almost three hundred potential dog actors, including six others from the Redington kennel.

"We used about ten," said Bacon.

The Redingtons had fun with the whole deal. When the movie opened, they went into Anchorage to see it.

Besides the Army salvaging, Redington found another way to make money from part-time work by taking clients big-game hunting. He started a guiding business in 1954, and the first client was a United States senator from Utah. The actual hunting took place in the Lake Louise area, near Glennallen, far from Flat Horn. The guy got a grizzly, a moose, and a caribou, which rated it a very successful hunt.

One thing Redington excelled at was shooting. He trained for hunting Alaska big game by hunting deer in Pennsylvania. Redington almost always used a rifle, though he was a deadeye pistol shot on the rare occasions he used one.

Redington's military operations took him all over Alaska, but there was always plenty going on in the Flat Horn neighborhood, too. As Vi put it, "Alls we did was mush dogs."

For a while, James Redington, Joe's dad, worked as a watchman at the Fern Mine, about twenty-six miles from Wasilla. The gold mine was shut down, but the owners wanted someone on the premises. During a particularly snowy winter, the flakes piled up to feet and left him snowbound. A person needed sturdy implements just to cut through the snow to reach James's front door. His job was nearing an end and he was anxious to get back to Knik. Joe had visited the week before and felt it would be an easy enough run for he and Vi to mush to the mine and back in a day to pick up Dad.

Only he picked the wrong day. The couple began mushing the six miles uphill to the mine, but the snow fell so fast and so thick they could barely see. Because they expected a milk run, they were ill prepared for a blizzard. They had no sleeping bags and no food. When they couldn't make the distance, Joe and Vi were suddenly at risk. The twenty-six miles, said Vi, "seemed like a hundred."

They came to an abandoned cabin at another gold mine that was nicknamed the Little Vee, after Vi, and it provided some shelter from the howling wind. A search discovered a little bit of coal and a crust of bread. They toasted the tidbit and split it. There was no true warming fire and no food for their two nine-dog teams. They spent a restless, chilled night squeezed between two old mattresses. "Dad was comfortable enough," said Joe. "He had plenty of food."

For all their devotion to dogs, mushing was not the only mode of transportation at Flat Horn. It might snow three feet and drop to thirty below zero, but the Redingtons broke out the snowshoes for fun.

"It was beautiful," said Vi. "We had a lot of snowshoe time."

Joe was always ready to try new things, so when he heard about the availability of snowmachines, he bought one. He says he owned one of the first in Alaska, if not the first. It was a model called a Ranger, with wooden skis. However, he didn't use the machine instead of hooking up the dog team. He used it to break trail so it would be easier for his dogs to run. The snowmachine had six horsepower, and while Redington said it was a good little machine, he also said it broke down a lot.

"It got stuck real easy," said Redington. "I trained three dogs to follow me. When I got stuck I had the dogs with me and I'd take them home, then send the kids out to get the machine and bring it in."

Although Joe had enough examples of bad flying or dangerous flying as a frame of reference, since he was the guy who often got sent in to pick up the pieces, that didn't prevent him from buying his own plane.

Bill Cotter, the veteran Iditarod musher who has known Redington for years, remembers Joe saying he was tired of being forced to take long, roundabout routes to Flat Horn Lake by boat all the time. One day, said Cotter, Redington announced, "I'm going to get an airplane." No idle thought, it turned out.

"The next day," said Cotter, "there he is with the plane. He went to town, bought a plane, and flew it home. Just like someone would buy a car."

Redington said he begged pilots for some instruction and after some quickie lessons, brought the plane home. By the early 1960s, Redington was using his PA-14 four-passenger floatplane to wing back and forth to Anchorage almost daily. He made a deal with the Piggly-Wiggly supermarket to obtain meat scraps. It was much easier to feed his hundred and fifty or more dogs that way than it was by catching fish by the thousands. Especially since the state Department of Fish and Game kept adding regulations that limited fishing on the Susitna River. Where once the fishing was plentiful right down the bank, now he was being forced to fish farther and farther north. The scraps did not replace fish and other sources of nutrition completely, but they were a key source of sustenance for the dogs.

One time Redington lifted off from Lake Hood in Anchorage carrying seven hundred pounds of scraps on board. On the way home, just as he approached the Susitna River, Redington ran into a surprise wind shear. The gust of wind hit the plane hard and flipped it upside down.

"I just barely recovered," said Redington. He dropped so low that the bottom of the plane clipped the tops of trees. And the violent jerking of the plane upset the containers of scraps, turning them over and flinging the bloody meat pieces all over the plane's interior.

Unsettled, Redington turned the plane around and returned to Anchorage. Only afterward did the man who said he has never been frightened during a hairy, life-threatening situation reflect that it might not have been the mess that bothered him.

"I don't know if it was the meat that made me sick, or the narrow escape I had," he said.

Redington normally exudes calmness, though he may display a flash of anger. But although he has been in innumerable dangerous scrapes in planes, on boats, and on the Iditarod Trail, he said he has the ability to push fear into the background.

"I don't get scared," said Redington. "I might get a little nervous later. I think that's good in order to be able to handle a situation. You get all shook up and you can't do anything."

Perhaps the lack of worry in the midst of circumstances is from simply handling things as they've come over and over. Vi said she doesn't fret about Joe because he has proven repeatedly that he has a capability of focusing on the task necessary when things get tense.

She doesn't worry about Joe, but she does get scared now and then herself. Once, in the 1950s, she and Joe were in a boat in Turnagain Arm and the waves were rough, tossing them to and fro. She was convinced the boat was going to break in half or sink. The water was coming in by the barrel full. The boat was taking on water and Joe told her to keep bailing.

"If it breaks, we'll get another one," he said. "Damn it, just bail."

On another occasion, they were in two boats near each other in Goose Bay when the water grew so choppy she didn't know what to do. Joe started motioning to her and Vi thought he was telling her to dive overboard.

"Hell no, I'm not gonna jump," she yelled to him. What he really meant was for her to sit down and things would sort themselves out. She did and they did.

The Redingtons tried to bring the same sense of equanimity to natural disasters.

One day in the mid-1950s, Joe, accompanied by Tim, took a load of fish to the cannery where they did business. The trip kept them up all night, so they went to sleep in the morning. Mount Spurr's eruption woke them about noon.

"Everything was getting dark," said Joe. "Pretty soon you couldn't see

Vi steadies little Keith atop Chinook, a 120-pound malemute in the Redington kennel. Chinook was among the burly dogs that Joe used for hauling heavy loads while working for the military.

a damned thing. It was the blackest black you ever saw. You couldn't see one foot away. You couldn't even see your hand."

It rained gritty, grainy, gray ash. Instead of raindrops, instead of snowflakes, what fell from the sky was solid. When they stepped outside, their faces were pelted by ash. About four inches of ash accumulated at the fish camp.

"We didn't know what the hell was happening," said Redington.

When volcanoes spew ash, all machinery is shut down. Jet planes can be toppled from the sky if ash insinuates its way into the engines. When the eruption ended and the ash ceased, it was still days before the Redingtons could use the outboard motor on their boat. They had five hundred seal carcasses hanging on their property. Native hunters caught them and kept the hides, and the Redingtons got the rest to feed the dogs. They had little warning when the eruption buried the yard. The seals were ruined.

The Redingtons were at Flat Horn Lake when the Good Friday Earthquake struck in March 1964. The most powerful earthquake in American history, which over time has been re-evaluated as measuring

9.2 on the Richter Scale, sent noticeable shock waves through the homestead. The trees shimmied and shook, their tops in some cases bent double over the water, which itself churned with tall waves.

"That was a dandy," Joe would say as another ripple of violence disrupted the earth. The dogs were so scared they shook, but the Redingtons suffered little damage to the large house that had replaced their tent. However, when the ground stopped vibrating, there was one large crack on the property and, Joe said, "the land was warm." The phones were out, but the Redingtons had a backup radiophone, and Vi was able to raise someone at Susitna Station to ask what was going on. The answer: "We were rockin' and rollin'." Over the radio they heard a boat captain shout that his vessel was taking on water.

Worried about Vi's parents, who lived in Anchorage's devastated Turnagain residential area, Joe climbed into his plane and flew into town to try to check on them. However, when he reached the city, the authorities would not permit him to land. From the air he saw the wreckage of the neighborhood. "There was not much there," he said. Vi's folks were OK, though.

During the 1950s, Joe's association with the military took him all around the state and he was gratified to see how important a role dogs played in the lives of Eskimo and Athabascan villagers. The windy community of Unalakleet, where the Iditarod race makes its turn to the Bering Sea coast, was a place that particularly entranced him. There was a dog team behind every house.

He worked at Moses Point, Elim, Granite Mountain—and everywhere there were dog teams. Except Nome. Nome, seat of all long distance racing and the destination of the famed Serum Run, seemed anti-dog to Redington then.

"There were no teams in Nome at that time," he said. "In fact, if a dog showed up on the street, they might shoot it."

Things began to change a little later in that decade when Howard Farley, who would play a critical role in the startup of the Iditarod race, moved to town. For years Farley owned the only dog team in Nome and gave tourist rides. In 1956, though, Redington, working with local teacher and historian Carrie McLain, got a small race going in the old gold rush city, and featured a two-hundred-dollar purse. Some mushers came from local villages, but the race died out after a few years.

It was in the mid-1960s, on other swings through the villages, that it dawned on Redington that dog teams were disappearing: "Instead of a dog team behind every house, there was a bright yellow snowmachine sitting in the front yard."

Dog teams were on the outs. You had to feed dogs, and that was more work and more costly than feeding gasoline to the machines. He could see the wave of the future. This was a trend Redington despised, but at that point he didn't know what to do about it.

Meanwhile, in 1957, Joe and Vi had a baby boy, Keith. Little Keith spent a great deal of his time outdoors in a homemade, wooden playpen that was set up in the yard. Sometimes the playpen was lifted into the thirty-foot dory that the Redingtons used while fishing on Cook Inlet. Once in a while, a fish would slip into the playpen through its walls and amuse him. In the yard, diapers fluttered in the breeze on the clothesline.

While Joe was an all-around resourceful fellow, one role he did not play was midwife. Vi gave birth in town and brought Keith to Flat Horn Lake when he was three weeks old. During the winter, she carried him on her back. Vi had a handmade squirrel parka, made by an Eskimo woman in Elim, and a white overgarment as an additional warming layer. Keith could be toted around in the hood-like pouch behind her neck.

As he grew, Keith was exposed to the same hunting, fishing, mushing lifestyle as the other boys. There were always many hazards accompanying wilderness living, but when things went wrong, they occurred unexpectedly.

The tragedy that stunned the Redington family was like that. A fluke accidental shooting killed Keith when he was nine years old. A gun thought to be empty discharged.

Joe Redington calls himself pretty tough, but there are times he lets his emotions free. He said he can cry over the death of a lead dog. But when his youngest boy died, he couldn't stop crying. "That hurt me real bad," he said. "I was bad for a long time."

Keith's death haunted the Redingtons and spoiled life at Flat Horn Lake for them. His loss was one of the main reasons they moved back to Knik in 1968.

8
WHEN SPRINTERS WERE KINGS

*—It was like you were Jesus Christ coming
for the last time. All the streets were filled.—*

**In this photo from June 1964, Joe prepares to haul a boatload of dogs
to Flat Horn Lake. By then, his kennel numbered in the hundreds.**

◼

Anchorage's Fourth Avenue was packed with people. Men wore heavy parkas on their backs and the skins of dead animals on their heads. Women wore fur coats. They came by the thousands, the locals and those who lived in remote villages spread across the northern tier of Alaska's vast territory.

It was a colorful mix of people, come to revel at the annual February winter festival and to cheer their favorites in the most important dog race of them all. The Fur Rendezvous winter carnival was all that the

Gareth Wright was among
the greats of the sprint-mushing
world when the Redingtons
began competing.

Redingtons guessed it would be from listening to the world championships on the radio.

When Gareth Wright of Salcha pulled his barking, straining dogs up to the starting line the applause was deafening. Fans called his name. A vocal man, Wright's outgoing personality matched his out-sized credits, and he had a following.

It took until the mid-1950s before Joe Redington fulfilled his long-held goal of bringing a team to the world championship sled dog race, and Wright was already a two-time world title-holder. In 1957, he won a third time. Coupled with his remarkable pairing of championships in the North American in 1950 and 1983, thirty-three years apart, his reputation was cemented as one of the great sprint mushers of all time.

And to be at the top of the game in sprint mushing in 1950s and 1960s in Alaska meant you were a statewide hero, a public figure at least as recognized as the governor, and certainly more revered than any politician.

"We were gods in those days," said Wright, now in his seventies. "It was like being Mark McGwire. It was like you were Jesus Christ coming for the last time. All the streets were filled. The bars were filled. When my lead dog Jennie died, people mourned the dog."

He was not alone in being accorded such esteem. In 1958, George Attla, an unknown young Athabascan Indian from the Koyukuk River village of Huslia, tilted the mushing world on its side when he not only upset defending champ Wright, but began the run that established him as the most honored sprint musher of them all. Attla electrified spectators for the next three decades and captured a record ten world championships.

That same year, a quiet and gentle musher arrived on the scene from Wayland, Massachusetts. Often mushers from other cold climates in the United States or Canada entered, but once the superior Alaskan mushers were done with them, they slunk off. Not this time. Dr. Roland Lombard placed fourth in 1958. And though no one suspected it at the time, he too was about to become one of the most dominant of racers. Lombard, who died in 1990, won eight world championships and his duels with Attla captivated a spellbound public.

The Rondy's route involved dashing through city streets. Snow was dumped onto thoroughfares and police held traffic back as mushers passed. They looped through the woods within the city limits and finished in the heart of downtown.

It could not then be imagined that some day mushers would start a race in the same Fourth Avenue location only to see it wind through the same streets and disappear into the rugged, inaccessible terrain of Alaska's Interior. Nor would anyone have guessed that the champions of the yet-unborn Iditarod Trail Sled Dog Race would attain the same stature as Wright, Attla, and Lombard. One day, Rick Swenson, Susan Butcher, Martin Buser, and yes, Joe Redington, would become equally bright stars in the constellation.

After his poor-judgment aborted training program with Stanley Collins in 1951, it took until 1956 for Redington to enter his first team in the world championship—and he scratched. However, the trips to town for the Rondy began earlier and were very much family affairs, even before Joe raced. The boys, who had been training and raising their own dog

From left, Raymie, Joee, and an unidentified man show off the beaver pelts and other furs they trapped at Flat Horn Lake. Joe notes on this 1966 photo that the furs were sold to furrier Perry Green in Anchorage.

teams for years, entered the kids races, and Vi even raced dogs in the women's world championship event. There were Redingtons sprinkled all over the start lists.

Neither competitive by inclination or by dint of hard training, Vi started racing mostly because Joe suggested it. In 1954, her first try, she was seventh out of seven finishers. Another casual foray in 1958 yielded a fifth place finish among five finishers.

"I hated racing," said Vi. "I did it because Joe put me in. One time he put me in with good, fast dogs, and they didn't listen to me at all. They dumped me halfway through it and ran away. I always was a freighter."

A freighter: someone mushing for fun or to get somewhere. So was Joe really. Redington took his dogs out in the backcountry for runs of thirty-five miles at a time. Usually he was hauling a heavy load. The dogs weren't running at high speed, and he never seriously considered putting them into an organized training program to try for the thousands in prize money offered by the big sprint races.

"I just loved being out there on the trail," said Joe. "It was great to be away from everything. To be under the stars, to be alone. I wanted to go and do some of it, but I knew I didn't have the racing dogs."

Not the words of a hard-core racer, though many years later, in 1973, Joe placed tenth in the Rondy. He also had finishes of fifteenth and twenty-second in the 1970s.

"It was not his cup of tea because he never had time to train," said Vi.

That assessment was echoed by Bill Cotter, now a top Iditarod musher, who raced in the Rondy: "Joe didn't do real well. He was always doing long trips. He didn't concentrate on going super fast."

Still, if you were a dog man, the Fur Rondy was the place to be. It is difficult to overemphasize the grip the Rendezvous had on people. There was no same-day live television programming in Anchorage. Professional sports

Raymie displays his trophies in this 1961 photo after winning a five-dog race in Anchorage. While Joe Sr. performed respectably in sprint racing, his sons excelled. Raymie placed fifth in the 1968 Fur Rendezvous races; brother Joee swept the Rondy and North American junior races in 1961, and as an adult, placed in the Rondy's top five from 1963-1966, winning the championship in '66. Younger brother Tim landed in the top ten of the Fur Rendezvous races three times during the 1970s.

ANCHORAGE MUSEUM OF HISTORY AND ART

Col. Norman Vaughan was first attracted to Alaska dog mushing in the Fur Rendezvous winter carnival dog races.

nationwide were not as widespread. And in Alaska live entertainment was at a premium.

"There was nothing else going on," said Dick Mackey. "You went to the dog races on the weekend." Mackey, who later became an Iditarod champion, got to know Redington through the Rondy when his own kids competed against the Redington boys. When Mackey talks about the races being where the action was, he means every winter weekend, not just the world championship downtown.

"It was *the* thing to attend them at Tudor Track," said Mackey. "It would be jam-packed. Everything led up to the Rondy."

It was a glorious period for sprint dog racing. The Rondy brought a contingent of New England racers to Alaska. Lombard was the best known, but Charlie Belford and Keith Bryar were successful, too. And the Rondy lured Norman Vaughan from Massachusetts.

White-bearded and stentorian-voiced, Vaughan become an Alaska legend as the oldest man to race the Iditarod (even older than

Redington). He solidified his reputation when for his eighty-ninth birthday in 1994 he climbed the 10,000-foot Antarctic mountain that Admiral Richard Byrd named for him when they explored the continent nearly seventy years earlier. But his first Alaska experiences involved being a handler for Lombard and others.

What a scene it was! "Anybody who could come, did," said Vaughan. "It was very important to everyone. It was the key event of the whole fair. People wanted to spend their money to see it in person."

The Rondy represented an annual convergence of the dog world. Villages combined their dogs to create super teams and entrusted them to a favorite musher, who represented the whole community. From his rural travels, Redington already knew some of the best Native mushers, men like Attla, Jimmy Malemute and Jimmy Huntington. If they were anonymous to the bulk of fans, Redington knew those racers, with a depth of village racing experience in popular spring carnival events, would do well.

Many mushers who later specialized in long-distance mushing, men like Dick Mackey, Jerry Riley, and Bill Cotter, tried their hand in the sprints.

"Sprint," said Cotter, "is a new word. We were dog racing. There wasn't any other kind. I loved the race."

Redington and Wright became good friends through meetings at the Rondy. Once, when Wright had to make an extended trip to the Lower 48, he left a dozen dogs with Joe to train. That was the ultimate sign of trust from Wright. When he dropped off the dogs at Flat Horn Lake, Wright simply opened the door of his plane and let the dogs run free. "They'll come back," Wright reassured a surprised Redington.

As payment for training rendered, Wright gave the Redingtons a lead dog named Freckles.

Much later, Wright said leaving dogs with Redington proved how much he appreciated his skill as a dog man. He said he always respected Joe.

"He's always been honest," said Wright. "He's always kept his word. The old days of the handshake have always been good as far as he's concerned."

Among those who race dogs, there has always been much wheeling and dealing. Mushers trade, buy, and sell dogs the way professional sports franchises swap players. In the 1990s, an Iditarod leader with a track record and out of good breeding lines might cost two thousand dollars. In the 1950s, when Redington first purchased dogs they cost less than movie tickets do now.

Once, Joe's old friend Jake Butler had five dogs for sale. Redington asked how much they cost and when he was told thirty-five dollars, he said, "That's a hell of a price to pay for dogs." Meaning they were too expensive. He was soon corrected. Butler wanted only thirty-five dollars for the group, or seven bucks apiece. Redington bought.

As the Fur Rondy caught on with the public and became a showcase event, and as the mushers grew more intensely competitive, the bidding for top dogs behind closed doors increased. After the races ended, mushers gathered to party, to tell stories, and to enjoy themselves. Often, the bull sessions turned into bargaining sessions. Redington knew the rules had changed when someone offered Wright a thousand dollars for his unusual, homemade eighty-pound sled and leader Venus.

"That was the biggest price I ever heard," said Redington, who was still paying a high of perhaps twenty-five dollars for a leader at the time.

Joe had some badly behaving fighting dogs in the early 1950s, one in particular named Cub he bought from Butler for seven dollars. Joe sold it to his Knik friend Clem Tellman, for twenty-five dollars. Tellman had better success in the Rendezvous, and better success with the dog, winning the world title in 1953 with Cub as part of his team.

A little later, a famous sale featured an Attla leader. Lombard, a veterinarian by trade, had more cash resources than subsistence living villagers, and when he made an offer of a thousand dollars for a dog named Nellie, Attla found it irresistible. Nellie became the key to Lombard's winning breeding line. Redington himself eventually ended up stepping up in class by buying an Attla leader for three hundred dollars.

Joee, Raymie, and Tim Redington all raced in the junior events, and as they aged they moved into the open class against the top racers. The names they first heard on the radio were brought to life up close and personal since they were now on the same playing field.

Raymie's first Rondy racing memories place him in the three-dog class for kids. Tim scored numerous top-three finishes, especially in the six-dog class. Just being there was a treat.

"It was a big deal to come in from Flat Horn Lake," said Raymie. A

A spacious trailer replaced the old tent at Flat Horn. It "rocked and rolled" during the 1964 Good Friday earthquake that ranked 9.2 on the Richter Scale.

rare and exciting excursion to the big city for Bush kids. When the Rondy came around on the calendar it always meant a good time.

If Joe was more of a plodder, the boys learned at a young age how to urge their dogs to run fast. They all recorded better overall Rondy results than Joe did. Tim's best placing was seventh in 1975 and 1977. He was also ninth in 1973. Raymie finished fifth in 1968. But Joee, the oldest, had the grandest success of all the Redingtons in the Rendezvous.

"At one time I might have been known more than my dad," said Joee, who still lives a subsistence lifestyle in Manley Hot Springs and commercial fishes on the Yukon River.

Probably so. Sprinting was the only dog-racing going and Joee excelled at it. In 1961, his last year of junior racing before he turned eighteen that summer, Joee was a dominant force. He swept all three days of racing in both the Rondy and North American junior events.

Joee switched to the open, adult class in 1962, showing promise against the seasoned older men by finishing eleventh. But just a year later he burst into the ranks of contenders with a fourth-place finish. In 1964 Joee moved up to third. In 1965, he was third again, trailing only Lombard and Wright. He was making the biggest of the big guns edgy.

In 1966, stationed at Anchorage's Fort Richardson, Joee was in the

U.S. Army and he represented the service in the race because a general thought it would be good public relations. "There was a lot of interest at the base," said Joee.

This was in the midst of American involvement in the Vietnam War. Instead of being sent overseas to fight, Joee performed patrol duty in Alaska's far north, near Fort Yukon and Venetie. It was a much preferable assignment and one perfectly suited to his background.

That year the Army bought some dogs for him and for the race itself Joee obtained a dog from Joe and two from Raymie. Those dogs, Happy and Windy, played a key role in the team.

On the first day, Joee took a twenty-second lead over Bill Sullivan and by the end of the third heat, his lead was a minute and six seconds ahead of second place. Joee accomplished what some felt was impossible—he broke the stranglehold Lombard and Attla had on the crown. "It was a thrill," said Joee.

For one year, Joee Redington was king of the world.

SEEDS OF A GREAT RACE

*—He was a man of vision
who could see twenty-twenty while others'
vision was often cloudy.—*

Clearing and marking the little-used Iditarod Trail was no small task.
Dick Mackey worked with Joe to re-open the trail for the Centennial race
in 1967, celebrating the hundredth anniversary of Alaska's transfer from
Russia to the United States. "We walked the entire trail from the Old
Skwentna Roadhouse to Susitna Station and marked it," Joe remembers.

■

In a roundabout way you could say that Bill Seward was responsible for
the start of the Iditarod Trail Sled Dog Race.

Everyone thought it was a steal when Manhattan was bought from
the Indians for twenty-four-dollars worth of trinkets. Practically no one

Joee Redington leaves the starting line of the Centennial Iditarod on
February 11, 1967. The trail covered fifty-six miles, or twenty-eight miles

each way. Promoting the race with Dorothy Page, Joe had enlisted fifty-nine

mushers to race, including himself. Isaac Okleasik of Teller won the race.

The late Dorothy Page originated the idea for the 1967 race, earning her the title "Mother of the Iditarod." She was a strong backer of the thousand-mile race, volunteering and helping with promotions. For fifteen years, she wrote and edited the *Iditarod Trail Annual,* a yearbook recognizing the mushers, the dogs, and the volunteers.

thought the $7.2-million purchase of Alaska from Russia negotiated by Secretary of State William H. Seward in 1867 was worth it. "Seward's Icebox," they called it. "Seward's Folly," the deal was termed. Originally.

By 1967, Alaskans, at least, recognized they resided in a special place. And they darned well planned to celebrate the 100th anniversary of the United States' acquisition of the Alaska Territory.

Dorothy Page of Wasilla had just been appointed to the chair of the Alaska Centennial Purchase Committee when Joe Redington brought Timmy in from Flat Horn Lake to enter the junior race at the Willow winter carnival in 1966.

Page, a short, heavy-set woman with a generous nature, approached Redington and casually asked if he thought it would be possible to conduct a dog sled race on the old Iditarod Trail. *Was enough of it open and useable?* she asked.

Joe said he thought so. After all, he and Vi mushed dogs on the trail every day.

How far could they go? Well, nobody was talking about mushing to Nome, that was for sure. Redington thought they could go at least twenty-six miles on the Iditarod Trail, from Knik, over Nine-Mile Hill, across Crooked Lake, over Mud Lake and into Big Lake. Twenty-six whole miles.

That was comparable to most of the racing that was taking place at that time during the daily heats of the Fur Rendezvous or North American championships. Redington and Page were members of the Aurora Dog Mushers club, a small club in the Mat-Su Valley. At the next meeting of the organization they suggested trying to hold such a race. Joe was elected chairman of the Iditarod Trail Committee, the first incarnation of the governing body of the Iditarod race, and an entity that endures to this day.

"I want to give Dorothy all the credit in the world for the Centennial race," said Redington.

In later years, Page, who died in 1989 at the age of sixty-eight, was called "The Mother of the Iditarod," not only for her original idea to stage the 1967 race, but also for her unstinting devotion to the longer Iditarod. She became a dedicated volunteer, and for fifteen years wrote and edited the *Iditarod Trail Annual,* a magazine-like publication that served as race program and early history book documenting the races.

Once the seed was planted with Redington, though, it germinated and flowered. As usual, once he gave a matter some thought, he concluded that if it was worth doing at all, it should be the biggest and best. At the club's meeting he announced that if there was going to be a race tied in with the celebration it should be the richest dog-mushing event of all time. The greatest purse ever paid out was $10,000 at the old Sweepstakes races in Nome. Joe said they should put up a purse of $25,000 for their Iditarod.

It would not be the last time Redington's grandiose thinking ran ahead of the pack. He was a man of vision who could see twenty-twenty while others' vision was often cloudy. Redington's pronouncement flabbergasted those in attendance.

"That floored everybody," said Redington. "They had never heard of anything like that." No wonder Redington was chosen chairman of the committee. It was a case of, *Your idea? Go raise the money.* He pledged to make it work.

Shelley Gill, an Alaskan writer who has observed Redington up close over many years and in many situations, said she learned that not only could Redington's word be counted on as gospel, he knew what he was talking about. "When he says it is so, you can take it to the bank," said Gill. "Even if the whole town says it's not."

That was true, she found, even if a Redington idea sounded goofy. Like paying out the fattest purse ever. Or starting up the longest race, for example. But that was later.

Redington, always a resourceful man in the wild, displayed the same type of ingenuity when it came to fundraising. He and Vi donated one acre of their land at Flat Horn Lake to the race and called it "The Centennial Acre." The acre was broken up into 45,000 one-foot-square lots and they were sold. The gimmick was that each buyer paid two dollars to receive his land, a deed with the title to it, and a certificate. This was not to be confused with the almost-free land offered to homesteaders. What could anyone do with one square foot of land? Maybe stand on it. Some $12,000 was raised toward the purse through Redington's donation.

The square foot that individuals bought to aid a cause was promptly forgotten by most of the real estate purchasers. But even now, thirty-plus years later, the Redingtons occasionally hear from people who come into possession of the title to chunks of the land. Maybe they don't realize how small the parcel is. Maybe they don't believe how small the parcel is. But they telephone and ask about "their land."

"Someone died and they inherited it," said Vi. "They want to know where their land is. The certificate doesn't say it's only a square foot. We tell everyone they can come and see it."

This was not Redington's only money-raising coup. The tribal chief of the Tyonek Indians committed $15,000, plenty to cover the remainder of the purse. However, shortly before the race, the man, who had been a close personal friend of Joe and Joee, died in a fire. That left Redington in a precarious position. He went back to tribal leaders and talked them into guaranteeing the payment anyway. There was a catch. It was a loan.

They wanted some security, too. So Redington put his Flat Horn Lake homestead up as collateral.

Meanwhile, Joe had a friend bring a big Caterpillar tractor out to the trail and bulldoze, clearing much of the debris that had grown up through the years of disuse. That was a help. But other sections had to be cleared by hand. For long hours, making slow progress, Redington and Dick Mackey literally blazed trail. They inched along, slicing through dense brush by wielding chainsaws. Mackey remembers that one big, fat tree had a block and tackle left over from old freight-sledding days grown into the tree bark itself.

"I did Nine-Mile Hill with Joe Redington," said Mackey. "We reopened the trail."

Only a small portion of the Iditarod Trail was accessible, but at least a genuine part of the trail was used. The Centennial Iditarod ended up covering fifty-six miles, or twenty-eight miles a day for two days.

One aspect of the festivities was particularly gratifying for Vi Redington. Beyond the pleasure taken in mushing the trail, the Redingtons always maintained a keen interest in the history of their region. In 1965, the Redingtons donated some of their own items to jump-start the collection of the Knik Museum and Dog Mushers Hall of Fame. The museum, now housed in an old pool hall built in 1910, really got rolling in conjunction with the Centennial. Vi helped nurture the collection and even today she retains a key to the place.

The big payday proved to be a great lure for the race, and when February 11, 1967, rolled around, fifty-nine mushers had entered, anxious to try out something different from the usual sprints around Anchorage and Fairbanks.

One of those entries was Joe Redington. Of course he had spent every available moment raising money and organizing the event, leaving little time to actually train a dog team for the race. This was to set a pattern for the future. With Joe the race always came first and personal achievement second.

"The dogs I ran, I hadn't even seen them," said Redington, who barely made the top fifty in the first day when they got ill. "The kids just pulled them out of their dog teams. They really fixed me up. They gave me their culls and cripples."

To put it bluntly, the young Redingtons didn't exactly turn over the pick of the litter. The dogs were not sharp racers. Some seemed to be lame. Hardly a first-rate group. No matter, the existence of the race counted the most.

There were some naysayers, mushers who worried how races along wilderness trails might impact sprint mushing. Orville Lake and Earl Norris, respected dog men with roots in the short-distance racing community, opposed it. They wondered aloud if the money could be raised—a reasonable doubt. And they felt long-distance racing might prove harmful to the long-term health of sprint mushing. As it turned out, that was a very reasonable fear, though one that was not realized for years.

The late Isaac Okleasik of Teller won the race, beating an all-star cast of mushers that included three Redingtons—Joe, Joee, and Raymie—plus Rondy champions Gareth Wright and Roland Lombard, and future Iditarod champions Dick Mackey and Jerry Riley. Oh yes, there was a less-heralded entry, a convict representing Palmer Correctional Center. Inmates helped groom the trail and were rewarded with a designated spot in the field. The man raced, then went back to prison.

Another musher who would later gain statewide renown and became one of Joe Redington's closest companions on the Iditarod Trail made the long journey from his home village to enter the Centennial Iditarod. Herbie Nayokpuk of Shishmaref, a village located on an exposed inlet by the Bering Sea on Alaska's Seward Peninsula, may well be the most revered Eskimo musher in Iditarod history. In his upbringing, Nayokpuk, a man built low to the ground with a powerfully wide body, had little in common with Redington, the Depression-era Okie come north. But their kinship was very real and to be admired. Both men fed their families with their wiles. To both men, the most pleasurable way to spend an evening was to mush a dog team under the stars, the only sounds in the darkness the padding of huskies' feet on the trail and the hiss of the sled runners. They were wise men of the trail and instantly seemed to recognize the same qualities in each other.

Nayokpuk, now approaching seventy, never won the Iditarod before being forced into retirement by two heart operations and a stroke. But he placed second in 1980, and is regarded by all as one of the toughest and

Herbie Nayokpuk of Shishmaref entered the Centennial Iditarod, traveling from his remote village on the Bering Sea to compete. Nayokpuk and Redington liked each other immediately and through the years have built a lasting friendship, often traveling together on the Iditarod. While Nayokpuk never won the thousand-mile race, he placed second in 1980, and earned the nickname "The Shishmaref Cannonball."

most savvy dog drivers who ever mushed a team off Fourth Avenue. He also has the most flavorful nickname of any musher—The Shishmaref Cannonball—bestowed upon him by reporters covering the Iditarod for his blistering early-race pacesetting.

An ivory carver who fishes and hunts to put food on the family table, Nayokpuk was so popular, as the stories go, that his fame actually prevented him from winning the 1980 race. It is said he would have won if he hadn't stopped to shake hands with so many villagers on the route. In 1976, Nayokpuk told reporters that mushing was a costly hobby and that he could make more money focusing on carving, but he wouldn't do it. He patted his stomach and said, "But I have a paunch and I decided if I quit mushing I would become a fat old man."

Nayokpuk said that he thought at the time that the 1967 Iditarod race would be the longest mushing event ever held. "Joe liked to see young people suffer," he joked.

Joe Redington said he and Herbie had some fine times on the trail together, camped out by the fire. Herbie said he and Joe indeed enjoyed a special bond and loved to swap tales about their adventures. Sometimes they took breaks, sipped their coffee and discussed how hard daily life must have been for early Alaskans.

"We talked about what they did long ago," said Nayokpuk. "How tough people were long ago without snowmachines and four-wheelers. They had to walk to get food."

There are some who will tell you Joe Redington is the toughest guy who ever set foot on the Iditarod Trail. There are some who will vote for Herbie Nayokpuk.

Terry Adkins, the Montana musher who made annual pilgrimages north to race the Iditarod for more than two decades, once visited Nayokpuk in Shishmaref and gained some insight into the man's character and hardiness.

In 1816, explorer Otto Von Kotzebue named Shishmaref after his chief lieutenant, Glieb Shishmarev, and in some ways the village remains as rustic and wild as it was when he sailed into the neighborhood. The harsh weather seems to beat a never-ending, nasty tattoo on the homes constructed facing the hard-blowing wind. Nayokpuk made Adkins welcome in a cozy, but far from elaborate one-room dwelling. When his host offered him a gift of a walrus skull, Adkins made the mistake of gently refusing it. Although he did not say so, he thought since Nayokpuk was not a rich man he could put the valuable item to better use as a carver. Nayokpuk was insulted, though. Adkins had previously sought to buy a dog named Patsy, but Nayokpuk turned him down. So instead of the walrus skull, Nayokpuk gave the dog to a chastened Adkins.

"Patsy became the foundation of my kennel," said Adkins. What impressed Adkins more than anything, though, was the ancient rifle Nayokpuk showed him. The weapon he used to hunt seemed to be falling apart. The stock was held together with strapping tape. When Adkins asked Nayokpuk what kind of range the rifle provided for his big-game hunts, Herbie replied that he got "close enough to shoot the polar bear in the mouth." From another, that might be thought to be a tall tale. Adkins believed him.

"If I got caught out in a storm, he'd be a guy I'd want to be with," said Adkins.

Nayokpuk has another thing in common with Redington: Both deny their age. Not their birth certificates. They know how old they are, they merely ignore it. Nayokpuk makes more jokes about aging than Redington does, though. "I'm too old," he might say. "Pretty soon I'm gonna buy me a rocking chair." Pause. "If I reach a hundred I'll buy a rocking chair."

Mostly, when the 1967 Iditarod ended, there were rave reviews. If Broadway critics wrote about the event their comments would range from "A Triumph!" to "Exciting!" and "Thrilling!" At the post-race banquet, Wright stood and proclaimed, "The Aurora Dog Mushers, the littlest dog club in Alaska, put on the biggest race in the world."

The results left Redington glowing. It seemed especially appropriate that the race took place in 1967. Not only was it a special anniversary for Alaska, but Leonhard Seppala died that year at age eighty-nine. After twenty-eight years in Nome and another nineteen in Fairbanks, in 1947 he had left the cold country and mushing behind him. He was residing in Seattle when he died. The spectacular success of the race left Redington more than ever committed to keeping mushing alive on the Iditarod Trail. Not that any of the mushers enervated by the event envisioned a future Iditarod that would last much longer than two days at a time.

"I never had any idea there would be a thousand-mile race," said Nayokpuk.

When the race ended, everyone went home, leaving Redington happy but with one problem: He still had to make sure the Tyonek loan was repaid. However, nobody but Joe, whose homestead was on the line, seemed to care about fundraising. He couldn't find anyone to make donations to a race that was already over. "They were going to foreclose on our property," said Vi.

It took the intervention of Governor Bill Egan and an act of the state legislature to save the Redington land. Once the minor financial problem was straightened out, Redington focused on turning the short Iditarod run into an annual event. He worked tirelessly toward that end in 1968, but there was a dearth of snow that winter, far too little to send sleds over the bumpy trail.

"The day the race would have started, Vi and I drove out on Knik Lake and took a picture of the truck sitting on glare ice," said Redington. "There was no snow around the lake at all."

Discouraged, but not deterred, Redington began planning for 1969. Believing he was still building on the excitement generated by the 1967 race, Redington touted the event to mushing friends. There were hardly any takers. He tried to raise funds for another significant purse. There were hardly any takers for that, either.

The Aurora Dog Mushers sponsored Iditarod II anyway. But the purse was only $1,000. George Attla, a marquee name, entered and won, but only twelve mushers had signed up. Joe was one of them and placed fourth this time. Disappointed in the turnout, Redington could not figure out what was wrong.

It was only a short time later that Joe traveled to Unalakleet, his favorite village, to work on a boat building project, and there he got a first-hand picture of the changes wrought in the sled-dog world. Snowmachines had taken over by then. There were only a couple of dog teams left. The transition from beasts to mechanized transportation was happening swifter than he imagined.

"I knew we were in trouble. They had thousands of dogs," said Redington, "and they didn't need both. This was still Alaska, though. I didn't want Alaska to be without sled dogs."

A way of life that linked the present with the past, a way of life Redington supported and embraced, verged on extinction. How could he bring sled dogs back to prominence in the Alaska Bush? What would it take?

"That's when we first started talking about a longer race," said Redington. "From Knik to Iditarod and back." For once, Redington didn't think big enough. Iditarod? Naw. Iditarod was a forgotten mining town. Why not ride the trail all the way to the end?

BIG DOLLARS AND COMMON SENSE

*—Those who listened were dumbfounded when
he suggested a guaranteed purse of $50,000.—*

Nome resident Howard Farley was a strong supporter of
Redington's "crazy" idea of a thousand-mile race. Joe's 1972 letter to Farley,
inviting him to join the Iditarod Trail Committee and participate in the
first distance race of its kind, is now an historical document.
"You could do a lot of good on the Nome end," Redington wrote.

◼

Joe Redington knew he still had some selling to do on his grand scheme
for an Iditarod Trail Sled Dog Race running from Anchorage to Nome
when his own son asked a pointed question.

"Dad," said Joee Redington, "do you think this thing is going to work?
If not, I'm going to change my name to John Paul Jones." In other words,

While traveling to mark the trail, Joe Redington and Dave Olson camped in extreme cold and heavy snow. Here, Olson hunkers down in the snow cave created by the previous night's roaring fire.

is this crazy idea of yours for huskies to race more than a thousand miles going to make us the laughing stock of the state?

Since the 1969 short Iditarod fizzled, and it seemed dogs were being phased out in the villages, Redington realized some broad, dramatic, galvanizing statement was needed to revive interest in dogsled travel.

Using the Iditarod Trail as much as possible was always in the forefront of Redington's mind. The disappointment of 1969 indicated it would be pointless to try to hold another race in 1970. But as a substitute the Redingtons organized a group of dog drivers to mush out on the trail and camp together during the first week in March. They called it a rally rather than a race.

Vi termed the brief adventure "symbolic."

The Redingtons followed the same format in 1971 and 1972, as well. While out on the trail, they worked it, smoothing and making small improvements with each trip. In 1971 the weather was distinctly inhospitable: minus fifty degrees. In 1972, they traveled only seven miles on the trail.

"But it kept the Iditarod spirit going," said Redington.

The Redingtons brought a tent and made a fire. "It got so hot I had to go out and get some snow to calm it down," said Redington.

By this time, the Iditarod Trail was special to all the Redingtons. Raymie even got married on the trail by Knik Lake. Vows were exchanged, then members of the wedding party hung a "Just Married" sign around his neck as he mushed off to his honeymoon.

Joe Delia, the Skwentna trapper who lives along the Iditarod route, said that in 1972 he scouted the trail with Joe Redington and found it overgrown with alders and brush.

"My trapline was the only trail through the country then," said Delia. "It had been fifty-some years since the Iditarod Trail had been in use."

The idea of a race all the way from Anchorage to Nome on rough, ill-marked trail metamorphosed slowly. Redington believed few Alaskans remembered the early-in-the-century Sweepstakes races of just more than four hundred miles (from Nome to Candle and back). By the 1970s, the only mushing event of any length was a two-hundred-miler between Fairbanks and Livengood. And that race left a bad taste because mushers didn't get paid what they had been promised.

Redington began by trying to promote the notion of a race from Knik to Iditarod, a race of eight hundred miles. It seemed logical to him because the old mining community and the trail shared a name. But long past its prime, Iditarod was a ghost town. The gold and people were gone, and the place retained none of its luster.

The reaction was discouraging. *Iditarod? Where's that?* Nobody cared. But when Nome was mentioned as a possible destination, people perked up. At the least they arched an eyebrow. Everybody knew Nome. It had a glorious and sexy history. Wyatt Earp. Leonhard Seppala. The Sweepstakes. It was the end of the trail, too.

The only thing was, the suggestion of mushing all the way to Nome scared the living daylights out of people. They thought Joe Redington and the dogs he rode in with were plumb loco. And even those who listened and didn't judge his enthusiastic spiels as wacko were dumbfounded when he suggested a guaranteed purse of $50,000.

Joe suggested the huge payout because he knew the big money

In preparation for the 1973 race, Joe's long-time friend

Dave Olson assisted with helping find and mark the trail.

lured mushers to the 1967 race. He hadn't thought much about a figure, though.

"I was just thinking big, I guess," said Redington. "I don't think I really planned it. It was probably on the spur of the moment. Someone probably asked me, 'What are you gonna pay'?" At this point, Redington was still chairman of the Iditarod Trail Committee, all members of the Aurora Dog Mushers club. As soon as he started talking about big bucks payouts, the committee disintegrated. Dorothy and Von Page, and others, said they did not want their names associated with a race promising fifty grand in prize money. They were afraid they would be held liable when the mushers weren't paid, were afraid they would lose their property and go bankrupt themselves.

"They said, 'Don't even mention our names'," said Redington.

The club went so far as to sever its relationship with the trail committee. Joe, Vi, and anyone who would stand with them, were on their own. It was a little bit like drawing that famous line in the dirt at the Alamo. It was believed that those who stayed behind the line were doomed.

After the haggling, after the fears were voiced, only Tom Johnson and Gleo Huyck, two Wasilla schoolteachers, were on Redington's side. They were excited and believed in the Iditarod and Joe Redington. The four of them—Joe and Vi, Johnson, and Huyck—became the officers when articles of incorporation were drawn up. Then they went to work seeking to make the impossible a reality.

Huyck remembers sitting at the Hotel Captain Cook in the fall of 1972 with Johnson and Redington after discussing holding a long Iditarod "some day." Feeling a sense of urgency, they concluded the coming March should be the time. It was Johnson, Huyck recalls, who said, "Not a better time than now."

In the beginning, the proposed race to Nome with the largest purse in history, was discussed in a quasi-private manner, and those who shied away may have muttered amongst themselves about Redington's lunacy. It was Redington himself, though, who raised the ante by going public. He announced his plan and his purse to the media. That merely provided a broader-based constituency to label him nuts.

"Fifty thousand dollars," said Redington. "It was unheard of. I figured it had to be a guaranteed purse. I wanted to make it the biggest purse in the world by far at that time."

Guaranteed? No wonder other mushing people ducked. After all, this was coming from the guy who nearly lost his homestead betting on the 1967 Centennial Race. Racing a thousand miles by dog team was unheard of, too. Of course Redington had never done it, but he believed in the ability of the dogs he'd worked with for nearly a quarter-century in Alaska. He'd mushed thirty-five miles at a stretch for a dozen days in a row. In 1956 he'd mushed from before daylight until after dark hauling supplies for men working on a trail survey in Skwentna. His pal Jake Butler took long trips in the Alaska Interior. In his heart Redington knew Alaska dogs were magnificent animals. Of course they could run a thousand miles.

People just had it stuck on the brain that the dogs couldn't race longer than twenty-five miles or so because that's all the Fur Rendezvous and North American asked of them. Some Eskimo elders, who had worked with dogs in the harsh northern environs all their lives, felt differently. They nodded their heads sagely and said to Redington, "I'll see you in Nome." Similarly, George Attla, maybe the greatest of sprint mushers, said that he, too, was told by Athabascan elders in Huslia that it could be done.

If Joe was the visionary, his flock of supporters was tiny to start with, though they were dedicated.

"I thought it could happen," said Johnson. "I really did. It was exciting starting something brand new that no one had done before. I thought if we stuck with it, it could happen."

Meetings were held at the Redingtons' home. Meetings were held at Johnson's home. Meetings were held at Huyck's home. And meetings were held in Anchorage. The phone lines burned up. The quartet felt it was they against the world, but the idea was to get the world on board. Inroads were made slowly as the word spread.

For every musher who thought a thousand-mile race was a fool's errand, another musher was intrigued. Ken Chase, from the Native village of Anvik, who raced in the 1973 Iditarod and in many since, relied on dogs to carry him along the trapline that he used to catch mink, otter, beaver, and other animals. One day, home from a trip, he turned on the radio and heard that Joe Redington was putting on a big race.

"I jumped up from the table and said, 'I'm going to go'!" said Chase. "I was excited."

Dick Mackey also saw the possibilities. Mackey grew up in New Hampshire and came to Alaska in 1958. Like Redington, he was enthralled by the Jack London stories he read. Summers, he served time as an iron-worker, a job that took him all over the state. Winters he mushed dogs on weekends when he could. When Redington told him what he was cooking up, Mackey said, "I'll be the second one to sign up." When Joe asked what he meant, Mackey replied, "Aren't you the first?"

As soon as it became known that he planned to race his dogs all the way to Nome, though, Mackey said he, like Redington, was harangued.

"People said, 'You're just throwing away the opportunity with your sprint team'," said Mackey. They felt running the dogs long miles would ruin his team. Mackey said he also spoke to Redington on the phone hour after hour. Always, he said, it was very late in the night, one or two o'clock in the morning, with Mackey in Wasilla and Redington in Knik.

Finally, the organizers obtained a central meeting place in Anchorage. The Ad Hoc Democratic Committee offered space in a place called "The Warehouse" on 15th Street. It was as much counterculture hangout as anything, dismissed and summarized as a commune, said Redington, a bunch of hippies. "Everybody hated them," he said.

When Redington showed up to explore the site he was greeted by a sign that read, "Don't Knock, Just Walk In." So he did. And standing right in front of him was a totally naked woman. She said hello. Joe said he must be in the wrong place. She said, no he wasn't, come right in.

"That's the kind of place it was," said Redington. But he was offered volunteer help, typing services, and telephone callers.

"They helped a lot, but they were a hell of a bunch," said Redington. Indeed, the word "colorful" seemed to apply. During one meeting the Iditarod group was chatting away when a half-dozen naked women ran through the room, chased by a group of men. When the apparition had passed, Redington asked what was going on. The answer? They had just come out of the sauna and were running outside to the jump in the snow.

"That interrupts a meeting," said Redington. It was not the only such occasion. At another meeting a naked woman began walking toward the group.

"Our eyes were riveted to this beautiful young creature going to the shower," Huyck said.

"My eyes were bulging out," Johnson said.

But Redington sat with his back to the beauty, oblivious. Finally, he realized nobody was paying attention to the issue at hand, and he turned around. The consensus of witnesses alleges that Redington's voice rose many octaves as his initially friendly "Hello" turned into "Hell-o-o-o." People rolled on the floor laughing.

"What business meeting?" said Johnson.

One day, Redington received a phone call from Governor Bill Egan asking if it was true that Iditarod organizers were meeting at The Warehouse. He apparently did not think it was so great for credibility. "I said, 'Not any more'," said Redington, who desperately wanted the support of the state's chief executive. Meetings were moved to the Gold Rush Hotel on Northern Lights Boulevard.

Dick Mackey said the governor was a real supporter and that was worthwhile.

"Dog mushing was already the unofficial state sport," said Mackey. "He stuck his neck out and said, 'This will be good for Alaska and it will go forward'."

Actually, in 1972, the Alaska Legislature took action, designating dog mushing as the official state sport.

Redington knew that the only way to make the race happen was to get solid backing in Nome, as well as in Anchorage. He set about finding a way to ensure that.

Howard Farley moved to Nome in 1959. For years, he had the only dog team in town. These days, just about anyone with a kennel tries to muster some kind of summer tourism business taking visitors for rides, but Farley has been doing that for the better part of four decades. Approaching seventy, Farley now gives rides to some five thousand tourists a season.

Farley's first-ever contact with Joe Redington predated the formation

Skwentna resident Joe Delia had long used a portion of the historic Iditarod Trail as his trapline when he joined the volunteer military personnel to help mark the 1973 race trail between Skwentna and Finger Lake.

of the Iditarod. Redington was working at a Unalakleet fish-processing plant, and one day Farley, a butcher, telephoned to place an order for some salmon. Redington answered. Farley said, "I know you." He recognized the name because of the 1967 and 1969 races. And Redington said, "You're that crazy guy who runs dogs up there in Nome in the summer."

A few years later, Redington wrote Farley a letter on "Iditarod Trail" stationery. The letterhead has pictures of the Alaska flag and of a musher racing a team. And beneath the "Iditarod Trail" marking is printed "International Championship Sled Dog Race, Anchorage to Nome, March 3, 1973. 1,000 miles—$50,000."

Dated December 9, 1972, the letter is the Magna Carta of the Iditarod Trail Sled Dog Race.

Handwritten, it read as follows: "Dear Howard: I thought you might be interested in this race. I need some help on that end. Let me know if you are interested. Also, I need to know how many teams will run such a race. I plan to enter and several others here in Knik plan it also. We have some teams already entered from the Lower Forty-eight. Can you get in touch with any of the nearby villages? Maybe radio. I would like to put you on our Iditarod Trail Committee. You could do a lot of good on the Nome end.

"Let me know how you feel about this as soon as you can.

"So Long for Now, Joe Sr."

Farley still has the original. A copy is mounted above a doorframe in the Nome store of Leo Rasmussen, a long-time Iditarod worker who later became president of the Iditarod Trail Committee.

Farley signed on and along with his wife, Julie, helped reconstitute the long-dormant Nome Kennel Club, which administered the old Sweepstakes races. He is very proud of that legacy. Farley too remembers huge numbers of midnight long-distance phone conversations with Redington. In fact, more than twenty-five years after the fact, he could still rattle off Redington's Knik phone number from memory.

One of Farley's achievements, besides ensuring that there would be a finish line and officials on hand to record times, was convincing the Chamber of Commerce that the race would be good for the town. He raised $1,200 to buy a first-rate trophy and awards for a race that was still on paper.

Redington wasn't having the same kind of luck in Anchorage. Banks turned him down. Businessmen turned him down.

They were galloping toward race time and rumors were hot among mushers that there was no money to pay for the guaranteed purse. Redington kept telling everyone the money would be there, but he was constantly challenged. Mushers George Attla and Jimmy Huntington were the most vociferous. They were also correct. There was no money for them.

"Right up until race time we didn't have a dime," said Redington.

Mackey said Iditarod supporters prepared for a mushers' rebellion. Local radio station operator Bob Fleming wrote out a $50,000 check, said Mackey.

"So if this question came up, Joe could hold up the check," he said. "It was a real check, but not a valid check."

It was never used. The money, however, still was needed.

Colonel Marvin "Muktuk" Marston stepped forward. Famed as the

Race organizers from 1973 recall that without the support and financial backing of old-time Alaskans like "Muktuk" Marston (pictured here), Frank Murkowski, and Bruce Kendall, the first Iditarod probably wouldn't have been launched.

man who formed the Alaska Territorial Guard, or Eskimo Scouts, during World War II, Marston was both a respected Anchorage businessman and as one might suspect of someone whose nickname stemmed from a whale-eating contest in a village, respected in the Bush. He publicly pledged $10,000 worth of land in the Spenard area of Anchorage toward the purse in the hopes that the gift would spur fundraising.

Marston's gesture was pivotal. A man with a booming voice, but regarded as a common-sense, down-to-earth man rather than flamboyant, Marston believed in old-time Alaska, the Alaska of dog teams and pioneers, homesteaders, and goldpanners.

In his autobiography, *Men of the Tundra*, Marston, who died in July 1980 at the age of ninety-one, wrote, "I was born and reared in the West. I have known frontier pioneer life. As a lad along Puget Sound I was perfectly at home on the water and in the mountains."

During his years assembling and monitoring the Alaska home guard, he traveled all over the Arctic by dog team.

"I used dogs for transporting supplies to the little villages along the Bering Sea, the Arctic Ocean, and up the great rivers," wrote Marston. "An average day's run is thirty-five to forty miles. I have made sixty-five miles in a long day's run with ten to fourteen dogs in a team."

If Muktuk Marston had been a younger man he likely would have been an entrant in a thousand-mile Iditarod.

"I had known him for years," said Redington. "He loved the dog races. He always made small donations to events, like a hundred dollars."

This time he committed a hundred times that much. *The Anchorage Times*, though, remained skeptical of a genuine payoff at the end. The newspaper sniffed a fiasco in the making and assigned first sportswriters, then a news reporter to shadow Redington and follow the status of fundraising. In the parlance of a more modern era, it was "Show me the money!"

Flip Todd, an Anchorage publisher, was the news reporter assigned to the story. The paper's perspective, he said, was "Does the money even exist?" Although many organizers kept telling him, "no problem, no problem," Todd was able to get at the truth—that the purse was not in the bank when the mushers left Anchorage.

Redington was annoyed, but tolerant of the media probing. It was Marston who blew up when he felt his donation of land was being ridiculed by some. "What are you going to do, give the mushers a square foot of land?" it was asked. Perhaps this wisecrack harkened back to the 1967 fundraising gimmick, but Marston didn't appreciate it.

So Marston told Redington to meet him in the Westward Hilton bar, which served food cafeteria-style. They walked in together, picked up some food, and deep in animated discussion, tried to eat. Redington was so distracted he had mashed potatoes and gravy spilling over the side of his plate and spilling onto his hands. Marston spied a young man at another table nearby. Mistaking him for a *Times* reporter, Marston marched up to him and yelled, "Look at this!" He waved a check in the air. It represented the $10,000 in lieu of the land. Then he ordered the young man to stand up and shake hands with Redington. Redington shook—with a hand slimy with gravy. The startled young man did so. The woman he was sitting with appeared scared. The guy never said a word, just complied with whatever he was asked to do, but he was not the reporter.

Then with a theatrical gesture, Marston handed the check to Redington. Only it was the wrong check. It was not for $10,000, but for $600 or so dollars.

"Made out to Standard Oil, or something like that," said Redington.

He paused, thinking of the innocent bystanders. "I always wondered what that man and woman thought."

Redington then pointed out the discrepancy in the checks and Marston produced the real one. A little later Marston bumped into the real reporter and shouted, "I showed you the wrong check!" The guy had no idea in the world what Marston was talking about.

However, even when Marston produced, it didn't solve all the problems. Much more money was still needed. One financier who helped out was Frank Murkowski. Then president of the Bank of the North, Murkowski is now one of Alaska's long-serving U.S. senators. He authorized a $20,000 loan.

Later, when the Iditarod became an established Alaska hit, Redington said Murkowski told him it was the best loan he ever made in the banking business.

One of Redington's fundraising plans was a goal of selling twelve thousand raffle tickets at a dollar apiece. He neglected to obtain a state permit, but Egan quietly rode to the rescue, making sure one was mailed to Redington with a note that said, "Here, I think you need this." Huyck said, "We wondered why we didn't go to jail."

The raffle ticket sales were not successful, though, and with the mushers poised to race, "We were really sweating it," Huyck said.

At least one deep-pockets businessman, though, did not want to see the Iditarod fail. Bruce Kendall, a former speaker of the Alaska House of Representatives, and owner of the old Roosevelt Hotel in downtown Anchorage, stepped up. Early on, Kendall made a financial pledge to Redington to use as security. He told Redington if he was short of funds that he, Kendall, would make up the difference. To deflect attention while he continued hustling for money, Redington told the media he had a businessman guaranteeing the purse. Kendall left for Hawaii.

When he returned, Redington told him he needed his support. Only when it came time to pay up, Kendall didn't have the cash handy. Redington said he twisted Kendall's arm a bit, told him he'd been counting on him. Kendall co-signed the loan with Redington for $30,000.

"He came through," said Redington. "He deserves a lot of credit."

One myth that grew up about the funding of this Iditarod race was that Redington nearly lost his homestead over it. That was not true and perhaps the circumstances have been confused with the danger his home was placed in after the 1967 race.

It was Kendall who wondered for a while if he was courting bankruptcy. Kendall moved to Alaska from Sioux City, Iowa, in 1939. He'd been a fur trader, prospector, worked on sternwheelers on the Tanana and Yukon Rivers and ran his hotel at Sixth and A Streets for twenty years. He worked for Alaska statehood in the 1950s and was proud of both old-time Alaska and developing Alaska.

"We were different," said Kendall, now in his eighties and residing most of the year in Palm Springs, California. "We felt it was 'My country.' I supported the Iditarod because I felt it would be a great thing for the tourist industry. People would come and see the grandeur and beauty of Mount McKinley. I thought it would inspire the towns and villages it went through. I could see a great publicity freebie for the state—and I was in the hotel business."

Kendall said he also believed in Joe Redington. The way Kendall saw it, Redington wasn't trying to make money, but to follow the spirit of the 1925 Serum Run. An Iditarod would revive that story. "His sincerity is unquestioned," said Kendall. "Then and now."

It took a couple of years, but Kendall dreamed up a way to get his money back. He sold thirty raffle tickets for a thousand dollars apiece and gave away a $15,000 prize. That brought in half the money. A year later he did something similar, selling five hundred raffle tickets at sixty dollars apiece to win $15,000. "I got it all back," said Kendall.

Among Marston, Murkowski, and Kendall, Joe Redington got his money, though not until after the mushers departed for Nome. At the time they quizzed Redington, all the doubters were right: He did not have the purse. But when Dick Wilmarth mushed down Front Street in Nome as the champion of the inaugural modern Iditarod, he was handed a $12,000 check. It did not bounce.

And Joee Redington did not have to change his name to John Paul Jones.

THE FIRST IDITAROD

—Joe Redington could only watch.
His idea. His race. Only he couldn't go.—

Robert and Owen Ivan, brothers from the Bethel area, traveled as a team
and finished sixteenth. Teams were permitted that first year of the Iditarod,
but never again. Only one other team started the race, but later split:
John Schultz and Casey Celusnik. Celusnik scratched and Schultz
earned the Red Lantern Award as last-place finisher.

The most forlorn guy on Anchorage's Tudor Road should have been the
happiest. As the dog teams raced away from Anchorage headed for
the unknown Joe Redington could only watch.

His idea. His race. Only he couldn't go.

On March 3, 1973, thirty-four dog teams galloped away from the
starting line toward Eagle River, Wasilla, Knik, and on to Nome. They
raced in the spirit of the Serum Run. They raced because people told

them a thousand miles couldn't be done. And they raced because they believed a thousand miles could be done.

Redington was the first one to sign up. He paid the hundred-dollar entry fee. He trained a team. The only problem was Redington couldn't afford to go. His race was short of money and his cohorts thought he was the only one who could save them from humiliation and disaster. Redington was the front man with the community. He was the only one who had a hope of raising the funds.

Tom Johnson and Gleo Huyck pleaded with Redington to stay in Anchorage because the organization was too unsettled. It was crucial to ensure that the money would be available, they argued. We need you, they said. When it came time to send food out on the trail to checkpoints, Redington did not send his packages. When it came time to start the race, Redington did send his dogs—with son Raymie.

"I wanted to go," said Redington. "I realized they did need me. It was a busy time."

So the loudest advocate, the truest believer in an Iditarod Trail Sled Dog Race, could not race. The guaranteed $50,000 purse haunted the organizers.

"I wasn't really worried," said Howard Farley, who traveled from Nome to Anchorage early, two weeks before the race. "People didn't trust Joe because this was outlandish. Joe was accused of chasing windmills. I believed he'd do it."

Farley followed Redington on his rounds as he hustled to pull details together. Redington, on his usual four hours of sleep a night, practically wore Farley out before the start. "It was incredible," remembered Farley.

Equally incredible, Farley thought, were those in the dog world who denigrated the race. Jimmy Huntington, victimized by the Fairbanks-to-Livengood race, complained there really wasn't any money. At a local sled dog association meeting, said Farley, "people were picking on us." Orville Lake, a great champion of the sport of mushing, who has a sprint race named after him, earned Farley's ire.

"He was going around saying, 'You'll go out and you'll fiddle around and be back'," said Farley. "He was real vocal about it. Those guys in Anchorage just didn't want it to rain on their parade."

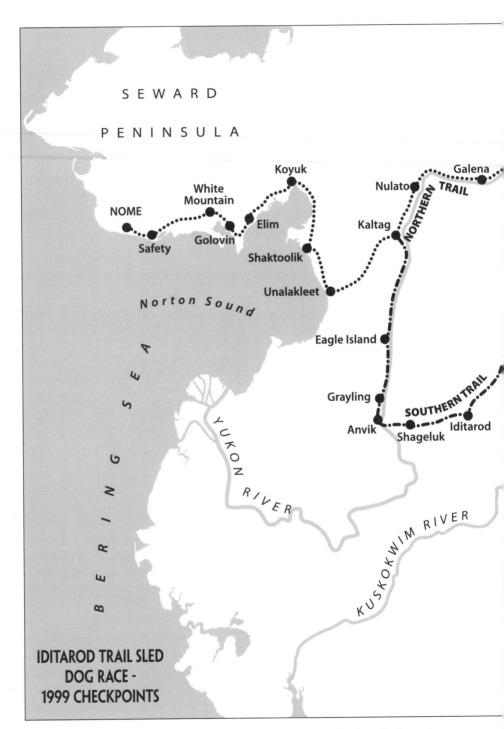

IDITAROD TRAIL SLED DOG RACE - 1999 CHECKPOINTS

Some say that compared to 1973, the trail today is a superhighway, but in reality it remains a challenging wilderness trek. The modern race route does not follow the historic trail

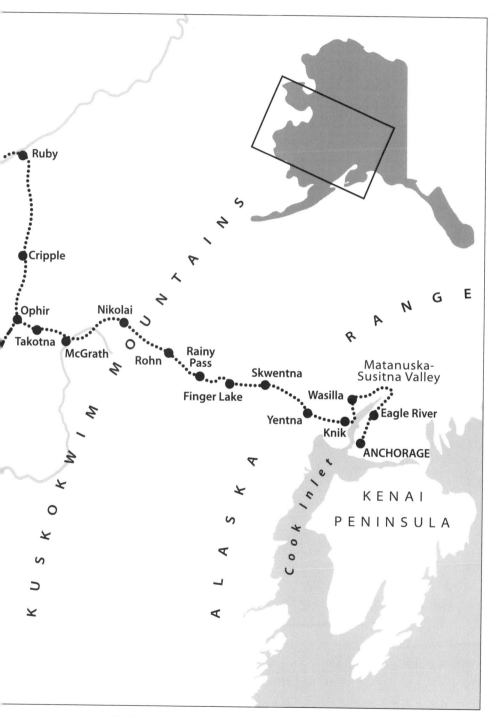

exactly, and it alternates annually between northern and southern routes to offer relief
from the crush of people who pass through the tiny checkpoint communities.

Maybe. Gareth Wright, to his credit, does not try to recast his views with the benefit of hindsight. He just flat-out didn't believe in long-distance mushing.

"Joe wanted me to back the race," said Wright. "I didn't want to back the Iditarod to begin with. I thought it would die out. I said it would never last."

True to his appreciation of history and admiration for his trail-user predecessors, Redington linked the Iditarod to the Serum Run. If no one remembered the days of the All-Alaska Sweepstakes, everyone recalled the Serum Run.

"The Serum Run is dog mushing's finest hour," said Farley.

In late January of 1925, Nome's Dr. Curtis Welch diagnosed children suffering from diphtheria. Instantly, he recognized that the disease would spread and decimate the population if life-saving antitoxin serum could not be obtained in huge quantities. Telegraph messages were sent to Fairbanks, Anchorage, Seward, and Juneau requesting aid. The only medicine in the state was stored at the Alaska Railroad Hospital in Anchorage. A supply of 300,000 units was available. But how could it be rushed to Nome?

No airplanes were handy. Scott Bone, the territorial governor at the time, ordered a relay of dog teams assembled. The vials of medicine were packaged into a twenty-pound bundle and began the journey north by train. The first of twenty mushers picked up the antitoxin at the station in Nenana, where it was fifty degrees below zero, and began mushing the six hundred and seventy-four miles to Nome in what really was a race against the clock.

Leonhard Seppala, considered the best of the mushers who volunteered, covered the lion's share of the distance, pushing his eighteen dogs, including his trusty leader Togo, some two hundred and sixty-eight miles of the way. However, it was Gunnar Kaasen, with a borrowed Seppala dog, Balto, in lead, who ended up hauling the medicine into Nome. Along the way, Kaasen had the heart-stopping experience of dropping the package in the snow. He searched frantically and blindly for it before recovering the medicine. Kaasen bypassed the last switchover spot where he was supposed to hand off the antitoxin to a fresher musher and team, because upon arrival at the place there was no apparent activity. So he plunged on.

The Serum Run was completed in five-plus days, and the event made worldwide headlines. All glory went to Kaasen and Balto, a forty-eight-pound brown Siberian husky with white forepaws, a development that irked Seppala. Later, a second shipment of 1.1 million units of antitoxin was sent to Nome and the epidemic was thwarted.

At the time of the 1973 Iditarod, the run was nearly fifty years in the past, but was still fresh in mushers' minds. If they were headed to Nome by dog team, how could it not be?

When mushers gathered on race day in Anchorage, the scene was gratifying. Until the mushers brought their trucks and dogs to town, it was impossible to tell how the public would respond. But a big crowd had gathered to cheer.

"Everybody spoofed the idea—until the race actually started," said Dick Mackey, who finished seventh in the event. "Everybody was just taken in by this. Nobody had seen big sleds and big teams. There was a sense of pioneering."

Even if Redington knew before the race actually began that he would not be going, few others did. Farley, who spent so much time with Joe in the days leading up to departure, didn't even notice his failure to mush out of Anchorage.

Leaving before the mushers was a team of thirteen Army trailbreakers from the 172nd Infantry Brigade, under the direction of Captain Harry Lockhart. The week before the first Iditarod began, a Chinook helicopter landed and disgorged ten snowmachines in Knik. They were white machines, for camouflage, and their coloring provided the official excuse to help out.

Redington said he was sure he heard a general tell the junior officer if he didn't get to Nome, not to come back. The Army was ostensibly testing the reliability of its snowmachines, but in reality, was just helping Joe.

At the starting line hung a yellow banner with black letters reading, "Iditarod Trail Race." Anyone who looked closely at the other side would find the words, "Welcome to Nome." The Iditarod certainly was a low budget operation that year. It couldn't even afford two banners.

The racers left Tudor Track, ironically enough the site of major sprint

The starting line of the first Iditarod long-distance race
was off Tudor Road in midtown Anchorage. As Dick

Mackey remembers it, the mushers had more confidence
in making it to Nome than did those they left behind.

races, and drove their teams north. First significant stop? Knik, Joe's home.

"I pulled up on Knik Lake there and he had all this dog food in his yard," said Farley. "Then I finally figured he wasn't going. He wanted to be in that race really bad."

Joe said he still feels badly that he missed out because of the historic nature of the first Iditarod. Vi said she too felt badly that Joe didn't race. Others bluntly state that if Redington had competed, the race would have sunk. Unspoken is the conclusion that it was a worthy tradeoff. The thing of it was, Redington really was in the race. If he couldn't mush it he surely could run it, and once the purse was secured he jumped in his plane and flew down the trail, trying to do everything at once and be everywhere as super race overseer.

The original Iditarod felt its way along the trail. Mushers did not know their dogs' capabilities, they did not have sophisticated equipment, they had little experience mushing at night, and the trail was poorly marked and quite rugged.

Robert Service's famous poem about life in the North commented on the strange things that occur under the midnight sun. But peculiar things always happen on the Iditarod Trail. Farley mushed out of Knik with Dr. Harold Bartko, who had delivered his twin girls. He pulled his team over at the Little Su River, twenty or more miles from Knik, to make camp and Bartko came in right behind him. Bartko wore green mukluks with five sets of insoles, but they were not protecting his feet.

"Howard," he said, "my feet are cold."

Cold feet are ruinous in the wilderness. If your feet are cold the rest of you shivers. Merely a glance at Bartko's feet told Farley that his friend needed better gear. Bunny boots, the outrageously plain, rubberized boots that were the stuff of legend, would save Bartko grief, he felt.

While they were parked on the Little Su, Knik musher Dave Olson rolled in. He looked flushed, sick. Dr. Bartko hauled out his black bag, examined Olson, and proclaimed, "You've got pneumonia!"

Bartko ordered Olson to give up the race, but he also placed an order for Redington. When Olson returned home, he was supposed to tell Redington, "Doc needs a pair of bunny boots."

Farley and Bartko mushed on to Finger Lake, arriving in the fog.

In 1973, the same banner was used at the start and finish lines. "We were so poor," Joe remembers. One side of the banner read "Starting Line," the other, "Welcome to Nome." A packet of berry-colored Kool-Aid was sprinkled across the snow for the line itself. Within a couple of years, Red Olson of Fox, Alaska, had created a carved wooden arch made of burled wood to mark the finish line.

Through the mists they heard the engine of a small plane. They parked their teams. The sound ceased and they saw a plane resting on a space the size of a tennis court. And then Redington appeared.

"Here's Doc's bunny boots," he said. Farley still can't get over how Redington even found them. Redington became the ace of the skies during the race, buzzing back and forth along the trail, swooping down where needed.

Poor Raymie, the late stand-in for dad. Given his lack of preparation, it made little sense that he even start the race, but at the same time perfect sense that he did because there just had to be a Redington out there.

"It was tough," said Raymie. "I had a week's notice that I was going. Nothing was flown out for me on the trail ahead of time. Dad was going to fly stuff out. I scrounged around."

Terry Adkins was the first Iditarod veterinarian and showed his

authority when he yanked a dog from a team on the starting line because it had been in a fight and had an open sore right where the harness was going to rub it. Adkins, who heard of the Iditarod startup because he was an Air Force man stationed at Elmendorf Air Force Base, autopsied

Dick Mackey crosses the finish line at Nome, placing seventh in a field of twenty-two finishers.

dead dogs, sewed up dogs that needed stitches and even sewed up Tom
Mercer, a musher with a problem who later finished eighteenth.

Adkins flew with Redington at the start of the race. Raymie's entire food supply at that point, said Adkins, was a dozen hard-boiled eggs. Another observer said Raymie carried only candy bars and cigarettes.

After the mushers were underway, said Adkins, he and Joe dropped a bag of Purina dog food to Raymie from the air. It contained Raymie's false teeth.

"We almost hit him with it," said Adkins.

Redington's flying sharpened Adkins' attention more than once. Leaving Knik, they flew at treetop level. Leaving Susitna Station, Redington flipped the plane upside-down, landing in deep snow. Adkins flew with Art Peterson the rest of the race.

"It got more interesting with Art than it did with Joe," said Adkins.

As the race was drawing to a close after nearly three weeks, the men took off from White Mountain, about seventy-seven miles from the finish line in Nome. They flew directly into violent weather blowing in off the Bering Sea and were forced to turn back. Grounded by the bad weather, they spent the night in White Mountain.

The next day, determined to see the finish of the race, Peterson and Adkins set out once again. And once again horrible weather shut them down, this time at Cape Nome. But instead of gliding to a halt, they glided all the way into Front Street on the trail, about twelve miles. "It's the longest airplane taxi ride I ever took," said Adkins.

They were too late to see the first six finishers. They showed up just in time for Mackey to mush down the street in front of cheering fans, and Adkins got a picture.

When he settled down in the finish, Adkins discovered he had no place to sleep. Eventually, he was offered a choice of two roommates, Joe Redington, race organizer, or Bill Egan, governor.

"I can say I slept with the governor," said Adkins. "I knew how Joe snored."

Captivated by the race, Adkins entered the next year after he'd been discharged from the service and moved to Montana. Adkins, a poker-playing, whiskey-sipping storyteller kept on coming back, too, racing more than twenty times.

All of the aggravation of making the Iditarod happen was forgotten as soon as mushers hit the trail. Then it became a grand adventure, a history-making event that spawned a repertoire of trail tales.

Bill Cotter, many years later a regular top-ten Iditarod finisher, was then a schoolteacher friend of Johnson's and Huyck's. They introduced him to Redington. Cotter makes it sound as if listening to Redington talk about mushing is akin to religious conversion.

"That was the end of my life as I know it," said Cotter. "He was just so charismatic. He was an evangelist for the sport." Cotter became the checker at the first checkpoint in the first Iditarod. And he was further smitten by the race.

"It just blew my socks off, all these teams coming in," said Cotter, who lives in Nenana, the site of the start of the Serum Run. "It was such a scene, exciting, different. I decided to do it."

Bud Smyth, who ended up twelfth, smashed up his sled in Knik and had to stop and build a new one. When Redington saw Smyth mushing into Susitna Station steam was pouring out of his sled. "Are you on fire?" Redington asked. Nope, said Smyth. He was cooking his dog food on the fly.

Since no one had ever raced anything of comparable distance, there was much experimentation. The only dog food readily available was designed for pets that hung around the house. But these dogs were burning up thousands of calories a day. Many Native mushers who had worked dogs in the Bush cooked up their own recipes, or improvised as they went. Outside of Rohn, Herbie Nayokpuk and Isaac Okleasik shot a moose and quartered it. They had meat for dinner.

Ken Chase of Anvik, the musher who leapt at the chance to enter the moment he heard about the Iditarod on the radio, placed thirteenth. He said watching mushers experiment with feeding was fascinating.

"Everyone had their own secret formula," said Chase, who used dried fish and beaver to fuel his dogs.

The Ivan brothers, Robert and Owen, from the Bethel area, baled dry fish, perhaps a hundred fish together, and carried five-gallon cans of Blazo. As Cotter put it, "They were going to be able to cook fish and light fires."

This was the only year in Iditarod history that teammates were allowed. The image of the Iditarod and its legendary challenge is one musher against the elements. However, in 1973, it was permitted to enter as duos with one sled. Redington said the initial idea was to encourage husband-and-wife teams to go together. The women were smarter than the men were, he said, and stayed home.

Two doubles teams entered: the Ivan brothers, and John Schultz and Casey Celusnik. The Ivans placed sixteenth.

"It was a hell of a deal," said Redington of the Ivans' circumstances. "It was a little, tiny sled and they had to carry the gear for two people." They looked like they were going out for a simple ride.

In an interesting development, Celusnik scratched, but Schultz continued. It took Schultz more than thirty-two days to finish, which brought him into Nome last and the claimant to the first Red Lantern award.

Posting a red lantern was already a tradition in mushing events for the last-place finisher. The Fur Rondy had one. In the mid-1950s, young Joee Redington won a red lantern in a junior sprint-mushing race. A decade later he was world open champion. The red lantern was a symbolic guide for the last musher in, a we'll-leave-the-light-on-for-you, caring message.

Getting to Nome at all has been an achievement that first year, and ever since. Raymie dropped out in Galena, unsafely clothed for fifty below zero, and unable to feed himself as he mushed. His was one of twelve teams scratched before the finish.

Again ill prepared for lack of experience, many mushers were halted or slowed because of their dogs' foot problems. Nayokpuk and Okleasik, the wise Native mushers, had dog booties made of sealskin. Few others had booties of any kind. The dogs' feet suffered worse than Doc Bartko's. Mackey bought cotton socks at a store in McGrath and taped them on his dogs' feet.

The feeling-out process meant that even though the Iditarod was a race with prize money, the event proceeded slowly. Now, high-quality headlamps make mushing by night almost as easy as mushing by daylight. Then, darkness meant pulling off the highway to look for the nearest motel. And since there were no such lodgings, groups camped together.

"It's five o'clock and getting dark," said Mackey of the way mushers thought. "We'd better find a place to camp." Dogs bedded down, a half-dozen mushers built fires together and cooked. They were competitors,

ANCHORAGE DAILY NEWS

Dick Wilmarth won the inaugural Iditarod in twenty days, forty-nine minutes, forty-one seconds. At the Nome Awards Banquet that followed, Orville Lake, right, offered the winner's check for $12,000 while Joe presented the champion's trophy.

sure, but more than anything else there was a feeling of a shared adventure. This was how Redington and Nayokpuk became such respectful pals. But they were hardly alone in developing shared comradeship. Such relationships bringing diverse people together from diverse parts of the vast state, began on the first Iditarod.

"We made lifetime friends because everybody camped," said Mackey.

Redington himself didn't have the slightest notion how long such a race would take to finish. It was merely prudent behavior for racers to be cautious.

"It was like taking a long trip," said Joe. "We'd wait until first light to go. Nobody got in a hurry until they got to Unalakleet." That was less than three hundred miles from the finish.

Dick Wilmarth, a miner from Red Devil, won the inaugural Iditarod in twenty days, forty-nine minutes, forty-one seconds. Bobby Vent of Huslia placed second. Dan Seavey of Seward, one of Redington's staunchest backers, and a man who donated much of his winning share of $6,000 back to the race, was third. Attla finished fourth, Nayokpuk fifth, and Okleasik sixth.

"I enjoyed the camping out," said Attla. "It was kind of fun mushing into the villages with a dog team. It was almost like turning the clock back."

Perhaps no one had as much fun during the first Iditarod as Farley. For all those years he had been mushing his dogs virtually in a vacuum. He had little company or support in Nome, and yet he enthusiastically backed the race from the first moment Redington approached him. Not only did Farley and his wife play critical roles in setting up the finish-line area and rejuvenating the Nome Kennel Club, but in the Iditarod he was surrounded by kindred spirits on the trail.

Farley was a slowpoke. Not a lonely slowpoke, but a musher at the back of the pack. He and others were way back in Ruby, on the Yukon River some five hundred miles from Nome, when Wilmarth finished. They were listening on the radio and said, "My God, this thing is over." But these mushers were mostly from small villages and they signed up to do a race and meant to complete it.

Farley was last coming into the village of Galena. When he went searching for his dog food at a bar, people laughed at him, saying, "I thought that race was over two weeks ago." His food was gone. However, he bumped into Roger Huntington of the famed mushing Huntington family. Roger had gone to school with Farley's brother-in-law, so he took him home, cooked him a steak and let him use the shower and a bed. Then Farley traded his extra-long, heavy freight sled for a racing sled, and ultimately mushed away on a full stomach filled with a hot breakfast.

Farley caught up with other mushers and finished in the midst of the back group, or twentieth of the twenty-two overall finishers. It took Farley more than thirty-one days on the Iditarod Trail to reach Nome. More than a month! Now the top racers finish in nine days and change.

Not that Farley regrets a moment of his journey. When he finished, reaching the main street of his hometown, Farley was greeted by tumultuous applause. Spectators and friends hoisted him on their shoulders and carried him down the street. Only when they put him down, timer Pam Randles whispered to Farley, "You're not over the finish line."

He got his dogs across the line and the glow of that scene has never

HOWARD FARLEY

At center, Joe joins a few finishers of the 1973 Iditarod to toast the birth of a brand-new race.

receded. Farley never raced from Anchorage to Nome again, but he got a lifetime of stories out of his one run over the Iditarod Trail.

At the finish-line banquet in a hotel function room, the atmosphere was electric. They had done it! *Showed those doubters a thing or two, didn't we? Alaskan dogs can too mush a thousand miles.*

Wilmarth was presented a trophy that seemed as tall as a Christmas tree. He got the winner's check, too, as promised, and everyone else in the top twenty got paid. Even Farley, last man in the money, collected five hundred dollars.

When Joe Redington stood up in front of the crowd, he did so this time not as the purveyor of a half-baked idea, but as the proud papa of a great Alaskan adventure. He shouted out his heartfelt feeling in the form of a question: *Does anybody want to do it again next year?*

The answer was a roar. In the space of a month, the Iditarod Trail Sled Dog Race had progressed from the dream of one visionary man to a happening that touched the lives of many. Now when Joe Redington talked about the Iditarod Trail, everyone knew what he was talking about.

NO RACE FOR SISSIES

*—This race is the most grueling contest
in the world, said "Muktuk" Marston.—*

JEFF SCHULTZ/ALASKA STOCK

**Artist Bill Devine is credited with designing the Iditarod logo that has
become so familiar all over the world. A long-time friend of the Redingtons,
Devine often painted Joe's dog trucks and sleds. His ideas for marketing the
Iditarod helped keep the race in the public eye.**

■

Just try to hold him back this time. Joe Redington was going to Nome
and he wasn't planning to fly. In 1973, Redington was determined that
there would be an Iditarod Trail Sled Dog Race. In 1974, he was determined to be *in* an Iditarod Trail Sled Dog Race.

The mood was different. An abstract concept—*Could men mush dogs a
thousand miles?*—was supported by empirical evidence. The skeptics were

134

squashed. Financiers who wouldn't take Redington's phone calls the first time wanted to sponsor the second race.

Not that raising a purse was a snap. The first-place payout was equal to the $12,000 of 1973, but it thinned out after that. Twentieth place paid only $196. But there was no griping about money. The Iditarod had an image now.

At the kickoff banquet for the 1974 Iditarod, venerable Muktuk Marston summarized what the event was all about. "This race is the most grueling contest in the world," said Marston. "It's the age-old desire to pit yourself against the elements and win."

Mushers named Redington were everywhere. Not only was Joe signed up this time, but Raymie and Joee also had their own teams. Just like the Fur Rendezvous. They all had their own dogs trained to race.

On race day, forty-three mushers lined up to run. There were veterans now, experienced trail hands of the first Iditarod back for more. Men like Herbie Nayokpuk, Dan Seavey, Ken Chase, and Dick Mackey were emotionally connected to the race. Other mushers with impressive resumes showed up, too, like Carl Huntington and Warner Vent. And women, too: Mary Shields and Lolly Medley became the first women to race—and finish—the Iditarod.

Seasoned Joe Redington was headed out on the trail he loved, the trail he mushed whenever he could since 1948. But most of it was a trail he'd actually never raced on, and he packed his sled as if headed not to Nome, but to Antarctica. He had the gear and provisions of a man sent on a mission to rescue a platoon rather than a man traveling light in order to win a race. The joke about Redington was that he not only carried the kitchen sink beneath the tarp of his sled bag, but the pipes, the flooring, and the stove from the same kitchen, too.

"I took off out of there and I must have had two hundred and fifty pounds of stuff," said Redington. Streamlined he was not. You would never catch Joe Redington unawares or ill-prepared in the wilderness. It's just that he might never catch a faster team with that kind of poundage. At Susitna Station, about forty miles beyond Knik, Redington began pitching excess equipment overboard as if he were traveling on a ship taking on water. He likely unloaded a hundred pounds of gear. Still, the

pattern was set. Throughout his mushing career, Redington was known as a guy who toted a lot of luggage. "I never did learn to cut down," he said much later.

Mushers were still trying to figure out the best feed for their dogs. Joe froze a mixture of fish, beaver and lamb with high protein supplement into big blocks. Big mistake.

The 1974 race was Joe's first Iditarod. "About six of us traveled together, and that's somewhere between Koyuk and Elim," Joe says.

"It was too hard to thaw out and the water weight in it made it heavy," he said. "It was not efficient carrying."

Redington and his neighbor Dave Olson concocted a mix of beef and lamb, another miscalculation. The dogs didn't appreciate the taste. Whitefish, though, that was a tasty snack food the dogs loved. Redington kept that perpetual favorite on the menu year after year.

When novice mushers or fans who do not know Iditarod history compare the slow times of early race days against the speed-demon times recorded now, they do so because they are ignorant of one critical fact: The trail is an interstate highway now compared to the 1970s. Picture a neighborhood street buried under five feet of fresh snow after a blizzard, with lanes blocked by fallen trees. That was the Iditarod Trail in the early 1970s. The only way mushers even advanced very far down the trail in 1973 was through the generosity of that United States Army group. The second year, however, snowmachines were at a premium. Often the trail was snowed under. Redington remembers traveling in a group of six mushers between the villages of Kaltag and Unalakleet and taking turns snowshoeing to break trail.

Earlier in the race, severe cold was an issue. Dogs do not like to run when it gets to be thirty degrees above zero. It may still be below freezing for humans, but it's too warm for them. They do love to run when it's well below zero. But there are limits. Even the tough dogs and tough guys who mush the Iditarod can be halted by extreme, overpowering cold, the type that makes exhaled breath freeze in mid-air.

Joe fell behind Raymie and Joee, and sought to catch up with them. In the harsh cold of fifty degrees below zero with a forty-eight mph wind, a stop at the Rainy Pass Lodge was tempting. But the others were beyond that point, so Redington kept going.

Someone at the weather station at Rainy Pass told the press that the chill factor was a hundred and thirty degrees below zero. Right about that time, Redington was passing a camped George Attla and Tim White. Cold or not, on he went, anyway, to Hell's Gate, outside of Rohn.

"I stopped and snacked the dogs," said Redington, who had been mushing all night. "I stopped because the dogs wouldn't run into the wind. I couldn't hold the trail."

He was working so hard that he was sweating at a hundred and thirty below. He climbed into his sleeping bag, boots and all. Redington rose when he saw Tim White mushing toward him, and he asked how long

White had been going. Fifteen minutes was the reply. Fifteen minutes! That meant Redington had mushed in circles most of the night.

The frigid cold snap hung on day after day for ten days and more. The mercury barely budged. It stayed at minus fifty all the way to Ruby on the Yukon.

"Fifty below really slows you down," said Redington. "I don't enjoy it. You keep going, so you use a lot of layers. I wore bunny boots, but when it gets to forty or fifty below, you've got cold feet anyway. It's hard on the dogs, too, hard on their feet."

Not many human beings experience fifty-below weather, and fewer still actually try to accomplish anything outdoors when it's that chilly.

Within the first few hundred miles of the race, Redington went through four hundred dog booties. Experience and better knowledge mean mushers might carry two thousand booties when they start the race now. By McGrath, about four hundred miles from the start, most mushers ran out of booties. An appeal went out and people in Anchorage sewed booties and shipped them up the trail.

"They made them out of every darned thing," said Redington. Even denim. Denim booties were good for about ten miles of loping before the dogs' feet worked through them. In Unalakleet, some blankets were discovered at an old reindeer camp, and they were cut up for booties. Of course, Redington had a sewing kit with him. Just in case.

Eventually, Joe did make up the ground between himself and the other Redingtons. It was a rare Iditarod for Joee, who wanted to try it, but then preferred to stick with sprint mushing as a specialty.

"I liked it a lot," said Joee. "It was great, but my dad was in it and my brother was in it, and it's hard to do both. I didn't want to see us give up sprint mushing. We had so much invested in it."

Redington learned first-hand how villagers warmed to the race passing through their hometowns when he ran low on fat supplies for his dogs. Good intentions, however, almost cost him his race. An Eskimo man threw some bearded seal to Joe's dogs and they swallowed it hungrily. Sounded like a good idea. Only about ten seconds later, they regurgitated it. It was too rich.

"What the hell did you do to me?" he asked. Nothing serious, it turned out. The dogs got over it quickly. The villagers fed the mushers, too, and friendships formed.

"You'd go in and they'd cook up a caribou steak and have a bed for you," said Redington. "You'd do some visiting and everyone would enjoy it. Everybody you stayed with was expecting you to stay with them again."

Indeed, mushers became regulars, for years staying with the same families until the rules changed, prohibiting it.

In Unalakleet, another system was used. The villagers drew lots to see which musher stayed with which family. "It brought people together," said Redington. "They'd come out and help you. They'd help you come in. They'd help you leave. They were part of the race."

Absolutely. That was a lure. Once a year this circus rolled through town, put up a tent, put on a show and rolled on. The people loved it right from the start.

Just when it seemed the brutal cold would last forever in 1974, the weather broke and the temperature shot up. By the time mushers reached White Mountain, close to the end, it was a stunning forty degrees above zero, a shift of ninety degrees on the thermometer. The sun was blinding. Creeks, frozen as solidly as asphalt roads only days before, were running wide open. Redington's dogs balked at one crossing of open water. He had to step in the water over his boot tops to tug the leaders forward. When they leapt ahead, Redington fell backward in a sort of slow motion, sitting right down in the creek. He was never able to get dry again. At fifty below, that would have been instantly life threatening. At forty above, he muddled through.

When Redington mushed into Nome, spectators lined Front Street and gave him a memorable and heartwarming reception. A real big welcome, he called it. Oh yes, when he mushed across the finish line, Redington could tell immediately how far the race had progressed. The Iditarod now owned a separate, distinct finish-line sign. The race somehow accumulated the wealth to acquire two banners. Raymie finished seventh, Joee ninth, and Joe eleventh that year.

"Three Redingtons, I was proud of that," said Joe. "I thought that was pretty good."

The race winner was Carl Huntington, "one hell of a dog musher," in the estimation of Joe Redington. It took Huntington twenty days and fifteen hours to reach Nome, a little longer than it took Wilmarth the year before. Huntington remains the only musher to win both the Iditarod and the Fur Rendezvous world championship. Not to mention the North American crown.

Huntington was a pretty tough guy. During the Iditarod he suffered an injury and a helicopter flew out to rescue him. But he said, "Hell, no, I'm in a race." He stuck it out and won.

When they finished, Joe might have thought there would be other times when three Redingtons—or even more with Tim—mushed the Iditarod simultaneously, but it never happened. Joee went his way and Raymie did not pursue Iditarod racing as avidly as his father. He skipped years, then entered again when he got the urge.

"I ain't done well at all," said Raymie, looking back on his sporadic Iditarod career, "but I'm still wanting to do it again. There are some challenges that make you want to do them again. You finish and think how hard it was and then a week later you want to do it again."

Raymie was far from the only musher to be consumed by Iditarod fever. Ken Chase, the Anvik musher, was back for more in 1974, and he was in the Redington bunch mushing toward Unalakleet when blowing snow and descending darkness obliterated the trail. Only short distances separated the three Redingtons, Dick Mackey, Ron Aldrich, and Chase. Chase thought it prudent to pull over and make camp. Within an hour, all of the teams were bunched up.

Joee turned around and saw Chase coming, though, and said, "Boy, am I glad to see you." Chase owned a dog named Piper in lead, and Joee said, "We hear a lot about your leader, let's see what he can do."

Chase gave the dog his head, and sure enough Piper dashed right between the other teams and sniffed out the trail. Chase pulled out and the others followed.

Not everyone on the trail was as experienced as Chase or the Redingtons. Terry Adkins, seduced by the Iditarod as veterinarian the year before, was a musher this time.

"I thought it looked like fun," he said. "I figured if some of these others can do it, so can I."

Adkins bought one dog for a hundred dollars and another for twenty-five. Then he borrowed a one-eyed dog he'd done surgery on and borrowed another he had treated. The rest of his twelve-dog team he picked out at the dog pound in Anchorage. He didn't go fast, taking more than twenty-seven days to reach Nome, but he got there in nineteenth place, and he finished with every dog.

"Joe's idea started it," said Adkins. "He's been an inspiration to everyone who's run it."

Another who tried the Iditarod that year, but scratched, was Tom Johnson, who like Redington was so busy the year before, he couldn't find the time to train.

Gleo Huyck never got closer to the race than organizational meetings, though in his heart he ached to race: "I was tempted," he said years later. "I just couldn't afford to go."

Redington feels badly that the critical roles Johnson and Huyck played in getting the Iditarod started are often overlooked.

"Tom Johnson was willing to put up his eighty-acre homestead for security," said Redington. "Gleo Huyck was on the verge of a nervous breakdown when the race finally got going. People don't know, or ever heard of them. They promised me they'd stick with me and they did. I think maybe they should get some kind of founder's award."

Proud of their own efforts and never begrudging of the attention lavished on Redington for his, Johnson and Huyck have receded into history. Even by the second year, new blood was infused into the Iditarod Trail Committee.

Bill Devine, a retired military man, listened to the first Iditarod on the radio and felt like a witness to history. "What a great race!" he thought. He also read the newspaper stories and heard the talk that this Joe Redington guy and a few others operated this thing on a shoestring. So some time after the first race ended, he went to Knik and met Redington. He told Redington something he well knew: "If you guys are going to do this again, you're going to need some help."

Redington, as his habit, immediately showed Devine his dogs, explaining this one was a leader, that one a wheel dog. But he had the wrong man. Devine didn't know what the hell he was talking about. He

RICHARD BURMEISTER

In 1974, Joe was able to enter the race that he founded the previous year. At fifty-seven years old, he trotted down Nome's Front Street en route to an eleventh-place finish. His sons, Raymie and Joee, finished seventh and ninth, respectively.

didn't plan to mush the Iditarod, he was volunteering some of his life experience, some accumulated in Korea, some in Vietnam, and some at Elmendorf Air Force Base. The message came across—here was a guy with a sharp mind, artistic talent, and photographic expertise.

Joe Sr. takes the platform at the Nome finish line after his arrival in the 1974 race. From left are Howard Farley, Joee Redington, Raymie Redington, and Doris Lake.

"They would welcome anybody," said Devine. "I didn't know anything about dog mushers." Soon, Devine, who took a job as a commercial artist, created an Iditarod logo. The design was stamped on the Iditarod mail, the cachets mushers haul in their sled during the race emulating the old mail carriers of the trail, and it was stamped on the famous red, white and blue shields that symbolize trail markers.

Year after year Devine made black-and-white pencil portraits of Iditarod winners, then presented the drawings to the champs the following March. In turn, the winners donated the pictures to the mushers Hall of Fame in Knik, where they still hang.

Devine was ahead of his time in envisioning Iditarod marketing. Once chosen to serve on the Iditarod Trail Committee board of directors he lobbied for the development of race souvenirs. A thriving, lucrative practice now, Devine initially couldn't get anyone to see it was a great idea.

"I just couldn't convince them you're going to make good money," said Devine, who became one of Redington's best friends. However, Redington, always looking ahead, did back the souvenir idea when others failed to see its merits.

"Joe was always a believer in it," said Devine. "He would say, 'Let's make Iditarod Christmas tree bulbs,' if he thought it would work. Joe is a promoter. That's why he goes to everything and shakes hands. You've got to get your name out there. Joe knew that right from day one. We've got to get out there and kiss babies and shake hands. He never gave up. It wasn't, 'If the SOBs don't want it, let somebody else do it.' I never heard him say that."

What Redington did do in his Iditarod Trail Committee capacity was listen to suggestions. Then if he thought the idea had a prayer of working, he put that person in charge of making it happen. Devine did eventually take charge of marketing and made the first souvenirs, buttons, and pins.

For the 1974 race, Devine also set up a table at the Hilton hotel, as a sort of public headquarters. Maps were posted and fans followed the progress of the race. The same procedure remains an important tradition and informational format for the race today.

At that very first meeting in Redington's dog yard, Devine was swept up in the race founder's enthusiasm. Over time, as he got to know Redington better, his respect for the man's commitment to the Iditarod increased steadily. It reached a point that no matter how far-fetched an idea sounded, if Redington proposed it, Devine believed it would happen.

"If he said he was going to climb the Empire State Building with a dog team straight up on the hottest day in July, I'd believe him," said Devine.

Redington had pretty much made believers out of Alaskans by the end of the second Iditarod. In 1974, the state House of Representatives passed a resolution congratulating all the participants. The mushers, the resolution said, "demonstrated that they are indeed men and women of great ability and possess characteristics that enable them to persevere under the most adverse conditions."

They got that right.

13

THE INFECTIOUS IDITAROD BUG

*—If you were interested in the Iditarod,
you were a friend of Joe Redington's.—*

Through the years, Joe's kennel has held championship bloodlines,
but one dog in particular stands out in his mind: Roamer, pictured here
with Joe in 1974. "Probably the best dog I ever had," he remembers.
Roamer sired Candy, who ran in seventeen Iditarods.

■

Not long after the 1973 Iditarod Trail Sled Dog Race made its debut, an
article about the event appeared in a mushing magazine called *Team and
Trail*. A young outdoorsman named Rick Swenson, who was living in rural
Minnesota, avidly read the publication.

Swenson may or may not have been born in the wrong era, but he most definitely was born in the wrong place. He was an Alaskan to the core. Growing up, he lived next door to a trapper, and he barraged the man with questions about living close to the land and about the way things used to be done. The man encouraged him and also gave him books to read. Those books contained stories about the All-Alaska Sweepstakes, and Swenson became the one-in-a-million kid not only captivated by the adventures therein, but also determined to relive them, or at least approximate them. His heroes were Iron Man Johnson, Leonhard Seppala and Scotty Allan, not the typical role models of choice during the 1960s when counterculture, anti-hero hippies, and rebellious musicians gained a foothold in the psyche of America's youth.

When Swenson, then in his early twenties, read the magazine article, he was jazzed. He was involved in skijoring, but long distance mushing sounded more challenging, more demanding, more thrilling.

"I thought, 'That's the deal for me'," he said years later. "It talked about the Iditarod and mentioned this guy named Joe Redington, Sr. I didn't know a soul in Alaska. The Iditarod forced me to come to Alaska."

Immediately he wrote a letter to Redington, introducing himself. He informed Redington that he planned to move to Alaska and as soon as he got to the state he would look him up.

Sure enough, months later, Swenson showed up at Redington's Knik homestead. Redington showed him around.

"He bought some dogs from me," said Redington.

Yes he did. Swenson ended up with a great group of dogs from Redington's dog lot. One of them, Nugget, was a star, and became the cornerstone of a kennel that produced Andy, the dog that became his super leader when Swenson won his first four Iditarods in 1977, 1979, 1981, and 1982.

"It was just luck, because I didn't know what I was doing," said Swenson. What Swenson learned and what became apparent to the entire world, eventually, was that if you were interested in dog mushing, and particularly if you were interested in the Iditarod, you were a friend of Joe Redington's. It didn't matter if he knew you. It didn't matter if he had never heard of you. He welcomed you into his home, to his dog lot. He

PHOTO COURTESY RICK SWENSON

In 1972, Rick Swenson was a Minnesota teenager with a hankering for adventure. After reading some of the same books that Joe Redington had read as a youngster, Swenson was bound for Alaska.

dispensed free advice and he was willing to sell you huskies to get you started. You might become the winningest Iditarod musher of all time, as Swenson did after he settled in first Manley, then Two Rivers. Or you might simply want to try the Iditarod once. Redington treated everyone the same, encouraged everyone enthusiastically.

"It's Joe's personality," said Swenson, "that no matter how swamped he is with stuff, he's always got time for people. I know that for sure he shared his knowledge and wisdom with me."

Redington's passion for mushing and the Iditarod was of paramount importance in his life. Dogs, dogs, and more dogs.

The Redington home off Knik-Goose Bay Road is surrounded by several storage buildings. Several vehicles that have seen better and more active days are parked in the yard. His hundreds of dogs are staked on their chains. As a visitor enters the long, dirt drive, a posted red, white and blue shield, the Iditarod symbol, offers greetings. It says, "Iditarod Trail, Alaska." Under that is a horizontal sign, black and yellow, with white letters, reading, "Joe Redington, Sr., Husky Haven."

There is also a sign above a doorway in Redington's living room reading, "Joe Redington Sled Dog Institute." It is not a cool joke. For a time, Redington actually operated a dog-mushing school. For a price of two hundred and fifty dollars, a beginner could obtain an introduction to the sport through five days worth of lessons.

"I never tried to discourage anyone from doing the Iditarod," said Redington.

On the contrary, he would always do anything he could to help. He had his doubts about some of the prospects who signed up for it, but they wouldn't hear a discouraging word from Joe Redington.

Although dog mushing is basically a solitary sport—from the human interaction standpoint—Redington is the kind of man who can't say no, even to strangers. It was once said that Hall of Fame baseball star Ted Williams could never break off a discussion about hitting, his number-one passion, even if he had a pressing engagement. Redington is the same. He never breaks off a discussion about dogs and he always, but always, tries to aid a musher seeking guidance.

DeeDee Jonrowe, the veteran Willow musher who has finished as high as second and become one of the most popular Iditarod racers with her repeated top-ten placings, said Redington was instrumental in helping her, too, when she was a novice.

At the time, nearly twenty years ago, she was living in Bethel. The Kuskokwim 300, the major local race and a challenging tune-up for Iditarod racers, was her first-ever race. Redington entered the event and stayed with Jonrowe and her husband Mike when he came to town.

Things did not go well in Jonrowe's debut. She had little support and was very frazzled after a poor finish, admitting she was in over her head. Her performance was easy to pick apart, but like a thoughtful coach gently critiquing a player's off night, Redington held back any harsh commentary.

"Joe sat down with me after the race and said, 'If you do this and you do that, you'll be just fine'," said Jonrowe, who went on to enter her first Iditarod in 1981. A pep talk, not a dressing-down, was exactly what she needed.

"He was encouraging when everyone thought I was nuts," she said. "And there are hundreds of people who could say the same. It meant a lot to me. Joe meant a lot to me. Joe was the guy who got me going in my first Iditarod."

Swenson was grateful for Redington's help. He also stayed in contact, and before he could develop his own breeding line, he bought more dogs from Redington. When Swenson captured his first Iditarod in 1977, nine of the eleven dogs in his team had Redington roots. Nugget was one of them, but he also used dogs obtained from Joee Redington.

The first year of the Iditarod, mushers were just feeling their way north. But it wasn't long before they began to recognize one of the main principles of sprint mushing also applied to long-distance mushing. Having a top-notch leader made a big difference. A smart leader kept your team on the trail, for one thing.

In 1974, Carl Huntington won the second Iditarod with a dog named Nugget (not to be confused with Swenson's Nugget) as his main leader. The animal was borrowed from Ruby musher Emmitt Peters. The next year Peters entered himself and using Nugget in lead, won the title.

"That dog won two different times with two different mushers," said Redington. "Lead dogs had an awful lot to do with winning."

While Redington always had the choice of a gigantic group of athletes in his densely populated dog yard, he did not always have great leaders. He had a memorable one in 1974, though, named Tennessee.

"Tennessee had the best feet of any dog in Alaska," said Redington. "I didn't ever have to put a booty on him. Susan Butcher once said, 'I think Tennessee could run on ground glass.' Raymie said if I had Tennessee today, I'd be rich. There would be that many people wanting to breed to him."

Concurrent with the awareness that a great leader could determine the caliber of a team was the startling increase in the value of good dogs. Roland Lombard had already driven the price of sprint dogs up with his judicious, though lavish purchases. Joe himself became conscious of the rate of inflation through an experience he had with a dog named Candy.

The story began in 1969 when Redington brought his dog team to Unalakleet to work managing the new fish-processing plant. Joee accompanied a friend and fellow musher they knew there named Victor Kotongan to Shaktoolik, where he wanted to buy a dog to breed to a

Joe erected this sign at his kennel during the early days of the Iditarod.

famous Redington leader named Roamer. Roamer ran in Joee's sprint team and was always eager to go, but the animal suffered from Attention Deficit Disorder. It only took a couple of blocks of running before he darted into the crowds at the big races.

In any case, Victor and Joee bargained with the family all night long. Periodically, the husband and wife would huddle in the corner. Finally, they decided they could let the dog go for the "premium price" of $6.50. Part of the deal for Victor breeding Roamer was that Joe was to get a dog.

"I was to get the pick of the litter," said Redington, "but I didn't. I left Unalakleet before she had pups."

Meanwhile, the dogs grew up and one, Candy, became outstanding. Candy was from the litter, but might not have been the one Joe was going to pick as a puppy. Instead, in 1974, Victor offered to sell Candy to Joe for five hundred dollars. Joe liked the dog well enough to borrow the money and he paid the bill. The dog kept getting better and Kotongan, who was eighteenth in that year's Iditarod race, had a good fishing season. He approached Redington, laid a thousand dollars on the table and offered to buy Candy back. Joe turned down the deal.

"Nothin' doin'," said Redington. No sale. Candy lived until she was seventeen years old. Redington believe she was part of seventeen Iditarod teams.

It was natural that those starting out gravitated to Redington. He was the most visible of the organizers, the guy who dreamed up the Iditarod and raced it, too. But not all of the attention was favorable. Several dogs died during the first Iditarod, mostly because the mushers did not understand proper nutrition. But that was a red flag for the Humane Society of the United States.

As early as 1973, the organization began poking its nose into Iditarod business from the Lower 48. Alaskans did not embrace the interest. Especially not Redington, who felt he knew more about dogs and how they should be treated and trained than bureaucrats who had never set foot in the state.

There was a telegram-writing campaign—Joe got his share—protesting the first Iditarod. *The Anchorage Times*, skeptical from the start about the Iditarod, even penned an editorial urging that the race be stopped. The Humane Society contacted Governor Bill Egan asking him to intervene. He ignored the suggestion.

"The Humane Society said, 'Stop right now!'" said Redington. "Naturally, we said, 'Go to hell'."

The Humane Society was not a major player in Alaska then and essentially did go away for a while. Perhaps because the Iditarod, despite the success of its inaugural race, wasn't yet such a big deal in 1973. While its uniqueness and freshness touched something in those predisposed to the sport, like Swenson, it was way too soon to take for granted a deep-felt hold even on Alaskans.

It might amaze the hundreds, or even thousands, of citizen adventurers who now take short- or long dog-mushing tours, but in 1974 nobody was particularly interested in doing anything but watching mushers drive their teams. Nobody actually wanted to mush for fun.

That year, Redington and a partner discussed going into the tour business. They printed up a first-class brochure and advertised all winter. They even planned to give away one free long trip, generating what they expected would be terrific word-of-mouth publicity.

"We never got any customers," said Redington. "And the people who won first prize never came to get it. That will show you where the Iditarod was."

The Iditarod, it was obvious, still had room to grow.

14

CRASHES AND SCRATCHES

*—His boots were still frozen and an
official had to cut them off with an ax.—*

By 1975, Joe had a deluxe dog truck that was hand-painted
by noted Iditarod artist Bill Devine.

In 1973, few believed the Iditarod could be completed. In 1974, most wondered if it would take place again. By 1975, the Iditarod was marked on calendars, first Saturday in March, taken note of just like any other holiday.

"People realized it was going to happen again," said Redington. "They started really getting behind it. We were getting more write-ups all the time."

By 1975, too, mushers had the thing half figured out. The thousand-mile race across the state had become just that. It was more race and less camping trip than ever. Emmitt Peters, "The Yukon Fox" from Ruby, made sure of that. The winners of the first two Iditarods spent nearly three weeks completing the race. By comparison, Peters was a John Glenn shooting into outer space. He won in fourteen days, fourteen hours and change. And it wasn't a romp. He dragged others with him.

Two Redingtons, Joee, third, less than an hour behind Peters, and Joe Sr., in fifth, were clustered near the front of a pack that included second-placer Jerry Riley and fourth-placer Herbie Nayokpuk.

This might have been the year of a Redington. It still lingers in Joe's mind as one race that got away. Peters went out fast and did not take his mandatory twenty-four-hour layover until late in the race. He took advantage of the race routing through his hometown, about six hundred and fifty miles from the start, to sleep in his own bed. He was able to rejuvenate himself that way. And, of course, Peters had the superior leader, Nugget, as captain of his team.

Long before Ruby, though, the Redingtons ran across an obstacle that does not present itself in too many sporting events—a moose.

It has often been said that anyone running a Boston Marathon, a New York Marathon, or any of the other 26.2-mile footraces of the Olympic distance, experiences an individual, personal adventure. Multiply that tenfold for the Iditarod. There cannot be a more unpredictable race on earth.

Joee was the first one out of Finger Lake mushing near Happy River, and Joe was in second when they came upon a moose in the trail. Joe was behind him and Joee flagged him down to alert him. Although the uninformed may see moose as big deer that are benign animals, in reality they can be very dangerous. Barking dogs tend to rile moose and the dogs don't ever seem to have the good sense to keep quiet and let them live in peace. Moose also can be stubborn, and this moose seemed quite content where it stood.

Standing uphill, off to the side of the trail, Joe and Joee threw sticks at the moose. This was the equivalent of yelling, "Shoo!" It had no effect but to anger the thousand-pound beast. The moose charged and feinted, and they backed away.

Often, for protection, mushers carry large-caliber handguns or other implements of destruction in their sleds. The Redingtons did not carry hardware that year, so they sought an alternative weapon.

"We taped a knife to a pole," said Joe. "We were trying to kill a moose with a spear."

Predictably enough, this cartoon-like approach to fixing the problem failed.

"It wasn't enough to handle him," said Redington in a notable understatement. A half-hour passed. Carl Huntington, the defending champion, mushed up the trail. *Do you have a gun?* Joe asked.

"Yeah," said Huntington, "but it isn't much of a gun."

It was a .38-caliber pistol with a one-inch barrel, something perhaps a private eye in the 1950s, or maybe in fiction, might carry under his coat.

The moose chased Huntington up a hill, but he took one clean shot and killed it. Only the moose fell into a dangerously steep area with an exposed drop-off, making it impossible for Huntington to bring his dog team near. In Alaska, the law requires hunters to gut and clean an animal shot in the wilderness. This even applies to a musher in the middle of a race. But Huntington did not feel he could safely do the job.

"Carl caught hell over leaving it," said Redington. "A .38 isn't much of a weapon, but it did the work."

A year after his championship, Huntington ended up not being a factor, dropping out of the race.

In Skwentna, only about a hundred and fifty miles into the race, Joe had to drop Feets, his main leader. A black husky, Feets stepped into a moose hole before the race, but seemed strong enough to start. The dog didn't last, though. After that, Redington did not have a top-flight lead dog to guide him when the going got sticky. At one point, said Redington, he was using musher Henry Beatus, who would finish sixth, as a moving human landmark.

"I needed him," said Redington. "I drove my team right up against him. It about drove him nuts."

For most of the race, the weather was fairly mild, with little of the extreme temperatures seen the year before. However, in Solomon, over the final stretch into Nome, the mercury dipped to thirty-eight degrees below zero. By then, though, the trail seemed fairly well defined, easy enough for his dogs to follow, figured Redington.

"I thought, 'It's time to pass him'," he said. So Redington stepped on

the gas and beat Beatus by less than an hour. The prize money differential was only five hundred dollars, but two decades later Redington still felt a little guilty overtaking Beatus in the standings after he had relied on him.

"That was kind of a dirty trick," said Redington.

On other occasions, where such help was needed, he chose not to mush hard in the homestretch. But this time Redington worked overtime to move up that additional place and finished on Front Street wringing

Several mushers, Joe among them, stop for a conference in this photo from one of the early Iditarods. "We ran out of trail," Joe says. "We wanted to know who wants to break trail."

wet with sweat. Fifth place. Good, but it might have been better. Redington had no way of knowing that in nineteen Iditarods he would equal that finish three times, but never better it.

Redington thinks it was Joee, though, who might well have matched

From 1969 to 1975, Joe worked seasonally with the Norton Sound Fisherman's Cooperative in Unalakleet. He acquired some of his best bloodlines from the village dogs he traded for or bought.

Huntington's achievement as champion of both the Fur Rendezvous and the Iditarod.

"I had a real good team, but Joee had a better one," said Redington.

Being on the Iditarod Trail means that mushers are traveling through remote and harsh territory, often far from civilization. They must rely on their own wits and preparedness, but sometimes emergencies occur. Oftentimes, other mushers represent the only help available. The code of the wilderness then prevails. That musher will jeopardize his own chances for victory or higher placing if another's life or health is in danger.

Late in the race, near White Mountain, Herbie Nayokpuk and Joee were traveling together. They stopped to eat lunch and soon Nayokpuk grew very ill, so sick he could not continue mushing. Joee, who would finish only twenty-four minutes out of first, would not go on, despite Nayokpuk urging him to race for the front.

"I'm not going to leave you here," he said to Nayokpuk.

The interruption certainly cost Joee a chance at the $15,000 first prize. He never hesitated in making his choice, and two decades later still did not second-guess himself.

"I would do the same today," said Joee. "Maybe guys depended on each other more in those days. It was long, hard and it wasn't good trail." Actually, Joee's selfless behavior is the rule, rather than the exception, even today, if a musher is at risk.

Joe said Joee would have won if he hadn't helped Nayokpuk. He thought he himself might have won if things had gone more smoothly. One thing always seemed to go amiss when Redington battled it out at the front. Remarkably, he remained a front-of-the-pack contender into his seventies. In 1988, one of the years he placed fifth, Redington was seventy-one.

Dick Mackey was forty-five, the oldest Iditarod winner, when he won the crown in 1978. Mackey wondered if it just wasn't in the cards for someone to defy the advancement of age in a young man's game. After all, Redington was fifty-seven when he raced his first Iditarod.

"If the race had started twenty years earlier, Joe probably would have won the first ten races," said Mackey. "He always had good dogs. He's as tough as boot leather. But the Iditarod came along too late for Joe."

Then Mackey revised his speculation slightly, saying even an older Joe might have won a title if he had divorced himself from the organization and devoted himself solely to training.

Similarly, race veteran Bill Cotter said Redington's time spent promoting the race, and handling its administration, cost him.

"He had some great teams," said Cotter. "If he had been the type of guy who went out to the boonies and trained, he might have won."

But it was not in Redington's makeup to abandon the race organization, especially when it seemed unstable. Once begun, the Iditarod became part of his fiber. This connection became so apparent to even casual race observers that the 1976 race annual biography of Redington included the following sentence: "Joe Redington, Sr. of Knik spends so much time promoting the Iditarod one wonders how he finds time to train his team for the race."

The answer was simple. Sometimes he really didn't train the way he should to race a thousand miles. Nonetheless, when the mushers left

With increased sponsorships came more patches on coats and hats, give-away promotional items, and photos in front of company logos. Ever the promoter, Joe is well known for his ability to slip a corporate logo into almost any picture.

Fourth Avenue each year, Redington always believed he had a chance to win. He didn't mope when he failed to win it, though.

"I probably enjoyed the race more than anyone did," he said. "I was well satisfied."

One way Redington had so much fun was passing through villages on the trail. From the start, the Iditarod was popular in the remote regions of the state. The Eskimos and Indians of rural Alaska were the people who knew dogs, worked with dogs, and had reveled in the notoriety gained when one of their own scored well in the heyday of sprint mushing. For them, the Iditarod was like a train making scheduled stops in Shageluk, Anvik, Shaktoolik, Koyuk, and Elim.

Redington spent years working in the fish business, making visits to the villages on the Yukon River and making friends with a lot of the Natives, so he knew people all over the north. Nowhere, however, was Joe more popular than Unalakleet. Less than three hundred miles from the finish line in Nome, this is the point where the race turns to the Bering

Sea. They say the wind always howls in this village of some nine hundred people, and indeed, its name in the Yup'ik language means "where the east wind blows."

In 1969, Redington became the manager of the Unalakleet fish-processing plant, an operation called the Norton Sound Fisherman's Cooperative. His boss was Leonard Brown, a man who with his wife Mary also managed Brown's Lodge since 1966. The lodge is a checkpoint in the Iditarod and stays open twenty-four hours a day at its otherwise quietest time of the year, just to accommodate mushers and officials.

"That time of year, when things are pretty slow, it livens the place up," said Leonard Brown of the annual mid-March visits from mushers and their followers. "People come out of the woodwork." The lodge's association with the race has made it world-famous, said Brown: "With Joe's help."

Brown, chairman of the Norton Sound Fisherman's Cooperative board, hired Redington in 1969. "Those were the best years we had," remembered Brown, who added that he was a little surprised when Redington showed up for the job with forty dogs. Had to have dogs to mush the Iditarod Trail, didn't he? Redington worked with the Browns between 1968 and 1975, living upstairs over their house at one point.

"He's just like part of our family," said Mary Brown, who had some Iditarod experience of her own. Born in the Yukon River village of Holy Cross, she remembered a dog-mushing trip with her father driving the team on the Iditarod Trail. She rode in the sled basket, bundled up in a sleeping bag, as her dad made a run to pick up radio parts and visit her grandparents in Anvik. She remembered, too, that in the store her family operated, the miners and trappers came for their mail. She worked in a corner counting the labels on canned goods, taking inventory, when they came off the trail.

Early on during the Iditarod Trail Sled Dog Race, a tradition was developed. When Joe mushed into the checkpoint, Mary Brown had a pie baked for him. Later, he brought his own Pyrex plates and she filled them.

"Apple pie," she said. "He had some of that on the trail. One time he said, 'I want to eat my pie here because the last one was squished'." The crust wouldn't stay firm packed in a loaded sled.

She remembers Joe talking about starting a big race on the Iditarod Trail even in his early days working at the fish plant.

"That was his dream," she said. "He should be proud of it because he's the one who put it together."

The dog drivers mush right up to the lodge when they check in, usually for a rest. Even if it's the middle of the night, a crowd shows up for the leaders. For the leaders, and Redington, if he is farther back. A lot of old-timers worked with Redington, and they make a point to turn out.

"Everyone wants to see Joe," said Mary Brown. "Every time he runs, everybody's pulling for Joe."

After three Iditarods, the enthusiasm was growing and spreading. Everything seemed to be going great. But that was a superficial impression. Soon after the 1975 race, the Iditarod faced a crisis. The Humane Society of the United States was back, campaigning on the platform that the race was cruel to dogs.

The Humane Society organized a letter writing effort among its members. Told the race was a bad thing, the members responded by complaining to major news organizations. Although they never admitted the correlation, ARCO, the oil company, and El Paso Alaska, a natural gas company, two major Iditarod financial supporters, yanked their sponsorship. *The Anchorage Times* reported that the Iditarod needed $80,000, or the race would die.

Demoralized by the abrupt action, at a meeting in Anchorage, the Iditarod Trail Committee board members felt it was appropriate to suspend the race for two years and come back later on firmer financial footing.

"Hell no," said Redington. "You can't do that."

So Board President Jay Bashor and others quit. The late Dick Tozier, another major figure in Anchorage dog mushing, also quit, saying, "I'm just a butcher. I can't help you, either."

Angered and disappointed, Redington feared his race was kaput. But he wouldn't admit it. Instead, after the meeting, he drove to Wasilla and woke up Dorothy and Von Page at two A.M., announcing, "I just re-elected myself president." They joined him on the board, determined to keep the Iditarod alive.

When Von Page went to the bank in his new capacity as treasurer, he

In 1975, Joe was the first musher out for the reenactment of the 1925 Serum Run from Nenana to Nome. With him at the far left is Nenana-based musher Jerry Riley. Bill Devine is at right.

discovered the Iditarod had $300 in its account. Shades of 1973, Redington once again threw himself into fundraising. He worked doggedly by day on race administration and at night, when he could, he trained his dog team. It wasn't much, but at least the dogs would have some miles on them.

The mushers still cared. Forty-seven of them started the 1976 race, even though the total purse was only $28,000, all Redington could gather. Winner Jerry Riley collected only $7,200 for finishing first, the lowest champion's share ever.

"But we had a race," said Redington. "That was the most important thing."

More important to Joe than how he fared himself.

Of course, Joe was lucky he was able to be part of the 1976 race. Redington has often said he has walked away from more plane crashes than he can count—the number is at least in double figures. One of his most harrowing experiences occurred in the fall of 1975.

On November 7, Redington took off from Knik, intending to fly his

PA-11 to Galena, three hundred and seventy-five air-miles north, for an Iditarod meeting. He was twenty-five miles south of Ruby, in weather registering nearly fifty degrees below zero, when the engine quit. He initially thought he caused it by backing off the throttle and cooling it. Redington brought the plane down on the tundra, nose up, and bent a propeller.

Redington had a sleeping bag and other gear, but he only had one meal of chicken soup that he found buried under some gear in the plane. Yet his outlook was simple: He had gotten himself into this situation, so it was his responsibility to get himself out.

"I sat down on a log and had a little talk with myself," said Redington. "I said, 'If you were dumb enough not to bring any food, I don't want to hear about it'."

Joe built a fire and spent the whole night warming the metal into malleable form so he could straighten it. That strategy worked. But to get out of the area, he had to clear a four-hundred-foot runway by chopping down spruce trees. It took four days, but he was able to fly out of the wild.

By that time, he had missed the scheduled meeting, so he turned back, planning to land at Nenana. However, not having remedied the initial mechanical problem, Redington had another forced landing. He was aiming for a lake, but fell about a hundred and fifty feet short. That landing broke a ski. He used a nail to punch a hole in the ski and wired it back in place beneath the plane. Then he cleared another runaway by hand. After being weathered in for another day, Redington was airborne again on November 13.

Four more times the engine fizzled on the way to Nenana. Redington would land the plane on a frozen lake, let it sit, and fifteen minutes later the engine warmed and started. He nursed the plane to the small airstrip in Nenana, and when he walked into the office he discovered he was the object of a massive search-and-rescue mission. He called the authorities to let them know he was safe. Then he walked over to musher Jerry Riley's house, phoned Vi, and asked her to come pick him up. He borrowed Riley's razor to shave. After all, he hadn't whisked off his whiskers in six days. He did lose ten pounds, but while others marveled at how resourceful this fifty-eight-year-old guy was, he did not consider himself to be the survivor of an ordeal.

"The only time I got cold was in the car going home from Nenana," said Redington. "The heater wasn't working."

When Redington was in another plane crash, he wasn't at the controls. He was a passenger in an overloaded plane. Part of the cargo was a freshly shot moose, and the carcass steamed up the windows. The pilot crashed on the Yukon River not far from Kaltag, hitting a bank upon take-off. Redington, who was not wearing a seat belt, was thrown all over the interior, and hurt his back.

That plane could not be easily repaired, and a Super Cub flew in to retrieve him. In McGrath, an aching Redington went to a restaurant to eat, but when he made an abrupt turn to admire a pretty woman, he cramped up completely and keeled over. Thump. He hit the floor. That crash was not his fault.

"I never crashed one I couldn't fly back out," he said.

In 1976, a snowy year, when the race slowed considerably (it took Riley longer than nineteen days), Redington discovered that the Iditarod Trail wouldn't always be as solicitous of him as he was of it.

Redington began superbly. Leaving from the No. 2 starting position, he was first to the Eagle River weigh station on the Glenn Highway. He was the first one out of Knik. He was in first place hundreds of miles later at the Kuskokwim River. At the river, he stopped to snack his dogs. Dick Mackey mushed up behind him, and for a while they stayed close. Redington's headlamp batteries shorted out, so Mackey said he would lead.

After a while, darkness fell. All of a sudden Redington, who was counting on Mackey's assistance, realized Mackey's team was out of sight. Mackey had made a hard left into the woods. Redington's dogs went straight.

Soon, Joe could no longer even see the glow of the headlamp. They were shy of the Rohn checkpoint, a trifle less than three hundred miles from Anchorage, but Mackey was gone. Mackey was using the same leaders who took him through the Iditarod the previous three years. They were knowledgeable and experienced.

"All of a sudden, they stop," Mackey said. "No more trail." He searched the area and saw a spot where snowmachiners had turned around and crossed an open channel. Mackey had to turn his team and lead it

As the old saying goes, unless you're the lead dog, the view never changes. In reality, the view from the runners never ceases to strike awe in the mushers who

begin the race route in the forests of Southcentral, cross the Alaska Range, traverse the tundra (shown here), and follow the Yukon River and Bering Sea coast to Nome.

through chest-deep water. He had a terrible time. He reached an ice shelf in the water and paused. Then he and the dogs crossed another open channel between knee and waist deep. He could hear Redington cursing in the darkness, but couldn't see him. Ice fog settled in, further obscuring visibility. And then Mackey's wheel dog became inanimate. He was sure the dog was dead.

Exhausted, Mackey mushed into Rohn, said he told the checker that Redington was coming, and reported a dead dog. Then he fell into a deep sleep for four hours. (Actually, the dog wasn't dead. It woke up and bounced back, eventually running all the way to Nome.)

"I was thinking, 'Joe's a big boy. He can take care of himself'," said Mackey. "I had my own problems." Plus, he thought of Redington as just about the best woodsman he knew.

Meanwhile, back down the trail, Redington was having a hellacious time. His dogs darted into the same stream, and he was pulled in waist deep. The water was moving so swiftly that it was dragging the dogs and sled downstream into an ice jam. Finally, Redington struggled out of the water, soaking wet, his dog lines in a wad. The harness was frozen solid. He was in trouble at fifteen degrees below zero and fearful of encroaching hypothermia.

There were alders by the side of the stream and without even swinging an ax, he broke off branches. Using a gallon of gasoline, he started a fire. Gradually, Redington warmed, thawed the harness, and got it back in working order. Very gradually. It took him eight hours.

Mackey awoke at six A.M., hooked up his dogs, and discovered Redington had not mushed in behind him. Initially, he figured Joe had just camped out. He was surprised so much time had passed, though, with no sign of Redington near the checkpoint. It was then that Mackey began to worry, with good cause.

Even when Redington reached Rohn, his boots were still frozen and an official had to cut them off his feet with an ax. He caught pneumonia.

"Joe said it was the worst night he spent on the trail," said Mackey. "It was a miracle he survived."

Despite the misunderstanding, the men stayed friends, and Redington was later best man at a Mackey wedding.

Feeling awful, Redington stuck with the race. He persevered for hundreds of miles, getting weaker. His dogs, with little race training, weren't faring much better. He kept dropping them one by one. In Shaktoolik, Redington was so ill, so short of breath, race veterinarians treated him instead of the animals. When he tried to sleep, he couldn't, moaning and groaning as he tossed and turned.

In Elim, only a hundred and twenty-five miles from Nome, Redington was reduced to seven dogs, and his energy was virtually depleted. When it was time to mush on, Redington stood over his leader, Bonnie, who acted as if she wanted to rest more than he did. She barely found the interest to open one eye.

"She looked so sad," said Redington. "I looked at her and said, 'We ain't gonna go'." So Redington scratched in Elim. "The trail is bad if you're sick," he said.

There are times when even the hardiest of men prefer soft sheets and a roof over their heads.

15

SEARCH FOR FINANCIAL STABILITY

*—It was just the sheer force of Joe Redington's
personality that made the Iditarod happen.—*

In 1977, Joe entered a "float" in the local Colony Days Parade,
keeping the Iditarod spirit alive even in the off-season.

It was an eye-blinking, jaw-dropping scene on Alaska Day in October
1976. There on Knik-Goose Bay Road, strung out for a thousand feet,
stood two hundred and one huskies hooked into a harness of two-inch
thick nylon rope.

The rope was eight hundred feet in length, and the dogs were tied to a
thirty-eight-passenger scenic-cruiser bus weighing twenty tons. Kind of a
Guinness Book of World Records atmosphere. Or a wagon train, roll-'em-
out scenario. Where was Ward Bond? Actually, Joe Redington was the
trail boss for this Bicentennial extravaganza. Of course.

In 1976, as the United States prepared to celebrate its two hundredth birthday on the Fourth of July, Tim Redington heard that people in another cold-weather state were going to hook seventy-six dogs to a sled. Seventy-six for 1976. That was one way to party.

When he told Joe, though, the president of the Iditarod Trail Committee immediately said, "Why don't we hook up two hundred?"

At that time the Iditarod was virtually broke. Redington decided instantly this would be a cool stunt that could double as a fund-raiser. The plan was two hundred for the two hundredth, but in the end, a bonus dog was hooked in. Jerry Riley, the reigning Iditarod champ, at the last minute brought his lead dog Puppy to town for the festivities. The first twenty-one dogs in line belonged to Redington. His dog Feets was hooked up in single lead. Joee's team served as wheel dogs.

A two-hundred-gallon pot of stew simmered at the Knik Bar, and spectators, dog owners and dog fans were asked to make donations of $4 for the Iditarod. The offbeat event raised $2,000.

"It was the biggest dog team of all time," said Redington.

It was a funky day and a major success. But the Iditarod wasn't going to last if it had to rely on weird events to raise a few bucks at a time, and Joe knew it. He kept hustling, but he needed help.

This was one time Redington himself worried about the Iditarod's future, and those around him knew it. Anchorage attorney John Norman, a member of the Iditarod Trail Committee board of directors, was present at the 1976 meeting that ended with the disintegration of the board and Redington's resumption of the presidency.

"We had just run a race on a shoestring," said Norman. "It was just the sheer force of Joe Redington's personality that made it happen."

Norman remembers members quitting, Redington pleading to continue the race and the others resolute in saying it was just not doable. The board members were exhausted by the fundraising pressures, and Norman didn't blame them for feeling it was hopeless. He didn't blame them, but he didn't join them, either. He retained faith in Redington and his vision.

"I was skeptical that we had the capability, but I could just not say no to Joe Redington," said Norman. "I really had no idea how we were going

to do it. When you have someone who's that decent a human being who is trying so hard, you try to help him. He just worked tirelessly. He should have been out there training, but he made the race happen out of sheer will."

If it seemed Redington was on a non-stop treadmill, there was truth to that. He had to find ways to fund a purse for the 1977 race. But he also took the long view. How could the Iditarod protect itself so the race organizers wouldn't have to go through this every year? His idea was to establish an endowment fund.

ROB STAPLETON

To commemorate the country's bicentennial, in October 1976, Joe went all out to organize the biggest dog team on record. The line stretched along Knik-Goose Bay Road.

And it was Norman who drew up the legal paperwork for a little-known arm of the Iditarod Trail Sled Dog Race. Little-known even today. At Redington's urging in 1976, Norman created The Iditarod Trail Race Foundation. This rainy-day bank account gets little mention in the press, but over the years it has served as a crisis reserve for the race.

On the trail in 1977, Joe prepares to break open the food drop boxes that he has shipped ahead. A tiny Alaska license plate, simply reading "Joe," graces the rear of his sled.

Initially seeded with six hundred dollars—donated by Norman—it was years before the Foundation blossomed and became a key element in Iditarod financial stability. The combined efforts of Greg Bill and famed Alaskan artist Fred Machetanz transformed the Foundation account from essentially an endowment-in-theory to an endowment-in-reality.

Even as late as 1984, when Greg Bill became executive director of the Iditarod, the race seemed to perpetually live on the edge. That fact disturbed him. A devoted fan of both the Iditarod and Alaskan artwork, Bill hit on the idea of a race fundraising print. He approached Machetanz and the Palmer, Alaska, artist agreed to a plan where one of his dog mushing prints would be linked to a promotion.

Machetanz was born in Ohio and came to Alaska in 1935 to visit his uncle who ran the trading post in Unalakleet. He fell in love with the Arctic, with the Eskimos, and the sourdoughs who preferred panning for gold to taking an office job. Not incidentally, he mushed dogs. In fact, he and his wife Sara mushed a dog team from Unalakleet to St. Michael in Western Alaska for their honeymoon.

The Machetanzes homesteaded an area in the woods about forty miles north of Anchorage in the early 1950s. But it was not until the early 1960s that Machetanz, already past fifty years of age, became an overnight sensation. By the 1980s, he was considered Alaska's greatest living artist. One of his favorite subjects to paint were mushers with dog teams in the snowy wild.

Bill's plan involved using a Machetanz painting for a print run of one thousand and forty-nine copies, matching the symbolic Iditarod race distance. All prints were signed by Machetanz and all of the Iditarod winners from 1973 to 1984. A blank space was left on the print for the signature of the 1985 winner. That winner was Libby Riddles, the first woman to capture the title, and that boosted the popularity of the print. Buyers paid $265 for the print, with an extra $200 premium going straight to the Foundation coffers.

Machetanz later donated the use of many of his other mushing paintings for the covers of the Iditarod annual programs. He was ninety years old in 1998 when he said offering up his work for the print was something he was happy to do because of his love for the sport. In turn, the Iditarod officially and publicly thanked him at the start of one race by giving him the honorary number one musher's bib.

The campaign raised $220,000 for the Iditarod and paved the way for future arrangements with other artists that Bill contacted as the race's development director. The Foundation is quite a bit richer these days. "Greg Bill is the one who made something out of that," said Redington.

And John Norman is still one of the administrators of the Foundation he helped invent.

By the time Machetanz was wooed into the fold, another younger artist, Jon Van Zyle, had long previously fallen for the event. Van Zyle entered and finished the 1976 race and was overwhelmed by trail life. He soon began painting scenes of the race and producing an official Iditarod poster, a tradition that has continued for more than twenty years. Over the years he has raised or donated large sums to the Iditarod.

Van Zyle finished thirty-third, or next to last, in 1976, and finished forty-second in 1979, his only two races. He was a back-of-the-pack racer and loved every minute he was on the trail, communing with his dogs, drinking in the solitude and quiet, or spending time telling stories with other mushers.

"To me, the Iditarod has nothing to do with being a race," said Van Zyle, "nothing to do with getting there first. It has to do with the experience, with mushers experiencing as much as they can."

Van Zyle may not have been fast, but he was still a Redington kindred spirit. Redington always cared just as much about participants as he did about winners, but that did not mean he had given up on the idea of winning himself. The next race proved that Rick Swenson had learned the fine points of mushing quickly. He was tenth in this debut in 1976, but was a champion by 1977, at the age of twenty-seven.

It was practically a stampede to the finish line. By then the finish line was more than just a line drawn in the snow with sprinkles of Kool-Aid, or a homemade banner. The famous burled arch was in place, a five-thousand-pound, hand-carved, wooden end-of-the-trail marker that did justice to a thousand-mile endurance contest.

The man behind the creation of the arch was Red Olson of Fox, Alaska, who entered the Iditarod in 1974 and finished last, taking home the red lantern. When he arrived in Nome, he was a bit disappointed. According to Howard Farley's recollection, Olson said something on the order of, "This isn't much fun. I've spent thousands of dollars and twenty-nine days, and there's nothing to say this is the finish line."

Olson told Farley he was going to do something about it. Time passed and he talked to Farley periodically, telling him progress was being made. One day Olson phoned and said, "I've shipped it."

Farley met a Wien Airlines plane and the pilot greeted him by saying, "That's some piece of lumber."

Farley had to shell out $1,300 for freight charges, but when he saw the piece that had five hundred man-hours of work from the Fox Lions Club invested in it, he was giddy.

"I knew this was the answer," said Farley. "My God, I would have paid $10,000 for it. It's become one of the symbols of the race."

Now when mushers arrive in Nome they are comforted and encouraged by the huge, rock-solid arch awaiting, carved with the message, "End of Iditarod Dog Race."

Joe Redington congratulates 1977 champion Rick Swenson as Alaska's Congressman Don Young, left, looks on.

A grinning and proud Swenson won by five minutes over defending champ Jerry Riley in 1977. Warner Vent was another twelve minutes behind and Redington was fifth again in another first-rate performance.

"I knew Swenson was good," said Redington. "He proved he was a good trainer. He set his mind on winning it. He knew what he wanted. He shopped for dogs. And there's one other thing about Rick Swenson. He'll tell you he's the best musher in the race and has the best team. He has confidence."

It was during this race that Redington hurt himself on the trail coming off the Susitna River. His sled dug in, he soared up in the air, and in the flip cut his knee, a three- or four-inch gash. In Skwentna, Redington was looking for first aid, but no one was around to help. So he called for his old pal Terry Adkins. The mushing veterinarian was nearby with his team and he sewed up Redington's cut.

"I was afraid I was going to get socked with malpractice for practicing human medicine," said Adkins.

Redington and Mackey were reunited on the trail for this race.

Mackey finished barely five minutes behind Joe in sixth place. The two men were compatible, enjoyed each other's company, and overall were good fellow travelers.

"He could always laugh," said Redington, "even when we were having trouble. You don't want to be with someone who's grumpy or miserable. It will pass right on to you and the dogs."

Mackey is about a dozen years younger than Redington, but he said for the decade of the early 1970s until the early 1980s, he considered the older man a father figure.

"We spent a lot of time together," said Mackey. "We have a lot of affection for each other."

They spent a little less time together on the trail in 1978. Once again Redington placed fifth, but the men he mostly mushed with were Ken Chase, Eep Anderson, Howard Albert, and Robert Schlentner, all of whom finished within five hours of each other.

Leaving White Mountain for the last run into Nome, the mushers were bunched. A storm blew up in one of the most frequently blasted areas of the trail. The winds ripped, the snow blew, and visibility was almost wiped out. Chase and Redington mushed together and passed Anderson and the others in swirling weather so soupy that Chase believes to this day that the trio didn't know they were being overtaken.

In Solomon the storm was vicious and Chase and Redington combined efforts. Redington did not want to leave Chase. At Topkok, Chase's headlamp went out, provoking more teamwork.

"He had a better leader than I did," said Redington. "I gave him my light and we tied our sleds together. We damned near got disqualified. It was one hell of a ground storm. I never have passed up anybody in trouble."

Chase had the best leader, Piper, but Redington's team was probably stronger. They mushed together between Topkok and Solomon in a ground storm.

"Outside of Solomon his team quit," said Redington. "I gave them honey balls. Pretty quick that got them going." At a cabin outside of Nome, Chase stopped for coffee and Redington waited for him.

"I could have been an hour or two ahead of him," he said. However, Chase finished ahead of Redington, taking third place.

Dick Mackey and Herbie Nayokpuk in Nome, exhausted and battered by the trail.

The real action in 1978 was at the front on Front Street. In a finish so stunning that it seemed scripted by Hollywood, Mackey and Swenson mushed the final few hundred yards of a thousand-mile-plus race side-by-side. Dogs strained, mushers climbed off their sleds and sprinted. Spectators lined the street screaming and disbelieving. When the men stopped, gasping for air—Mackey fell over on his sled, his legs too wobbly to hold him—the older man claimed victory by one second over the cocky defending title-holder.

One second. No Iditarod race has come close to matching it for drama. Mackey, who had gone off into the hills to train what he believed was a special team, knew this was going to be his big chance.

"Before he ever left Anchorage," said Redington, "Dick said, 'Rick is going to think I'm his shadow.' It was true for most of the race."

Swenson, who had conquered the field the year before, was certain he had the goods to do it again. All along the trail he talked a good game, telling Mackey it looked as if they would go one-two. He would be first, Mackey second. Mackey smiled at the psyche job and ignored it. He hung close. He knew his dogs were still full of pep.

The scene in Nome was unforgettable. Fans and officials debated who

Dick Tozier, left, was 1978 race marshal in Nome for the most exciting finish in Iditarod history. He made the call when mere seconds split Dick Mackey and Rick Swenson's finish.

won. Mackey's lead dog was the first across the finish line. Swenson's entire team and sled crossed ahead of Mackey's entire team and sled. Both men were sure they had it.

Like a horse race with a tight finish, the officials tried to sort out who, what and why. Race Marshal Dick Tozier provided the answer. In famous judicial words that might be classified as an Iditarod Supreme Court opinion, Tozier said, "In a photo finish, you don't look at the horse's behind."

The descriptions of the finish, photographs and words, brought worldwide attention to the event. The wild and thrilling happenings represented a milestone that Redington believes catapulted the Iditarod to the next level of recognition.

"Dick caught Swenson off-guard," said Redington. "That helped the race. It will probably never happen again. Everybody was talking about it."

Too bad he didn't see the end of the race in person. Redington was busy trying to fight his way in the final eighty miles. "Joe was in White Mountain when I won the race," said Mackey. "He said, 'If I knew what was going to happen, I would have flown to Nome to see it'."

The magnitude of Mackey's triumph became even clearer over the next few years when a stronger-than-ever Swenson won again in 1979, 1981, and 1982. The man who only a few years before soaked up any advice available from Joe Redington lived up to his own hype.

16

TRAINING THE UP-AND-COMERS

—Butcher arrived driving a Volkswagen
bug crammed full with fifteen dogs.—

Joe posed with a favorite dog, Feets, for this promotional photo that
had him dressed in his best parka near what he calls "a fancy tent."
Feets was less cooperative when a camera crew came to Goose Bay to film.
The dog actually lifted his leg on Redington while the camera was rolling,
setting off a slapstick series of events that was captured on film.

■

Susan Butcher was working on the calving program at a musk-ox farm
about seven miles outside of Unalakleet in the fall of 1977 when someone
said she should meet Joe Redington, the Iditarod guy, who was working in
the nearby fish-processing plant.

"Any Iditarod musher was like God in my book," she said.

In 1978, Joe arranged for Susan Butcher to camp and train dogs from a base camp at Point McKenzie. Dick Mackey, Shelley Gill, and Varona Thompson were other mushers who lived in wall tents and benefited from Joe's assistance.

Butcher grew up in the community of Cambridge, Massachusetts, the home of Harvard University, right next to Boston. As soon as she was old enough, she fled west to Colorado, then to Alaska, determined to build her life around dog mushing and a rural lifestyle.

She and Redington chatted, and he said, "Why don't you come to Knik to train?"

What began as a planned few-week stay evolved into an off-and-on training mission over a few winters and culminated with Butcher's elevation into the top echelon of Iditarod mushers. Just as he did with Rick Swenson, Redington became a mentor to a comparatively raw musher, helping her develop into one of the best mushers in the history of the sport. Butcher wore her dark brown hair in braids, had an appealing smile, and was just twenty-two years old.

Butcher arrived in Knik as a poverty-level musher, driving a Volkswagen bug crammed full with fifteen dogs and her meager belongings. It was dark when she began unloading. She'd dropped off five dogs when Redington approached and said "Great to have you."

Redington talked and talked about mushing and a bashful Butcher hated to interrupt him, but finally she said, "Joe, I've got another ten dogs in there."

16

He looked on disbelieving as dogs poured out of the tiny car. It was just like the circus trick where clown after clown climbs out of an impossibly small vehicle.

Butcher moved in. Not to the Redington house, but to a tent on Joe's property, about ten miles away at Goose Bay. Dick Mackey would come by and train for a while, then move on. Varona Thompson set up a tent there, too. And Shelley Gill, training for her first Iditarod, shared Butcher's tent. Redington told Butcher that Gill would pay for her food, a good thing since Butcher was broke.

"I had zero money," said Butcher. "Joe paid me in dog food in exchange for helping to train his dogs."

Redington always did have that come-one, come-all outlook. He had the space on his land, the dogs in his lot, and the know-how to pass on to the novices. Back then Butcher was inexperienced in racing. But Gill was a true beginner in October 1977, when she decided she'd like to give the Iditarod a try.

Gill was in the construction business with her then-husband, a rock mason, and taking classes at the University of Alaska Anchorage. There she met Norman Vaughan, at the time an employee at the school. Vaughan took her for a dog sled ride and she loved it. Vaughan also told her he was training for the Iditarod and said she should, too. Vaughan, however, was in no position to provide her with either dogs or intensive instruction.

"I thought, 'If I'm going to do this, I'd better get a real teacher'," said Gill, now an author and publisher of children's books in Homer, Alaska. "I just went out and knocked on Joe's door."

Didn't they all?

Gill recalls Redington's reaction when he asked where she was originally from and she told him Florida.

"He bust out laughing," she said.

Her classwork began swiftly. Redington told her the first rule of mushing was not to fall off the sled. She promptly fell off. Gill had this notion that training for the Iditarod was going to be a something of a lark, a part-time hobby while she lived and took classes in Anchorage, about sixty miles away. It took about ten seconds to realize that plan was hopeless. Butcher already was ensconced at Goose Bay when Gill joined her in the tent.

Gill was completely ill prepared for wilderness living. And this was just a training camp, never mind the Iditarod Trail, where a musher had to fix food for herself and the dogs and contend with a thousand unforeseen elements. Redington and Earl Norris, the veteran sprint musher, watched Gill in action as she tried to master not only the fine points of mushing, but the necessary skills for winter camping. They made great sport of ridiculing her, joking all the time about her lack of fundamental culinary talents.

They would shout, "You can't even boil water!"

She kept at it, though, boiling water and mushing dogs, even if it was a very rustic living arrangement. They slept on caribou hides. Residing in a tent for an Alaskan winter definitely meant being frequently chilled.

One day, Swenson showed up. He was the reigning Iditarod champion and just starting his run of dominance. Swenson rarely hesitated speaking his mind. When he saw all the women running dogs and training for the Iditarod, he announced that if a woman ever beat him to Nome he would walk the trail back to Knik.

Butcher shot right back: "I'll just have to give you the sneakers."

In later years, Butcher and Swenson became intense rivals. Butcher certainly would beat him to Nome, though if he ever walked hundreds of miles home it remains a secret. She never gave him any Nikes, either. The two, who in one way or another both graduated from Redington's dog lot, were the king and queen of long distance mushing for more than a decade. At the height of their rivalry, fans were either pro-Rick or pro-Susan. It seemed impossible to root for both. The outlook was polarized. Once, *Alaska* magazine printed a dual cover. Held one way, Swenson was on the cover. Turned around, Butcher was on the cover. In 1991, when most mushing observers felt Butcher would surely win her record fifth title, a blizzard rearranged expectations and the standings. Instead, Swenson braved the inhuman conditions to take his record championship.

Redington said Swenson certainly captured the chauvinist vote.

"The public liked that thing with him and Susan," said Redington. "It appealed to a certain population."

Swenson's boast that he'd walk to Knik if a woman ever beat him stuck to him like tarpaper.

"He had to eat his words several times," said Redington.

All of that was in the future, though. Butcher was a hungry novice during the winter of 1977-78, but one who impressed Redington with her desire, improving ability and intense focus. Redington likes to tell the story about when he first recognized that Butcher was going to be something out of the ordinary. He drove over to the Goose Bay campsite on a bitterly cold day.

"It was colder than hell, and she was out there chopping wood in the droopiest drawers you ever saw," said Redington. "I said, 'Where the hell did you get those drawers?' She said, 'They belonged to my dad'."

When Butcher came to Knik, she told Redington she had mushed dogs in Colorado, and for three years in the Wrangells, but he sensed she was less experienced than she let on. What he saw, though, was a woman with an innate touch with dogs, someone who absorbed knowledge eagerly, learned fast and listened intently when Redington said something.

He quickly observed she had a phenomenal work ethic, something later reinforced when Butcher and Redington worked in the same fish plant in Emmonak. The Susan Butcher others would later characterize as driven to succeed in mushing, brought the same approach to the slime line.

"She could cut two heads to everyone else's one," said Redington. "At the end of the day she couldn't pull her fingers off the knife. I pried her fingers off."

Once, Redington was sent a replacement worker from another plant and told she was the best "header" in Alaska. After working near Butcher, she quit.

"She lasted one day," said Redington.

Butcher had never even tried the Iditarod when Redington began publicly proclaiming that she would someday win the race.

"I knew she was determined to do good," said Redington. "I thought there was no doubt she would do damned good. I figured she would win it. That's all she had on her mind."

People thought he was nuts. Redington's friend Rob Stapleton, a well-known Alaska photographer, even told him to tone it down.

"You shouldn't say stuff like that," Stapleton advised. "It will seem that you don't know what you're talking about."

Redington, of course, always knew what he was talking about when it came to dogs and mushers. He was just like a Hollywood scout or a football coach. He knew talent when he saw it.

Butcher was gung-ho to race the 1978 Iditarod, but she didn't have the money for the entry fee and supplies. Not surprisingly, Redington, who after all had managed to finance an entire race more than once, came up with a novel fund-raising scheme. He convinced Butcher that if she jumped into Knik Lake—after a hole was cut in the ice—the publicity would pay off.

"Joe said if I took a bath someone would sponsor me," said Butcher.

So Butcher mushed down to the lake wearing a bathing suit under a parka. She jumped in three times. And someone did sponsor her to the tune of $3,000.

Another time, in his continuing efforts to raise money for the race, Redington told Butcher and Gill that he'd convinced Channel 2 in Anchorage to come out and film a piece on him on Christmas Eve.

"That was the time he destroyed our camp in thirty seconds," said Gill.

The idea was that Redington would give an interview while standing on the back of the sled, then mush off over the horizon doing the Miss America wave.

Redington hooked up twenty-one dogs with Feets in lead. This was for show and Redington wanted to show well, but putting a full team in harness with no ballast was a mistake. At the Iditarod starting line a team of that size needs several handlers to keep it under control. An empty sled with only lightweight Joe to pull was a recipe for disaster.

Things began badly when Feets relieved himself on Redington's leg—on camera. An irked Redington shoved the dog away—on camera. The dog got even madder—on camera. So when it came time for Redington to yank the snow hook and give his little wave, he actually was barely holding on. Feets bolted from a starting position, exciting the team, and the dogs darted off the trail immediately.

For Redington, it was the equivalent of riding a bucking bronco. The dogs plowed through the ladies' camp. Butcher was in the tent and it collapsed on her and caught fire. She fought to escape the fallen tent. The razor-sharp snow hook bounced along. Redington hoped it would catch in the snow, only instead it merely bounced off of glare ice. Gill's Toyota Land Cruiser, complete with new tires, was parked nearby. The hook ricocheted off the ice and lodged in a rear tire, wrecking it.

The dogs swung wide and as they turned towards the trees, in a whiplash effect, the sled, with Redington on it, slammed into the vehicle. Redington was hurled off the sled as the dogs ran on. Covered with snow, he jumped up, climbed in his car and gunned the engine. Only he promptly stalled the vehicle in a drift. All of this took place on camera.

The well-intentioned Iditarod story turned into a slapstick comedy. No one ever said hanging around Joe Redington was dull.

Butcher found that out soon enough. Later, when she worked at the fish plant in Emmonak and Redington worked as a fish buyer on the Yukon River, they concluded the season of seven-day, twelve-hour work weeks by taking a flight back to Knik carrying receipts of more than $30,000 for delivery to company headquarters. They were essentially sneaking out a couple of days early to get back to dog training, so they did not publicize their departure. They didn't alert anyone when they were leaving, or when they expected to reach Knik.

The pilot had another task and detoured the red-and-white Cessna 185 to St. Mary's. Then it was on to Knik. They were homeward bound when suddenly the plane began to lose power.

"At fifteen-hundred feet, you get this lump in your throat," said Butcher, whose first reaction was "Oh, no." Redington was in the front passenger seat. Butcher was in the back seat, holding a baby fox she had acquired. By this point in his flying career, Redington had been in as many plane crashes as sled crashes. When things started turning bad, Butcher tapped him on the shoulder seeking reassurance and he said, "Everything's going to be fine."

The sentiment was nice, but Butcher did not quite believe a happy ending was imminent. At one point she thought, "This is it."

Trying to make the impact softer, the pilot turned sideways and when they hit, the plane flipped upside down. They crashed in a remote area of the Beaver Mountains in the general vicinity of McGrath, landing in the middle of a berry patch in an area thick with grizzly bears. Bears love berries. As a bonus they were carrying fish. Bears love fish.

Joe remembers the day he and Susan Butcher went down in this plane. As Joe tells it, when the engine quit, the pilot said, "What do we do now? I've never done this before." Joe said, "I have. I'd put it in those little trees over there. They'll bend right over." The pilot didn't take his advice and ended up flipping the plane. No one was injured, and the trio camped while they waited for rescue. Several times they had to climb atop the up-ended floats to avoid bears.

"We were there with everything bears liked," said Redington.

Nobody was seriously injured, but they were marooned with no outside communication. Butcher handed the fox to Redington and it bit him. They had no supplies and no water and only one low battery for their emergency locator transmitter.

"We were very isolated," said Redington.

Ordinarily, without a flight plan and without leaving notice of departure and scheduled arrival, no one would have begun a search. However, they were lucky. Soon after the plane left Emmonak, Vi Redington telephoned the plant seeking to talk to Joe. She was informed he had left. When he never showed up in Knik, she sent out the alarm. A rescue mission was organized, though initial probes explored the wrong area.

It is not uncommon for small planes to crash in Alaska's vast open spaces and disappear forever despite the persistence of rescuers. A day passed, then two. All the while Redington and Butcher were conscious of the big bears sniffing in the area.

"It was something to watch for," said Butcher with more of a light-hearted tone than she felt at the time.

Finally, on the third day, a helicopter appeared and lifted them out. Happy ending? Well, sort of.

"We both got fired," said Redington. The penalty for leaving the plant a couple of days early.

Those who attended the informal, but quite serious training camp at Goose Bay during the 1977-78 winter all had different goals for their Iditarod. Dick Mackey wanted to win it and felt he had his best chance ever. Joe Redington wanted to win it. Varona Thompson wanted to improve on her thirty-fourth-place finish of the year before. Susan Butcher hoped to do well. And Shelley Gill simply hoped to finish.

Just about everybody except Joe got what he or she was after. This was the year of the astonishing sprint down Front Street between Mackey and Swenson, so Mackey got his prize. Redington raced well, but was fifth, just behind Ken Chase in that storm along the Bering Sea Coast. Thompson took twentieth, right behind Butcher, who made a notable debut in nineteenth place. Gill crossed the line in twenty-ninth place. She even beat her friend Norman Vaughan.

Redington said he mushed with Susan as far as the Rohn checkpoint. They chose a trail on the glare ice of the Post River while other teams chose a land route and passed them.

"She hollered to me, 'We're gonna be last! We're gonna be last'!" said Redington. "In McGrath, I said, 'You're doing good. I'm gonna do a little racing now'."

He pulled away, but Butcher could not complain about a first-rate, first-race effort.

"Susan was really driven to do well," said Gill. "Joe didn't think I was gonna survive it."

It took Gill more than nineteen days and fifteen hours, but she reached the finish line at three o'clock in the morning. There was Joe, roused from sleep to greet her.

"Welcome to Nome," he said. "I never thought you'd make it."

Redington had no such doubts about Butcher. He knew she was a comer. Over the next few years, Butcher helped him train his dogs and he offered pointers. As she improved and made a little money, they cut several deals revolving around dog raising and dog sharing.

The next year Redington said he gave Butcher a gift of Co-Pilot as a birthday present, a dog who became a top leader for her. She said she doesn't remember it being a birthday gift. But she does remember bugging him for eight months, asking for the dog, going "Please, please, please," until he made the transfer.

"We had so many dog deals going," said Butcher. "Joe was generous."

Butcher said she was trying to establish her own home in Eureka by 1979, but still trained mostly with Redington in Knik. There were ninety-eight dogs in training that year and when puppies were born, they split the litter. Joe got the pick of the litter and Butcher got the second choice. She said that's how she acquired Granite, her most beloved and outstanding leader, and the dog who would take her to Nome faster than anyone else to date.

"Granite developed very slowly," said Butcher. "It didn't even seem like he'd be a good sled dog." When Granite became famous Butcher told stories about how she nursed Granite along from near-reject animal into champion leader. Redington was offended because he felt she made it sound as if Granite was a mangy mutt. Redington said to his recollection there was never anything wrong with Granite, that he simply let Butcher have him because she wanted him so badly.

There is no dispute that the core of Butcher's kennel came from Redington's dog lot. Granite, Dandy, Boomer, Co-Pilot, and others made a difference for her and she is grateful for that.

By Butcher's second Iditarod in 1979, she had stamped herself as someone to watch, proving Redington's astuteness. That year Swenson won again, but Butcher broke into the top ten, placing ninth, one slot ahead of Redington. It was a startling improvement and for the first time sparked debate on whether or not a woman could ever win the Iditarod.

"We ran a lot together," said Redington. "I knew she had better dogs. To show you how stupid I was, we were a mile out of Nome and she said,

By 1979, Butcher broke into the Iditarod's top ten, and even placed one spot ahead of Redington. Her successes as a novice marked the beginning of a much-watched career. Butcher and Rick Swenson would dominate the race during the 1980s.

'Oh, you're not going to go in ahead of me, are you?' And I said, 'Oh, go in ahead of me. Go ahead.' That was dumb."

Redington forgot that Iditarod racing involves all sorts of techniques, including not letting yourself get psyched out.

Another year later, with her team filled out with even more dogs from the Redington yard, Butcher placed fifth. She was on her way to greatness. Working with Joe Redington, living with Joe and Vi Redington, enabled her to make her long-held dream of living in the Alaska Bush and mushing dogs come true.

"I was a good musher, but I wasn't a good racer," said Butcher two decades after the younger version of herself showed up at Knik in that VW. "What I found in Joe was a soulmate. He never, ever tired of talking about dogs. I had never found anyone else like that. Clocks didn't matter, and that suited me perfectly."

Butcher recalls the period of the late 1970s as a special time in her life because she learned so much from the Redingtons. She admired not only

Joe's only daughter, Shelia, helped Butcher train dogs in the early years at Goose Bay.

Joe, but Vi in particular because she was a role model for any woman who wanted to be tough enough to succeed in the wilderness, plus all of the Redington sons and daughter, Shelia. Shelia, who lived in Anchorage, often came out with her two sons and helped Susan with her mushing.

"I became entrenched in the family," said Butcher. "I learned from the whole Redington family. Having grown up in Cambridge, Massachusetts, there weren't a whole lot of people like the Redingtons there. The biggest treat I had was that they were amazing people. My respect for Joe is for the life he's led and what he's done. I was at least equally impressed with Vi."

The Redingtons never panicked when something went wrong. Not even when a plane crashed did Joe Redington get flustered.

As much as anything else, that is what Susan Butcher took away from her time spent in Knik: There is going to be adversity in your life, but you must be patient and you must deal with what comes. No one can compete in the Iditarod Trail Sled Dog Race year after year and avoid adversity.

Butcher's greatest triumphs lay ahead, but not before her greatest frustration. And not before she and Joe Redington shared one of the most incredible dog-mushing adventures anyone ever undertook: In 1979, Joe Redington and Susan Butcher would mush a dog team to the summit of Mount McKinley, the tallest mountain in North America.

17

TO THE TOP OF MOUNT McKINLEY

*—I kept hearing people say dogs couldn't
go that high. I believed differently. —*

Susan Butcher, Ray Genet, and Joe Redington were photographed
on the afternoon of their descent. Ray's swashbuckling
appearance and attitude lent him the nickname "Pirate."

Joe Redington had his fishing boat anchored at the mouth of the Susitna
River when another boat pulled up beside him. A man he had never seen
before asked for a ride into Anchorage, jumped over the side of his boat
and said, "I'm Ray Genet."

Redington thought he had heard the name before, but couldn't quite
place it. He asked Vi, "Who the hell is Ray Genet?"

The year was 1969 and only a couple years earlier Ray Genet made
his name famous all across the state. A Swiss mountain guide who
migrated to Alaska, Genet, Dave Johnston and Art Davidson were the

first men to climb Mount McKinley in winter when they reached the summit in February 1967. They battled terrible storms, were trapped by the violent weather for days at a time, suffered frostbite, and in the end achieved a climb of mythic proportions.

Oh, that Ray Genet, Redington's mind almost spoke out loud.

Genet had turned McKinley's snowy slopes into a personal playground. A man of swashbuckling style, indomitable stamina, and bold and mischievous vision, he essentially was the first guide to bring the masses to the 20,320-foot peak. His slogan was, "To the Summit!" and he dressed and lived the part of wilderness mountain man to the fullest. He had a bushy beard and wore a colorful, trademark bandanna. His nickname was "Pirate." Genet was on the cutting edge of the modern age of citizen adventure.

In a sense, he was a man after Redington's heart. If Joe was more circumspect in his speech and more restrained in manner, he too was always thinking big, always thinking ahead, always trying to dream up ways to popularize his sport and his Iditarod race.

The boat ride from the Susitna River to Anchorage took just two hours, but by the time Genet disembarked, the men had cemented a pact.

"We decided we'd take a dog team up Mount McKinley," said Redington. "We got to be good friends right off the bat."

Genet never told Redington why he agreed to guide him and his dogs, though Redington figured Genet saw it being good for business. He was, after all, a promoter, and that was something Redington could identify with, too.

When to go? The next climbing season. The weather on McKinley is never benign, but most mountaineers attempt to climb the peak between April and July. Just right for Redington. The Iditarod ends in March, and the long-distance mushing season is pretty much over then.

Time passed and the next spring Redington received a postcard from Genet—from Paris. He was writing to say he was going to be late getting back to Alaska that year so the McKinley trip had to wait.

Redington's desire to mush dogs to the roof of North America was rooted in twofold purpose: He thought it would gain needed attention for Alaskan huskies, but he also wanted to show to naysayers just how tough the breed was.

"I wanted to show what dogs could do," said Redington. "I kept hearing people say dogs couldn't go that high. I believed differently. I just felt there wasn't anything a man could do that those dogs couldn't do."

Genet was on board and he was the man for such a climb. A problem arose, however. They never could get their schedules to mesh. Year after year passed with no forward progress. Genet kept telling Redington that he had too many climbers to shepherd up the mountain and didn't have time to devote to their endeavor.

In 1978, Redington heard that someone else tried to drive a team of dogs to the summit and reached about the 14,000-foot level. The musher froze his feet and turned back. But the fact that he was in danger of being scooped did not sit well with Redington. He announced in the Anchorage newspapers that he was going to mush a dog team to the summit of Mount McKinley in 1979. The reaction was instantaneous. Everyone thought he was bonkers. Even Vi.

"I thought it was a nutty thing to do," she said.

Joee Redington was another who wondered what in heck his father was doing.

"I figured, 'He'll do it, or he'll be there for several years'," said Joee. Not a subtle observation. People do die climbing Mount McKinley. During a single climbing season in the early 1990s, eleven people were killed on the mountain. By going public, Redington was pretty much trying to force Genet into a commitment, too. And he also put pressure on himself to follow through.

"Pretty soon I had to do something or shut up," said Redington.

Mount McKinley is in many ways the symbol of Alaska. It is a huge, broad mountain, perpetually snow-covered. It towers over the nearby peaks of the Alaska Range. Although located roughly one hundred and thirty air miles from Anchorage, on clear days it can be seen from downtown city streets.

Called "Denali," the high one, by Alaska Natives, the mountain was first climbed in 1913 by a party led by Hudson Stuck, the Episcopal archdeacon of the Yukon. The first man to actually set foot on the mountain's summit, though, was Stuck companion Walter Harper.

In 1951, an expedition led by Dr. Bradford Washburn of Boston's

Museum of Science, pioneered the West Buttress route. This became the so-called easiest way to reach the summit and is the path most often followed by the thousand or so adventure climbers who attempt to scale the mountain each spring.

The era of amateur vacationers tackling McKinley was just being established in 1979. Genet was in the forefront of this new tourism business. Redington, then sixty-two years old, was never one to shrink from a challenge, but he had never before expressed much interest in making the climb for the climb's sake.

This was the time period when Susan Butcher was training extensively with Redington and he asked her if she wanted to accompany him. Dogs and McKinley. Sounded good to her.

"I'd always wanted to climb McKinley, so it put my two favorite things together," said Butcher. "It just seemed perfect. It seemed exactly what I wanted to do and I'd never known it. People kept saying it was crazy. They kept saying dogs couldn't do it. I just kind of knew they wouldn't have any trouble. That was Joe's big thing."

After the 1979 Iditarod, Butcher and Redington began preparations back in Knik to bring a team of seven Alaskan sled dogs to the summit of Mount McKinley. Four of the dogs belonged to Redington, three to Butcher.

"Seven of our best ones," Redington characterized them.

Mushers might use sixteen or twenty dogs to race along the Iditarod Trail, but these mushers were not going to be driving the dogs along a trail at all. They did not need dog power so much as dog wisdom.

"I learned a long time ago you could get in trouble with too many dogs," said Redington.

Anchorage photographer Rob Stapleton was friendly with Genet and he heard about the likelihood of this adventure before it became public knowledge. He wanted to go along and document it. He was also aware the trip had been in the works for years, so he couldn't be sure if 1979 would bring it any closer to reality than the discussion stage.

Stapleton was not a mountain climber and he did not train for a journey he didn't trust to happen. Then, one day in April his phone rang. The voice on the other end was unmistakable.

"Stapleton, this is Genet. Are you ready to go?"

"Am I ready to go where, Ray?" answered Stapleton.

"To the summit!"

Well, of course.

The trip was scheduled to begin in two days. Some mountaineers train a lifetime for a climb of McKinley. Some train and prepare their supplies for a year. Two days!

"So many people had bet against it ever happening," said Stapleton, who then worked for the *Anchorage Daily News*. "The newsroom was betting against that I'd come back alive. They thought I'd be killed on the mountain."

By living to tell about it, Stapleton said he won a case of Jack Daniels from a reporter.

"Except I don't like bourbon," he said.

Right before Redington and Butcher left for the mountain, they visited Joe's friend Bill Devine. He photographed them together, made a drawing of Genet and created a postal cachet to commemorate the occasion. A total of one hundred and thirty-two of the cachets were made, and the adventurers intended to use them either to promote the Iditarod, Genet's climbing business, or both. Genet got the envelopes canceled at the Talkeetna post office before the trip got underway and later he got them canceled there again. One was eventually auctioned off, Devine believes for about $30. The others are still sitting in storage.

The small community of Talkeetna, located some hundred and twenty road-miles north of Anchorage, is generally the jumping off point for McKinley expeditions. In the spring the air fills with the buzzing sound of small planes. Busy pilots ferry climbers and their gear back and forth to the Kahiltna Glacier, at 7,200 feet of elevation the base camp for those who make their way up the West Buttress.

However, Redington and Butcher, then twenty-four, and Stapleton, a broad-shouldered man who stands well over six feet tall, began their journey by mushing, or in the case of Stapleton, hiking, to Pirate Lake. The lake was the site of Genet's cabin, located about twelve miles from Talkeetna.

Stapleton came in for instant abuse from this group of hardy wilderness travelers when blisters the size of silver dollars formed on his heels. He carried a heavy pack for twelve hours and was greeted by Genet saying, "I've had a lot of women who've done it better than that."

Genet, as was his habit, booked several climbs at once. Not only was he supposed to be leading Redington and his dogs, but there was a group of German climbers on the mountain, and another group of Americans. He dashed off to the mountain to get those climbers started before Redington's group. The next day he flew over and dropped a note to Redington. It read, "Joe, we've got to wait until next year. I've got too many climbers."

That was unacceptable. Redington had never been on Mount McKinley before, but if Genet wasn't going to guide him, he was going to guide himself. He turned to Butcher and said, "We'll have our own expedition."

Redington, Butcher, and Stapleton joined forces with two climbers from Europe, one a woman named "Blondie." They were friends of Genet's. As it turned out, they were far from experts and quit the climb by the 10,000-foot mark.

Once Genet realized they were going to climb, with or without his guidance, he said he would try to support them.

"Genet said, 'Great, you're doing it'," said Redington. "'I'll help you every way I can'."

In this way, Genet was like Redington. Redington would offer aid, advice and assistance to any musher who wanted to race the Iditarod. Genet would try to help anyone who came to "his" mountain. He wanted everyone to reach the summit.

Redington flew to the Kahiltna Glacier in a Super Cub single engine plane. Butcher flew to base camp in another plane. The aircraft were packed so tightly there was barely room for humans. They carried eight hundred pounds of dog food.

When the five climbers in the party departed the Kahiltna Glacier, mushing a dog sled pulled by seven barking, energetic huskies, Genet was nowhere around. He was busy elsewhere on the mountain with another group. Genet had such phenomenal endurance, though, he could dash up and down the mountain, racing between parties, tucking in one group, so to speak, and then coaxing another ever upward.

Brian Okonek of Talkeetna, now one of the most respected of McKinley guides, was working for Genet as an assistant guide at the time and that got him involved in the trip. He helped Redington and Butcher carry loads at different times, mostly dog food. Initially, Okonek viewed the expedition as a stunt, something just for attention. He didn't think it was at all practical to mush dogs up McKinley. But once immersed in the journey he enjoyed and appreciated it.

"It was fascinating just to be there with Redington and Butcher," said Okonek. "It was a hoot being with the dogs. You'd forget where you were. It was like being at a camp on the Yukon River. It was just a picnic for the dogs, especially given what they'd trained for."

The West Buttress route on Mount McKinley is known as a "walk-up," an expression that often plants a misleading picture in climbers' minds. It makes them think the climb is an easy one. That is not so. The term walk-up really refers to the limited amount of technical climbing involved in scaling the mountain. Yet McKinley is steep, has exposed ridges, and can often produce the worst weather in the world—worse than the Iditarod Trail.

Genet met them at 10,000 feet and assessed their progress. They were doing fine, he said. Later, at 14,200 feet, he put in fixed ropes for the group, making it possible for them to scramble up one of the steepest sections without much pure mountaineering experience.

It was in this area that Butcher was nearly swept away. Ferrying loads between camps, she found herself being dragged by a runaway sled. The dogs ran full throttle downhill. She held tight, hands knuckle-white in their grip on a sled turned sideways. She remembered well that first rule of mushing—never let go of the sled. But the dogs might easily have dashed over a ridge and carried her to her death and killed themselves.

Butcher bounced along like a sack of potatoes, bruises forming as her body banged against snow berms and frozen ground. The dogs sprinted, and she screamed at them to stop. They kept running. Until they saw the man standing in the trail ahead, two ice axes planted in the snow, arms spread wide. It was Genet, brilliant against the white snow in an orange jumpsuit. Tekla, Butcher's leader, and one of her favorites in a long mushing career, turned the sled and other dogs right into the man.

"It was pretty wild," said Butcher.

Redington said that was a terribly dangerous moment and that

RAY GENET

Joe Redington and Susan Butcher pause before their final ascent to the peak of Mount McKinley. With help from famed climber Ray Genet, and joined by newspaper photographer Rob Stapleton, they drove a team of sled dogs to the summit in 1979, marking a first in climbing history.

Butcher was close to a crevasse when the dogs were running all out.

"Genet just happened to be in the right place," said Redington.

This was definitely a risky expedition for novice climbers accompanied by frisky dogs. Redington and Butcher, though, were wily outdoors experts, used to extreme weather conditions, and unlike many groups which climb with guides nowadays, they were not on a three-week timetable with plane reservations in place to whisk them back to work in an office thousands of miles away. They had patience and time on their side, so they could outlast McKinley's temperamental conditions when necessary. At times, it was needed. An amazing storm blasted them at 16,500 feet. Sometimes McKinley is buffeted by hurricane-force winds and in conjunction with extraordinarily low temperatures that creates an astonishingly cold mix. The book written by Art Davidson about that first winter ascent is titled *Minus 148*. That is as low as the temperature/windchill readings go, and Davidson is sure it was colder on the trio's bodies. In other words, off the charts.

Redington likes to say he never gets cold on the Iditarod Trail because he dresses for the weather and has good boots. But McKinley offered new extreme weather lessons to a man who thought he had seen it all.

The storm that hit at 16,500 feet carried winds of a hundred miles an hour. Butcher was melting snow for water for the dogs. Redington was in a tent. The wind rose, more and more powerfully, gusting stronger and stronger. The tent blew over and the wind sucked gear and clothing right out of it. Butcher and Stapleton clung to rocks and huddled with the dogs. The wind roared like that for a half an hour.

"It was one hell of a wind," said Redington. "It was so damned strong you couldn't stand up." The storm also dumped snow in feet on them. Not the first time on the mountain, nor the last.

If there was one piece of useful advice Genet offered that Redington never forgot, it was stressing the value of an ice ax. The tool can be a lifeline if a man slips and begins to slide down a slope. It can be dug into the cliff. It can be dug into the side of a crevasse if the earth opens beneath your feet.

"I never laid the ax down," said Redington.

Stapleton went along as both chronicler and interested observer.

"I was trying to be there as a team member, but not be part of the mix," said Stapleton. "I believed in Redington's theories that dogs would be fully capable of doing it. I knew he took care of his dogs."

Stapleton had heard the description of McKinley as "a kind of a walk" and believed he would condition himself to the altitude as they went. He did well by just putting one foot in front of the other slowly, until they reached the 16,500 area. He was so fatigued he could barely stand, and it took Genet's exhortations to get him to the 17,200-foot elevation.

"Ray dragged me to 17,200," said Stapleton. "I was too gassed."

Genet impressed Stapleton mightily with his ability to move up and down the peak and shift from one climbing group to the other. Stapleton said Genet was "Twinkletoes" on the mountain: "He was like a damned mountain goat."

As an untrained climber, Stapleton depended on Genet's help off and on, but later he resented it when other observers said he never would have been able to reach the summit if Genet hadn't kicked his butt up the hill. He got so sick of hearing it that in 1988, Stapleton went back to McKinley and climbed it again. Everyone pretty much shut up then.

Stapleton never doubted that Butcher, Redington and the dogs would reach the summit. No matter how gnarly the going got, no matter how rough the weather got. He was with Redington. He was sure the dogs were at least as tough as the people were, and at least as capable of making the summit.

"I always admired Redington and had great respect for Susan Butcher because they always mastered the winter," said Stapleton.

On McKinley they had to do that even more creatively than they did along the Iditarod Trail. They changed harnesses, parkas and other cloth-ing to suit the moment. They modified sleds whenever necessary.

Redington discovered the snow's consistency was different on McKinley than it was on the Iditarod Trail. Bering Sea snow was finer. McKinley snow was wetter. In both places, it got down to fifty degrees below zero. There were other times when the sun was bright and offered a kind of artificial warmth. Working hard to haul loads of supplies or set up camps, a climber sweated so much there was no need for a parka. They stripped off the heavy coats then. That coat stayed nearby, though. The moment the sun began setting, the temperature plummeted, and all hint of warmth evaporated.

"As soon as the sun went down, you'd grab it," said Redington.

The mushers hauled three sleds to McKinley and McKinley was not kind to the hardware. There were times the snow was smooth and times the snow was rough. There were times the path was clear and times the path was broken up. While Stapleton walked, Redington and Butcher drove. Redington said he hoped Stapleton would make it all the way to the top, but the primary objective was putting the dog team on the summit.

The dogs never faltered, only the machinery. When the first sled cracked, they replaced it. When the second sled broke, they patched it. When the third sled broke, they cannibalized it for parts, totally demolishing it. When they ran out of useable interchangeable parts, they tore up a pair of snowshoes to patch the third sled. In the end, they did carry the remnants of two sleds back to civilization. One is located in the Knik Museum. The other is in the Iditarod Trail race headquarters.

Stapleton, the tagalong member of the team, said the journey was a dog expedition more than a people expedition, and a scientific expedition without hard scientific study. Yet it proved Redington's point.

If there was a certain fascination with the trip by spectators in the flatlands, the same enthusiasm was not evident on the mountain. They were pretty darned unpopular with other climbers, who just thought dogs on McKinley were a nuisance.

"They were bitching about the dog turds on the trail," said Stapleton. Well, it was kind of tough to curb your dog in this environment.

There were scary times. Between 17,000 and 19,000 feet, the group crossed a narrow ridge that leads to McKinley's summit. The ledge was not wide enough for a sled to pass over with both runners flat, so when they mushed across the area, one sled runner stuck out in the air. The climbers could look over the edge and see thousands of feet down to solid rock. It was the kind of view that could leave hands and knees trembling.

"Genet wouldn't rope up to us there," said Redington.

Normally the dogs were fine, but here they were scared. Tekla would lunge ahead but whenever she stopped, she clung to Butcher's legs. Lucas, another dog, appeared suicidal. Butcher said the dog was trying to jump

The climbing party followed the popular
West Buttress route to the summit. "I kept

hearing people say dogs wouldn't go that
high," Joe said. "I believed differently."

off the mountain. It took some effort to calm him. But that was the last obstacle to making the summit.

After the sled-dog expedition reached the 17,200-foot camp, Genet notified Devine by telephone. They spoke for about twenty minutes, Devine recalled, and he was told the dogs were fine.

Devine gathered his camera gear, contacted Vi Redington, and they drove to Talkeetna. They jumped in a plane, loaded oxygen bottles for use above 14,000 feet, and set out for the mountain. The goal was to locate the climbers and photograph them.

Somehow, the pilot of the small plane got them up as high as 19,500 feet on the stunningly clear and beautiful day, but their heads throbbed the whole time in reaction to the swift altitude climb.

"All the headaches in my life were equal to that," said Devine. "I would pass out and come to."

The plane circled and circled, but against the vast expanse of rock and snow the climbers were merely ants. Devine or Vi would shout, "I think I see them," only to discover it was a false sighting. That happened again and again.

Finally, Devine just aimed his camera with its large lens at the summit and clicked. He shot many pictures, but never thought he captured Redington and Butcher on film. Only a few years later did he closely examine his slides and see a few specks of dark blue against the white that grabbed his attention.

"What the hell is that?" he said as he scanned the pictures. "I couldn't hardly believe what I was looking at." Magnified, blown up to a size of eight-by-ten, he could tell that he had a photo of Redington, Butcher, and the dogs just a few feet shy of the summit.

On Memorial Day, May 28, 1979, they mushed their sled onto the highest point on the continent. Redington, Butcher, Stapleton and four of the seven dogs made it. Those four completed the trip only because the mushers didn't want to take more of them over the final scary stretch. The other three rested at 14,000 feet.

On the summit, it was minus-eight degrees, with bright sunshine and no wind. It doesn't get much nicer than that on McKinley. The view was breathtaking. They could see off to the Interior, to McGrath. They could

On Memorial Day 1979, Joe came off the mountain windburned and happy, having proved once more that sled dogs were exceptional creatures.

BILL DEVINE

see the city of Anchorage. They could even see the Kenai Peninsula, hundreds of miles distant. Butcher sat down to rest, but Redington kept moving, walking around in the small area. Genet joined them. He wouldn't miss that moment.

And the dogs? They seemed as fresh as the day they started. They were at the end of the road and didn't even care.

"The dogs looked around like, 'Where's the rest of the trail?'" said Stapleton.

The climbers laughed and exulted and celebrated. Then they realized they really didn't have a good idea for getting the dogs safely down the mountain. Stapleton said Genet flailed his ax in a fit. Everyone said *Joe, we thought you had a plan.*

"Joe had trained the dogs to go," said Stapleton. "They hadn't been trained to stop."

Okonek later commented that "the downhill stuff was real tricky." And he admitted that Genet worried about Redington, Butcher and the dogs the whole time they were there because he knew the mountain so well and understood how easy it was to get into trouble on McKinley.

But they all retreated safely. To base camp. To Talkeetna. To home. Men, woman, and dogs. The sleds took the worst beating. It was a journey of epic effort and scope, lasting forty-four days in all.

Devine met them upon their return bearing a box of strawberries, and Butcher thought it was the best thing she'd tasted in her life.

People still thought they were crazy. But the tone of voice changed, least. Now there was admiration and applause, as well.

"Everybody embraced it then," said Butcher. "Everyone thought it was neat."

Stapleton, come back alive, was pretty proud he was able to keep up with such a group of strong-willed adventurers. But remembering the origin of the trip itself, he retained a sense of perspective about the achievement.

"Joe Redington had a vision," said Stapleton. "He wanted to prove what dogs could do. He did it in the Iditarod and he did it on the mountain."

When they returned triumphant, Genet told reporters, "I underestimated Joe Redington." Turns out for all of his backing, he was always skeptical that they could pull it off.

Sadly, later that year, Genet, a nearly superhuman figure on McKinley, a guide who climbed the mountain forty times, by some counts, perished on Mount Everest at the age of forty-eight. He was on his way down from the 29,028-foot summit. His body rests on the world's highest mountain to this day.

In 1984, Butcher returned to Mount McKinley to climb it again, this time in the company of Dick Bass, the man who became the first climber to conquer the seven summits, the highest peaks on each continent.

Satisfied with the accomplishment, Redington said he was later tempted to go back and climb Mount McKinley in more conventional fashion, too. Just by hiking. No dogs. But he never did. For one thing, Vi was not so keen on the idea.

"I would have had to get a divorce," said Redington.

Besides, he had already climbed Mount McKinley on his own terms. Really, that was enough.

PROTECTING AN HISTORIC TRAIL

—The Iditarod Trail? Joe got his trail.
No sweat.—

Joe and Dick Mackey post Iditarod Trail markers for the 1980 race.
During the previous decade, Joe was determined to draw attention
not only to the race, but also to the preservation of the trail itself. With help
from U.S. Senator Mike Gravel, his aide Pat Pourchot, and many others,
the Iditarod was added to a short list of National Historic Trails.

■

W*hy not?*

Why couldn't the Iditarod Trail be like the Appalachian Trail?
Protected forever by federal legislation.

The Iditarod Trail had become Joe Redington's playground as soon as
he moved to Alaska. And almost from the first moment he learned of its
significance to previous generations, he began working to preserve it for
future generations.

Redington was not merely interested in history for history's sake. He was interested in the Iditarod Trail as a living entity. Even if its original purpose—transporting gold to market—was long before eliminated, the Iditarod Trail's revived purpose as a travel route, then a race route, was worthy enough to keep.

From the 1950s on, any time Redington had a chance to buttonhole a politician, he took advantage of it. Save the trail for the future, was his message. Joe always could talk sense. It's just that people weren't always listening.

Redington's low murmur of a campaign to preserve the Iditarod Trail was episodic more than concerted, erratic more than linear. When he got the chance, he planted a seed. When he had an opportunity, he put in a word. This went on for years. And years. Decades.

"It was about protection of the trail," said Redington. "So we would have a place to mush dogs all the time. And the history was very important. I wanted to rebuild some of the roadhouses. I waited and waited and they said there was no money. I initially wrote to Congressmen in the 1950s."

When Redington first broached the idea of labeling the Iditarod a National Historic Trail, Congressmen did not even know what he was talking about. They had not heard of it and did not get excited enough to take action. When Redington educated them, they could no longer say they hadn't heard of it, but that didn't jump-start things, either.

"Eventually, they wrote back and said it was a good idea," said Redington. "But they didn't do anything."

But in the 1970s Redington found someone with a receptive ear, as well as the power to make something happen. United States Senator Mike Gravel, helped mightily by his aide, Pat Pourchot, spearheaded a drive to make Redington's program law.

Between 1974 and 1976, Pourchot worked for the Department of Interior's Bureau of Outdoor Recreation. He did some of the original groundwork and research for the government in the initial foray to save Alaska gold rush trails.

Pourchot went on a scouting mission with Redington in 1974. They flew along the trail, Redington at the controls of a small plane, highlighting points of interest and key areas. Back and forth they went, banking and swooping, crisscrossing the trail and the wilderness.

"He damn near made me sick," said Pourchot, who called the adventure "a remarkable time."

That was one way to meet the Iditarod Trail. Pourchot undertook other journeys, via land, to explore the trail up close. One winter he camped in a hollow by Susitna at thirty-two degrees below zero. That kind of intimacy with the trail meant going beyond the call of taxpayer-funded duty. Another time he slept out at Ptarmigan Pass at twenty below. Good training for racing the Iditarod, just in case he was ever interested in taking up a hobby.

After his stint with the Department of the Interior, Pourchot, who now lives in Anchorage, joined Gravel's staff. Between 1977 and 1980 he was Gravel's legislative assistant in Washington, D.C. When he switched jobs, Pourchot transported the save-Alaska's-trails agenda. He prodded Gravel to act, but Gravel was interested in the subject anyway.

In the mid-1970s, Redington and Gravel had a long powwow in Nome. The meeting lasted most of a day. Redington pled his case and Gravel listened. They plotted strategy.

Redington wrote to other officials, and in his scrapbooks has letters of support from such prominent men as former United States Senator Dale Bumpers of Arkansas and ex-Senator James Eastland of Mississippi. In June 1976, Alaskan Congressman Don Young wrote Redington a letter saying he would introduce the necessary legislation in the House of Representatives.

In one way, Redington and Gravel were lucky. There was already a mechanism in place to give the Iditarod Trail national historic preservation status. In 1968, Congress passed The National Historic Trails System Act. At the time, only the Appalachian Trail, running between Maine and Georgia, and the Pacific Coast Trail, three thousand miles west, were designated with special status. But the government did request that gold rush trails be studied for possible inclusion. That's where Pourchot came in at his Interior job.

Redington was relentless in his long-running campaign to protect the Iditarod Trail because he could see a day when Alaska's growth would encroach even on remote areas and villages. He did not know how long it would take, or how development would come, but he could easily see the trail being broken up, interrupted by some project. Redington well understood that Alaska's population would continue to mushroom and that between airplanes and snowmachines, even rural areas could come under stress. Better to protect it early rather than try to reclaim it.

In a sense, Redington was as much a visionary to see the future trends that could affect the Iditarod Trail as he was in being able to foresee a wildly successful Iditarod.

Although Alaskan Senator Ted Stevens was also a sympathizer, Redington gives Gravel the main credit for making the Iditarod part of the national system.

Gravel, who now lives in Virginia, said he had a fondness for the Iditarod, right from the first small race in 1967. At that time he was working for a real estate company that sponsored musher Isaac Okleasik, the man who won that inaugural event.

"I had a certain fondness, or emotional association with the Iditarod," said Gravel.

When Gravel introduced the bill to make the Iditarod Trail part of the national trail system, it was sent to the Senate Energy Committee. In a speech made in late July and reported by *The Anchorage Times*, Gravel sold his bill by emphasizing the gold rush period.

"The rush to the Iditarod in 1910 was the last major gold rush in North America and closed out one of the most colorful eras of American history," said Gravel. "The trail served as the only communications and transportation link with the outside for Nome, Iditarod and many other gold mining boom towns during the six to eight months when the rivers and seas were frozen."

For all of the inertia and inaction rooting Redington's idea in place for so many years, once it found a sponsor, it rolled. When Pourchot, doing the legwork, asked for input, he discovered that just about everyone he talked to in Alaska was in favor. Everyone from trail users, historians, nature groups and people in the villages along the trail were "generally supportive," said Pourchot. "Everyone liked the idea of recognition of the Iditarod. There was no opposition. It was thought to be a good thing to do."

Once it was cleared and reopened, the Iditarod Trail once more served as a major transportation corridor for subsistence fishers and hunters as well as recreationists. In this 1981 photo, Joe camps sixty miles out at the traditional turnaround spot for the Junior Iditarod.

Gravel recalled that Redington made it easy for him. Redington was a visible, popular advocate of the idea who worked to drum up all kinds of support wherever he went.

"Joe was a very good political manipulator," said Gravel. "He was outspoken. It was easy to latch on to that. He provided citizen leadership. On any legislation, you need a patron to weigh in. That's all it took, a patron to take a stand on it. You had the Serum Run and that added a lore to it. This was able to move through without a great deal of difficulty."

Of course, there was one other very good reason why the Iditarod Trail could sail through Congress without much attention. At the same time, Gravel was working on the issue of whether or not to rename Mount McKinley formally as Denali, using the Athabascan Indian name. Now that provoked intense debate. In the end, when that furor died down, Mount McKinley retained its old name, but the surrounding national park was named Denali.

The Iditarod Trail? Joe got his trail. No sweat.

"This wasn't very controversial," said Gravel.

Members of the Knik Trailblazers Club traveled to Seward to help open another chapter at Mile 0 of the Iditarod National Historic Trail.

When the bill passed the Senate and House in 1978, President Jimmy Carter signed it. Redington was tremendously excited. Gravel wrote him a congratulatory letter saying in part, "Joe, we made it. I couldn't have done it without your help."

In the years after the Iditarod Trail received its protective designation, Redington worked to make it an even higher profile thoroughfare. He did not want the trail to be exclusionary. Although mushing was the sport closest to his heart, Redington was thrilled when athletes who specialized in other sports took an interest in the trail.

His friend Bill Devine said the trail should be called "The Iditarod Trail—A Trail for All Seasons," though there wasn't much travel on the trail in the summer when the rivers and creeks were open.

Dolly Lefever, an Anchorage adventurer who later became the first American woman to climb the tallest mountains on the seven continents, skied the length of the Iditarod Trail, a thousand-plus miles all the way to Nome.

"She's a tough woman," said Redington.

Then Redington, and the Iditarod Trailblazers' Knik Chapter, lent a hand in getting the famed Iditaski underway in 1983. Billed as "The Longest Cross-Country Ski Races in the World," the Iditaski made its debut in February of that year with companion races of 123 and 150 miles. Soon enough, racers in snowshoes, racers on foot, and racers on bicycles were traversing the trail each February as part of the vastly expanded Iditasport challenge. This type of activity continues to grow and Dan Bull, one of the main organizers, predicts that one day the racers will routinely compete in events taking them the length of the trail. Redington loves it.

"It gave more publicity to the trail," he said. "I always wanted to see people use the trail."

Redington is less enamored of the "Iron Dog" snowmachine race to Nome along the Iditarod Trail, though. He feels the machines pound the trail too hard and do too much damage. In his mind it looks ugly. Ever since he felt the threat of snowmachines replacing his beloved huskies, Redington has been slow to warm up to snowmachine activity.

In March 1990, two men in their thirties, Tim Kelley, a former member of the United States ski team, and his friend, Bob Baker, a four-time past champion of the Iditaski, decided to do the "Dolly trip"—cross-country ski from Anchorage to Nome. The trip was roughly eleven hundred miles long, and they experienced everything from rain and snow to hallucinations and joy. It was sunny at times, and it was thirty below zero at times. By finishing in twenty-three days and change, Kelley and Baker skied the trail almost as fast as the first Iditarod mushers traveled by dog team.

"This is the ultimate trip I've ever done," said Kelley. "I've climbed Mount McKinley and that's a picnic compared to an ultramarathon."

Calling their trip "The Nome Odyssey," the skiers actually overlapped with mushers on the trail during the 1990 Iditarod. One of the best moments occurred when Redington mushed past them and hailed them. He told them they were tough guys, and he was betting they would make it all the way to Nome. By then, Redington was known as "The Father of the Iditarod," and Kelley was only half-kidding when he said, "We got blessings from the Father."

Redington applauded their achievement and noted that there has never been any conflict between mushers and skiers on the trail. Skiers

PRESIDENTIAL TREATMENT

—The dogs that were stolen,
they received the biggest cheers.—

Waiting for the inaugural parade to begin, Joe and Vi posed with
a dogsled that was fitted with wheels to roll down Pennsylvania Avenue.
The Alaskans were cheered along the parade route as Washingtonians
showed their support for the victims of the "dog-napping."

■

It was late at night when the mushers heard the ruckus. Barking dogs,
squealing tires. By the time they ran outside, a pickup truck was peeling
rubber and some of their dogs had been kidnapped.

In 1981, Joe Redington, Herbie Nayokpuk, and Norman Vaughan
were selected by Alaska Governor Jay Hammond to represent the state at
Ronald Reagan's inaugural parade in Washington, D.C. What a crew.
Nayokpuk called them "The Three Stooges."

Redington always would go anywhere, anytime to publicize Alaskan huskies, dog mushing, or the Iditarod. Besides, this sounded like a kick. They all figured it would be a good time. What they didn't count on was losing their leaders to a gang of dog-nappers a few nights before the event.

A group of mushers and their dogs constituted a different animal when it came to preparing floats for the parade. So the men and beasts were quartered at a horse farm on the outskirts of the nation's capital in Maryland, away from downtown and city traffic.

The mushers arrived at their accommodations to some fanfare. When they parked their dogs and set them out on long chains, a crowd of perhaps a dozen curious people surrounded them, chatting, asking questions, gazing at the huskies with admiration. Vaughan said he noticed one young man in the group who was wearing a sling. He asked a few questions, including which ones among the dogs were the leaders.

Of course, no one saw any significance in his inquisitiveness. Just typical stuff from a cheechako. It turned out later that this young fellow was a key player in the brouhaha.

The dogs were bedded down, the men were bedded down, and then loud noises and unhappy dogs broke the night's silence. The mushers came running out of the house wielding flashlights, but no one got the license plate number of the disappearing truck.

All three of the dogs taken were leaders, two belonging to Redington and one to Vaughan. Immediately, the theft was reported and publicized. The mushers—three of the most colorful men to race the Iditarod—were interviewed in newspapers and on television.

"That created a hell of a lot of excitement," said Redington. But no leads. The guys from Alaska came to the big city and got fleeced. However, the locals felt badly because of the incident, and the attention focused on the robbery remained intense. Radio shows mentioned it. TV shows brought it up. Newspapers highlighted it. Descriptions of the dogs were broadcast.

Although depressed by the development, the mushers prepared to go through with the appearance and make the best of it. They had brought nine dogs apiece with them, so they still had plenty of dog power, and in

Alaska's Senator Ted Stevens and Congressman Don Young met members of the Alaskan delegation who traveled to Washington, D.C., in 1981 for the inauguration of President Ronald Reagan. From left are Dick Mackey, Joe Redington, Sr., Don Young, Norman Vaughan, Ted Stevens, Vi Redington, Elizabeth Nayokpuk, Herbie Nayokpuk, and Jan Masek.

the days leading up to the parade they gave sled-dog rides to congressmen on the grounds of the Capitol.

Then the day before the parade, the dragnet produced results.

"A woman was cooking in her kitchen and had the television on, and she saw the description of the dogs," said Vaughan. "She said, 'Oh my God, they're in my cellar'!"

The culprits were three sixteen-year-old boys—friends of the injured teenager in a sling who issued all the questions when the mushers first got to the farm.

"The kid's mother turned him in," said Redington. "We got the dogs back just in time." The dogs were reclaimed and were in good health. Vaughan said he was under the impression that the teenagers planned to hold the dogs for ransom, but got caught before they could make any kind of financial demand.

The sleds were specially made by Alaskan Vern Hill with big, toboggan-style frames. It was January, but January in Washington, D.C. is nothing like January in Alaska. A lack of snow meant the mushers had to attach wheels to the sleds to roll down the street.

"It was a good job putting wheels on them," said Redington. Indeed, dog sleds are supposed to glide, not ride.

The special occasion turned those sleds into special commemorative vehicles in the same way that a bat used to club a special home run makes that baseball equipment a coveted collectible. After the inaugural, in fact, former executive director of the ITC, Burt Bomhoff, bought one sled. Another sled was put on display at Iditarod Trail headquarters. And the third was donated to the state transportation museum.

A few friends and fellow mushers came along for the journey to help out at the starting line, handle the dogs, and snap pictures. Dick Mackey came east to participate. So did Bill Devine. And Mat-Su Valley musher Jan Masek. They all helped prevent the excited, straining-at-the-harnesses dogs from darting into the crowd when things got underway.

This was hardly supposed to be an all-out sprint. In fact the cadence was quite slow. Vi joined Joe in the sled for the ride. Herbie's wife Elizabeth rode with him and Norman brought a date. The Redingtons decked themselves out in mushing finery, a wardrobe complete with fur hats and mukluks.

As their sled was pulled down Pennsylvania Avenue, they waved at the thousands of people lining the street and people shouted back, *Alaska!* "We had a lot of fun," said Vi.

The mushers' slot amongst the parade participants was right behind a group of horses. The rules stated that they must remain at least twenty-five feet behind. Accompanying the welcome to the line-up was an admonition that they could be pulled from the parade for getting too close, or veering off track. Anyone who has ever watched the start of a dog sled race knows that the dogs are so hot to trot that they strain their tug lines and actually yank handlers off their feet. Redington remembers how hard it was to control the dogs in the parade, but the mushers did so without a major snafu.

"We were right behind those horses," said Nayokpuk. "I had a good

The Redingtons and other visiting Alaskans dressed to the nines for a Washington ball. "We were just dog people," remembers Dick Mackey. "But we cleaned up real nice."

brake. The dogs got excited." Nayokpuk said he thinks the dogs believed the horses were moose. A reasonable theory. And moose are dog magnets in Alaska. Not always with healthy results. At the least, even in this foreign environment, the dogs would be curious enough to sniff at the strange, large animals ahead of them.

It was a memorable trip for the man from Shishmaref. Pennsylvania Avenue. Inaugural parade.

"That was fun," said Nayokpuk. "I'd never seen that kind of life before. We saw a lot of people."

Nayokpuk joked that he, Redington, and Vaughan, should band together more often. Perhaps for some kind of entertainment venture. "Maybe we could make more money," he said, "so then we don't have to work hard."

They probably would be the hardest-working men in show business.

Everyone would argue these mushers were wise choices to represent Alaska and the sport of mushing in an event of this magnitude, but it was hardly a surprise to anyone that Redington was involved. Not only was he singularly identified with the Iditarod race, but anywhere there was any kind of activity that could help mushing, that's where you'd find Joe.

Gareth Wright, who made his reputation by racing dogs short distances, is blunt in his assessment of how long-distance mushing has eclipsed his specialty in the public eye, and he gives much of the credit for that development to Redington's prowess as a promoter. To Wright, Redington is the P.T. Barnum of mushing.

"I think he is a hell of a promoter, a hell of a dog man," said Wright. "He is the greatest promoter in the world that I've ever known. Going up Mount McKinley. He did things no one imagined doing."

Unless you witnessed it first-hand, it was pretty hard to imagine this grizzled bunch of daring wilderness mushers guiding their dog teams down Pennsylvania Avenue, that's for sure.

Vaughan said the reception of the spectators, cheering, waving, hollering for Alaska, gave him a memorable thrill. But more than that he said the graciousness of the people responding to the near-loss of their dogs, struck home.

"They were yelling things like, 'Sorry it happened to you fellas'," said Vaughan. " 'Hope they're all right'."

Vaughan tied pink ribbons around the necks of the dogs that were stolen, and the public address announcer singled them out. Those dogs received the biggest cheers. Except for maybe the old human dogs who were driving them.

20

TRAIL WOES, HIGH HOPES

—The public perceives Joe Redington
as the Iditarod.—

Following a scratch at Unalakleet in 1980, Joe arrived in fourteenth
place for the 1981 Iditarod, but still found the energy to display his sponsor's
logo and the apt message: "Staying on Course." Too busy to train, he had
started the race with only three hundred training miles on his dogs.
He had decided to "take it easy and train these dogs on the way to Nome."

■

Even after all these years, Joanne Potts remembers how she was struck by the old guy's incredible passion.

Potts is the race coordinator of the Iditarod Trail Sled Dog Race and she has held a number of positions with the race over the last two decades. When she first met Joe Redington in 1976, she was a volunteer. As the years passed, and she advanced to become a full-time employee, she spent more and more of her time at the old race headquarters above Teeland's store in downtown Wasilla.

In those days, race headquarters was not nearly as large, or plush, as it is now. There were just a few chairs and a few tables.

"We didn't have anything up there," said Potts. "But Joe used to hang around a lot."

The race headquarters was indeed Joe's second home. He never stopped talking about dogs and he never stopped trying to come up with ways to increase recognition of the race.

"I've never heard Joe say it was 'his race'," said Potts, "but I know he feels some sort of ownership. The Iditarod, that's the most important thing to Joe. The public perceives Joe Redington as the Iditarod. He probably attracts more attention than a champion. People tend to have a lot of respect for age."

As the 1970s turned to the 1980s, Joe Redington was approaching retirement age. For someone who had worked nine-to-five in regular society, that is. But he was hardly the type of guy likely to sit around collecting Social Security. Redington was still a full-time musher, a full-time racer, and a full-time promoter of the Iditarod. And it didn't seem as if he was running short on energy, either.

At age sixty-two he had just taken a dog team to the top of Mount McKinley and later that same year the Los Angeles Times published a story about him headlined, "The Toughest Man in Alaska." In that story, writer J. Michael Kennedy called Redington's life, "a good, but improbable movie script."

However, Redington was showing wear and tear on his body in one area—he was losing his hearing. Redington now wears hearing aids in both ears, and he cannot use a normal telephone to communicate any-more.

Redington believes the initial damage done to his hearing probably occurred during World War II when he was around airplanes, other loud machinery, and artillery. Later, he worked in many fields where loud engines were prominent. Everything from automobiles to boats. "It gradually worsened," said Redington.

One job he had placed him on a boat in Homer, Alaska, and standing right between two large, churning, noisy engines. He first started to realize his hearing was a problem in the 1970s, but he was either too proud, stubborn, or busy to do much about it. He adopted that approach for years. When he finally went to have a test, the doctor immediately said, "You can't hear, can you?"

The hearing aids help quite a bit and Redington can understand conversation in person with little trouble. And the hearing problem didn't slow him on the trail. Unlike some sports where exploits are passed on by word of mouth to up-and-coming stars, who never get to see some of their predecessors perform, Redington was right there, live and in-person, still active. New stars could actually get to know him.

Martin Buser of Big Lake, a three-time Iditarod champion who turned forty in 1998, said when he tells stories about the trail he always uses Redington as an example of someone with a special spirit.

"I tell people that when I grow up I want to be as tough as old Joe," said Buser.

Jeff King of Denali Park won the Iditarod in 1993, 1996, and 1998, but when he competed in the race across Alaska for the first time in 1981, he was more novice than contender. King's first meeting with Redington took place at Teeland's, at the headquarters office. King was there to take care of his entry paperwork and was standing at the foot of the stairs when Redington bounded up the staircase. He didn't recognize him at first.

"I thought, 'Who is this guy'?" said King.

At the time, the story going around was that Redington was once again so busy promoting the race he didn't even have time to train. King, the beginner, asked veteran mushers for advice and was warned that a key element in making it all the way to Nome was ensuring that his dogs had enough training miles on them. He fretted about that constantly, and when the race began his training log showed his toughened-up dogs were approaching two thousand miles on the odometer. Not bad, he thought.

King thought he was prepared—then the racing began.

"I got to Skwentna in a daze," he said of the checkpoint only a hundred and fifty miles in. "I was whipped. I hadn't slept."

King, who is known for his meticulous ways, said he spent weeks preparing his food packages for drop-off at the checkpoints along the trail, then watched in amazement as Herbie Nayokpuk dug into the goods shipped out for him and pulled out a whole seal carcass. So much for neat

The Iditarod Trail Sled Dog Race had gained a loyal following but was still not stable enough to grow without Joe's heavy involvement. As a result, he sacrificed time training with his team, and it showed at race time.

packing jobs.

The Skwentna checkpoint is Joe Delia's all-purpose cabin, and whenever Redington shows up during a race, the two have a mini-reunion. King was astonished by the conversation he overheard between Delia and Redington.

Delia: "How's it going?"

Redington: "I've only run the dogs three hundred miles."

"That's impossible," King thought. "You can't get there." At least not according to all the mushers he talked to; he was totally baffled.

Redington: "I'm going to have to take it easy and train this team on the way to Nome."

King mushed into McGrath nearly twenty-four hours ahead of Redington, and once he heard that he doubted Redington would even make it to the finish line.

Several days later and much farther along the trail, a hardworking, but somewhat frustrated King was making slow progress in the hills outside of

Jeff King was dumbfounded when Joe Redington passed him near Ophir in the 1981 race. Only a couple of days earlier, King and his well-trained team had a twenty-four-hour jump on Redington. The elder musher wished King good luck as he passed.

JEFF SCHULTZ/ALASKA STOCK

Ophir when out of the darkness behind him he saw a headlamp closing.

A voice called out: "On by. On by." King pulled over, and the dog team sped past. The musher riding the runners hailed him. "Good evening," he said. "Who's there?" King gave a hello. "Good luck," said the musher. "See you later."

The dogs never slowed, and King was left far behind.

"I was in shock when I realized it was him," said King.

When King completed the handful of remaining miles into Ophir, Redington's team was already bedded down and the musher was asleep.

"I never saw him again," said King, who finished twenty-eighth in his rookie year.

Redington? He kept gaining speed and placed fourteenth that year. With a team training on the job.

What any skeptic of Redington methods overlooked was that the trail was his second home. It was part of him. And besides, as he proved year after year, Joe Redington wasn't really like anybody else. Not that

Redington was perfect. What King had not known was that Redington was searching for redemption in 1981. He was angry with himself, angry at the way he let himself go soft in the 1980 race. It was so uncharacteristic of his entire life.

There is no disgrace in scratching from the Iditarod. It is a long race, with many hardships. But there are appropriate circumstances when it is best to pull the plug. Best for the musher, best for the dogs. There are also times even the savviest of mushers can learn a lesson. That was 1980 for Joe.

Redington's woes began early in that Iditarod. The Farewell Burn is an aptly named section of the Iditarod Trail in the first quarter of the race. A 1978 fire scorched 345,000 acres of land, devastating the trees and terrain. It is often very rough going through this area, especially in light snow years, and especially in the dark.

Redington reached the Burn at night and trying to make headway he repeatedly ended up off the trail. He termed this stretch a nightmare. It was a disheartening run, but Redington was still not out of contention.

The 1980 race was captured by Joe May of Trapper Creek, but Redington was in the group of front-runners plodding over slow trail for hundreds of miles. Redington knew he had a good team that year—he had placed third in the Kuskokwim 300 in January. For a long time in this Iditarod he was with May, Rick Swenson, who would place fourth, and Sonny Lindner, who later dropped out, too.

The weather was a factor. It went from hot to cold quickly. Around Kaltag, about nine hundred miles into the race, and the last community checkpoint before reaching Unalakleet, Redington had problems.

"It was just miserable going," said Redington.

For days it had been unseasonably warm, higher than freezing. Then abruptly the temperature dropped to forty degrees below zero. Hard on the dogs and not good for the musher's mental state, either. All of Redington's gear got wet. The zipper on his sled bag wouldn't work. It was all discouraging. He pulled into Unalakleet and said "Enough." There was no really good reason. It just felt too hard to go on. Indeed, if he had only waited out the night after a rest, Redington probably wouldn't have scratched.

"I could have kicked myself the next morning," he said. "I got up and the dogs were screaming to go. I was foolish to quit. There was nothing wrong with me or my dogs except my head. We could have stayed the whole night in Unalakleet and still caught up because the whole race slowed down after that."

But there was no taking the decision back.

"I was even mad at him," said Vi Redington.

Redington learned that it was best to sleep on any drastic decision before doing anything irrevocable. In fact, he now routinely offers that advice to mushers starting out in Iditarod competition.

Eagle River musher Bob Ernisse, who took up the sport in the 1990s and first met Redington during a qualifying race, said that indeed is the very first morsel of advice Redington gave him.

"Finish what you start," is what Redington told him, said Ernisse, who adopted that as a personal motto. "Sleep on it," said Ernisse. "Don't just say, 'I'm done.' He told me he made a mistake once."

The 1980 mistake. When Redington gave up in Unalakleet that year he was at least in a friendly environment.

"When Joe arrives," said Leonard Brown, "I always say to him, 'Welcome home.' We sure love this guy."

However, Redington was supposed to be a short-term guest, just stopping by before hitting the trail again. Redington's dogs went home and Brown ended up flying him to Nome in his plane.

Not a good ending.

The 1980 race was the one deemed Herbie Nayokpuk's best chance, the one where observers cracked he would have won if he hadn't taken the time to be so gracious to so many villagers on the way to Nome. Nayokpuk, who did place second, was just that kind of guy.

"He was a real jolly fella, always laughing, always telling stories," said Redington. "He had an old Eskimo way of doing things. You always learned a little something when you talked to someone like Herbie."

Or maybe you just had unforgettable experiences hanging out with Nayokpuk. Redington and Nayokpuk mushed together through a storm near Golovin Bay. It was a vicious storm, snow swirling, wind screaming. Blackie, Nayokpuk's leader, got them through the ground blizzard, leading both sleds the right way.

"Herbie looked like he was floating on a cloud," said Redington. "It

JEFF SCHULTZ/ALASKA STOCK

At the starting line in 1982, Joe had high expectations, and would finish in the money at seventeenth place. In first and second places were rivals Rick Swenson and Susan Butcher, separated by not quite four minutes.

was blowing eighty miles an hour."

Redington vowed to show that he was still a for-real threat in 1981. Then he ended up having little time to train because he was still so devoted to fundraising and organizing. Others could focus on their own kennels, Redington's kennel was all Iditarod dogs. He did not feel secure enough about his baby to let go, to let it stand on its own feet quite yet.

In the early 1980s the Iditarod was better known than it was during the exciting, but shaky first years of the 1970s, but nowhere nearly as well known as it would become.

"People were just learning about it," said Redington. "There were no sponsors from outside Alaska. We didn't have much of an image in those days. People were still asking, 'Are you going to have a race next year'?"

Not that Redington admitted any skepticism publicly. On the contrary. In the 1980 trail annual, editor Dorothy Page quoted Redington as saying, "There's no doubt about it. The Iditarod is here to stay."

The big picture always took precedence over his own racing. Yet in the 1981 race Redington wanted to prove he was far from washed up.

Swenson was the champion again in 1981, but Redington thought he should have finished a little higher than fourteenth. Leaving White Mountain, his dogs had a lot of pep, but the group of mushers right in front of Redington wouldn't let him pass. Eventually, he stopped trying to get by.

"I just went in behind them," said Redington.

That year he received a congratulatory letter from United States Senator Ted Stevens of Alaska after seeing him in Nome. "Congratulations on your finish this year," Stevens wrote. "Your ability to run the Iditarod every season is an example for all Alaskans. Perhaps next year you will win it all."

Redington wanted to make Stevens' wish come true. He had high hopes again in 1982, but Swenson won for the fourth time. Redington finished seventeenth, in the money, but was looking for more. Most of the buzz was about the front of the pack, for a unique reason. Susan Butcher finished second, not quite four minutes behind Swenson. *Could a woman win this race?* It seemed inevitable. This is what Redington predicted years earlier. Besides, Butcher placed fifth in 1980 and fifth in 1981. Her improvement was steady.

"I knew she was a good dog musher and had what it took to do it,' said Redington. "I fully expected her to be the first woman to win."

And he fully expected to be up there racing against her for the title

SIDELINED, NOT STOPPED

*—Redington was mushing home when
he was jumped by a killer moose .—*

At the finish line of the 1984 Iditarod, Joe's face was a mess.
"That would be the time I fell asleep and hit the tree-low branch at
Unalakleet," he remembers. "You know, I was always pretty lucky. I hit that
tree, I broke my light, but I recovered my dogs. Went two miles, here's two
nurses on their way to Nome, camped at Old Woman. One patched me all
up and I was on my way. Another time I got banged up near Rohn and
I didn't go five miles until Dr. Martin was camped on the trail."

The moose came out of nowhere.

A few weeks before the 1983 Iditarod, Redington was mushing home
to Knik on a training run. Whooshing along, glad to be almost finished,
he was jumped by a killer moose.

Moose do not like to share the trail. In summer, they tend to blend
into the trees, and they thrive on devouring vegetation. In winter, when

the tree branches are bare, moose move around more and forage for anything they can get. Deep snow makes it hard for them to move in comfort, so any time they find an open trail, they love it. And once they claim a place, they also get stubborn and refuse to budge.

One thing that is sure to rile a moose, though, is a pack of barking dogs. And one thing certain to create curiosity among dogs is a large, recalcitrant moose. Bad combination.

The moose was protective of its territory and Redington barely saw it coming. The moose charged head-on, plowing through the dog team and leaping at a ducking Redington. Anyone who believes that moose are friendly, tame beasts has never met with the animal's flying hooves. Moose have trampled men to death and have many, many times put dogs to rout.

Redington almost sidestepped the moose, but he couldn't quite get clear. The moose actually jumped over the sled and Redington. As the moose hurtled him, though, it flailed out with its hooves and struck him. Redington was sent sprawling. "One hoof caught me," he remembered. The impact of a kick on his back broke three ribs and the spill damaged his right knee.

The dogs were terrified and they fled, leaving behind a sore Redington lying in the snow. He had to be rescued by friend Dave Olson. One dog was severely injured, too, also suffering broken ribs, although it recovered.

The injury, coming shortly before the race start, ruined Redington's hopes of a good finish in 1983. He had to scratch before reaching the starting line.

"I was the first to sign up and I couldn't even go," he said.

The ribs healed in due course, but the knee injury bothered Redington for a long time. He bought knee braces and experimented with them steadying his leg, but for a long time nothing worked.

"It took me a year to get my leg better," said Redington.

This was one year Redington had a well-trained team. At the time, Roger Legaard of Norway was staying at the Redington homestead and training for his Iditarod debut. He was in the forefront of what would become a foreign incursion in future years and, as so many others would do, he came to Redington for help. Using Redington dogs, Legaard placed tenth in the race.

Joe poses with a lead dog named for one of his sponsors: Tang.

BILL DEVINE

Not only did Redington miss racing in the Iditarod for the first time in a decade, he also missed out on a special mushing celebration in Nome. The seventy-fifth anniversary of the inaugural 1908 All-Alaska Sweepstakes prompted the mushing world to stage a re-enactment.

This is the race that made folk heroes out of Iron Man Johnson, Scotty Allan and Leonhard Seppala. Redington admired those old-timers who made their reputations in the Sweepstakes races before World War I. The 408-mile round-trip race between Nome and Candle represented the origin of long-distance mushing in Alaska.

While those well-known victors were historical figures of some note, everyone figured that a modern-day musher would easily eclipse the best times of the past. Nutritional knowledge was vastly improved. Sleds were lighter in weight. Dogs were better trained. Fewer and fewer Alaskan huskies were both work dog and racing dog. The old records figured to be obliterated.

The prime candidate for besting the old bests was Rick Swenson. A man who knew and respected the Sweepstakes history, Swenson was the dominant Iditarod musher of the moment. He set out to better the mark, but with his long-held respect for his esteemed predecessors, wasn't as certain as others it would be accomplished.

The Sweepstakes was the highlight of winter activities in Nome after the gold rush ended. It was a major event from 1908 to 1917, but the race that lived on in lore was the 1910 competition.

The race began on Front Street—where the Iditarod finishes—on April 6, 1910. It was snowing hard and severe winds blew directly in the mushers' faces. Candle lay more than two hundred miles to the northeast, and no matter what type of clothing a man wore, the wind penetrated to the bone.

John Johnson, a.k.a. Iron Man, seemed impervious to the weather, though. The first musher out, he would be the first musher back. Lead dogs Kolma and Sandy took him on the run of his life. Johnson set a standard that was still intriguing three-quarters of a century later. Johnson's finishing time of seventy-four hours, fourteen minutes, thirty-seven seconds, was the target for the mushers of the modern day.

The special Sweepstakes was held after the 1983 Iditarod, won that year by Rick Mackey, Dick's son, and Redington hoped to be healthy enough to race. But that didn't happen. He wanted to go, but his body said no.

"I wanted to be in it," said Redington. "I just couldn't make it."

Redington's knee was far from healed and prevented him from doing many chores, such as carrying buckets of water for his dogs. The knee buckled constantly. Sometimes it gave out and he fell to the ground.

"I think it was the worst pain I ever had," said Redington. "It collapsed all the time. It buckled and I'd go down. I'd hit the deck."

Many well-known mushers signed up for the new Sweepstakes. Jerry Austin, Jerry Riley, Roger Nordlum, and Herbie Nayokpuk joined Swenson among the twenty-four racers on the starting line. It was a touchstone with history for them, a chance to retrace the steps of the greats. The 1908 Sweepstakes awarded a prize of $2,400. Winner take all. That was the philosophy back then. Unlike the Iditarod, which has always paid prize money down to many placers, if you finished lower than

In 1983, Joe served as a Race Judge at Council, Alaska, for a new race commemorating the 75th anniversary of the All-Alaska Sweepstakes. A bum knee kept him out of the running.

JEFF SCHULTZ/ALASKA STOCK

first in the Sweepstakes, you got a pat on the head. Keeping with the spirit of the original race, the 1983 Sweepstakes featured a $25,000 winner-take-all payoff. However, Nayokpuk did win a $1,500 halfway prize for being the first into Candle. He dropped out before the finish line, though.

Swenson was the steadiest and the fastest, adding the championship of the Sweepstakes to his glittering resume. Swenson defeated Nordlum by two hours, but he never caught the ghost of Iron Man Johnson, finishing in a time of something over eighty-four hours. He was about fourteen hours off the record pace.

"That was a hell of a race," said Swenson. "That's awesome country up there."

Rugged country, too. Country that the original racers negotiated without headlamps.

Redington's son Joee raced his dogs for him, and Joe had to be content to participate as a race judge along the trail. A part of him seemed quietly satisfied that the old guys proved so enduring. The new mushers had been fooled into thinking a record time was in the bag.

"They didn't do it. The trail was a lot rougher," said Redington, adding that it was hardly surprising who won the new Sweepstakes. "Swenson was right in his glory then. He was hot."

There was some talk of holding another Sweepstakes commemorative event in 1998 as a kind of tie-in to the founding of Nome as a city during the gold rush, but that never occurred. The next time to hold a big anniversary Sweepstakes would be in the year 2008, a hundred years after the first Sweepstakes. Redington would be ninety-one years old then.

"I'll probably never make that," he said.

If they schedule the race and he is able, no one would bet against him trying it, though.

Redington's bothersome knee haunted him for a full year, but in 1984 he was back in business, back in his rightful spot near the front of the Iditarod pack. He was driving a strong team and felt good when he pulled into Unalakleet, still running seventeen dogs. As part of his strategy, Redington plan to drop five dogs, trying to keep the fastest of the fast going. But more than one bad thing reared up and sidetracked him. At one point, Redington dozed off on the back of his sled and mushed himself right into a tree limb. It cracked him in the face and blasted him right off the back of the sled.

"It was like getting hit by a two-by-four," said Redington. He rested six hours to recover from that headache.

Another big mistake cost Redington when he was leaving the village. Misinformed about the proper way, Redington found himself mushing on the sea ice instead of the marked trail.

"I was out front and gaining," said Redington.

He heard a radio broadcast with Susan Butcher. During her interview she said the musher she was most worried about was Redington. Butcher was near the front, along with Joe Garnie and Dean Osmar. A commercial fisherman from Clam Gulch, Osmar had invested heavily in new dogs and without much preamble or build-up, had turned a contender.

"He picked out the best," said Redington. "He knew what he was doing. I figured he'd be pretty good."

Precedent indicated Redington would be pretty good, too, and here he was, making a run at the biggest prize in his sport. Until Unalakleet.

He fell back then and lost time he never regained. In the end, Osmar

Vi was no slouch when it came to running sled dogs, but she never had the same competitive fever that affected her husband and sons.

won the championship—and didn't race the Iditarod again, turning over the family responsibilities in that realm to son Tim, who has been a regular top finisher. Butcher placed second, Garnie third, and Redington seventh.

Disappointed, Redington said, "I had a hell of a good team."

The 1984 race was one of those coulda, woulda, shoulda years for Redington. He was sixty-seven, much older than other contenders. It was one of his almost-did-it finishes, one that raised the issue of whether Redington might have won if he had been younger when the Iditarod began, or if he had separated himself from race organization.

Top contender DeeDee Jonrowe believes Redington had it in him to win even as a much older than average musher. "Joe denies his age," she said. Jonrowe believes his perpetual involvement in the race administration weighted him down.

Indeed, the early 1980s were a time of turmoil for the Iditarod. Outside circumstances had to be distracting. The first-place winner took home $24,000 a year, starting in 1981, but the purse didn't increase.

Alarmingly, the race was courting bankruptcy, rather than growth.

Bill Devine and Gareth Wright are among those who said Redington had a great promotional mind. He was always willing to undertake any activity that brought attention to dog mushing and the Iditarod. The Bicentennial Mush in 1976 was one of those offbeat events that had grabbed people's attention.

Much later, in 1991, Redington helped create the first musher cards. Taking the cue from the baseball card industry, he thought, "Why can't we do it?"

Redington and Norman Vaughan are perhaps the most prolific and generous distributors of personal mushing cards. "I carry them around all the time," said Redington. Good publicity.

There is also a pretty rare Joe Redington doll out there. It wears a blue parka snowsuit with black mitts and black boots. There's a real fur ruff on the parka hood and an Iditarod pin on the hat. The doll has an Iditarod patch on its back. It looks quite authentic, very Joe-like. Redington has one standing on a chest of drawers in his living room and said maybe as many as fifty were made. They sold for $295. Again, good publicity.

However, there is a difference between goodwill-good publicity and paying-off-in-cash-money good publicity.

In 1984, the Iditarod was hurting for money. Redington credits Greg Bill, currently development director, with transforming the Iditarod trust fund into a money-making financial boon to the race through his deal for the use of Fred Machetanz's "Reaching the Pass" painting as a limited edition print. The success of the Machetanz sale also pointed Bill in the right direction for future fund-raising projects. He developed a decade-long tie-in with Eagle River artist Charles Gause to produce an annual, official Iditarod print, and that connection raised nearly $1 million dollars for the race.

The profits from the Machetanz print enabled the Iditarod to pay the winner of the 1985 race $50,000, more than double the 1984 winner's share. Given the dividends that result paid in publicity, it was quite a bargain.

The astounding, mush-through-a-storm, milestone triumph by Libby Riddles outshone any Redington publicity-seeking venture for the Iditarod.

Yes, a woman could win.

A WOMAN TAKES THE TITLE

—If Joe was a dog, he'd be the best dog you ever had. He works harder than any dog.—

Libby Riddles won the 1985 Iditarod, staking a place in history as the first woman to claim the championship.

W hen the 1985 Iditarod began, the only Alaskans who knew of Libby Riddles were intense race fans, the kind of fans who know the attributes of the eleventh pitcher, or the twenty-fifth man on a baseball roster.

An increased presence of national and international media put "The Last Great Race" in front of a worldwide audience and fans increased by the thousands.

When the 1985 Iditarod ended, everyone in the nation had heard her name, even the most casual of fans who barely knew such a dog race existed. Riddles imprinted herself upon race history with a single bold maneuver. Her daring stupefied the dog-mushing world and her success electrified the world at large.

"Libby did more for the race than anyone," said Redington. "Here's a blonde-headed gal out in a blizzard beating all the men."

What an unbelievable development. The toughest, most ornery, most rugged men of the wilderness were beaten by a woman. Of course, most Iditarod observers—Joe included—thought the first woman to win the race would be Susan Butcher. But early in the 1985 race, a moose in the trail halted Butcher's dog team. No amount of shooing would scare the moose off. Then the moose got really mad. Sadly, the big animal crashed through her team, killing some dogs, injuring others, before musher Dewey Halverson, who was carrying a gun, arrived on the scene and shot it. The moose wrecked Butcher's hopes and she had to scratch. Hundreds of miles farther down the trail, Riddles emerged as the one to beat.

Riddles, then twenty-eight, was living in Teller, Alaska, some ninety miles north of Nome with her partner Joe Garnie. They shared the dog raising and took turns competing in the Iditarod, using the best from their dog lot. Garnie was third in the 1984 race, and 1985 was Riddles' turn.

Most of the race drama centered around a vicious storm blown in from the Bering Sea Coast. So violent and powerful was this storm that even the best mushers hesitated to push out of the village of Shaktoolik.

The choices were limited: Stay in town and wait out the storm's worst. Or mush ahead and hope it would be possible to break trail. That might give a musher a big enough lead so that others would never catch up in the pursuit of the $50,000. Such a move might also burn out the dogs and ruin that musher's chances. Stay or go? Go or stay? Riddles debated. Then she telephoned Garnie long-distance and asked his opinion. He suggested she try it.

Redington was nearby. He was at the old Shaktoolik village site just three miles down the trail with a local old-timer, the only one still living in what was otherwise a ghost town.

"It was one hell of a storm," said Redington. Then he heard an Iditarod update on the radio reporting that Riddles was going out.

"I thought she'd be all right because she had trained in Teller, and she was storm-wise," said Redington. "I didn't think she'd get very far, and she didn't. Everyone said it would stop and they'd catch right up. But as long as it was blowing, you couldn't find the trail."

Redington is the one who truly did not get very far from Shaktoolik. At least not by dog sled. When he mushed over to the main town site the next morning, he did not see dug-up trenches beside some homes. He fell and when he stumbled he landed on the handle of his ax. He had left it standing straight up in the sled, something he never did. The blow broke some ribs and collapsed a lung. The injury forced Redington to scratch from the race at the Shaktoolik checkpoint.

"I couldn't even stand up," he said.

Riddles fared better. It was a controversial move, but she mushed out of Shaktoolik. The other contenders stayed. As Redington predicted, she didn't get far, only a dozen miles down the trail. The weather was so extreme, so overwhelming, that Riddles decided to park her team and zip herself into her sled bag, and spend a fitful and frightening night in the horrendous cold. Later, Riddles spoke with the publishers of the *Iditarod Trail Annual* about her feelings during that long night.

"Sure I was scared," she said. "You'd have to be stupid if you weren't scared in those conditions. But fear helps keep things in perspective. And I just kept telling myself that if you win the race, it's worth it."

When the snow stopped flying, Riddles was out front, and no one could catch her. Riddles kept looking over her shoulder, waiting for someone to pull alongside her. Even with less than eighty miles to go, when she left White Mountain, she refused to declare victory.

"We could have an earthquake or a tidal wave," she said.

Halverson, the good Samaritan who helped Butcher, was the closest pursuer. He placed second, nearly two and a half hours behind Riddles' slowed-by-weather, eighteen-day winning time.

Not only did a woman win the Iditarod, but she mastered Alaska's worst elements and outdid those tougher-than-nails men. Suddenly, Riddles was a celebrated star. Not only in Alaska, where women gloated over the scope and style of her victory, but nationwide. Her triumph touched a chord in all women.

Redington is among those who state unequivocally that Riddles' championship put the Iditarod on the map worldwide. Indeed, there is little doubt that the double cachet of being the first woman to win the thousand-mile-plus race and the way she won it, created more excitement about the event than any previous development.

Riddles received a letter of congratulations from President Reagan. Alaska Governor Bill Sheffield proclaimed a Libby Riddles Day in the state. She received the professional sportswoman of the year award from the Women's Sports Foundation. She authored a book. *Sports Illustrated* featured her and dressed her up in a frilly dress, presumably to show off her feminine side. If anything, the fact that Riddles was an attractive blonde, and that could be emphasized in some photos, merely added to the If-she-can-do-it, so-can-I sense of resolve that she sparked in many women.

Since that 1985 breakthrough, women and girls have been telling Riddles how much she inspired them. It comes up everywhere she goes, even when she's getting her hair cut at the beauty shop in Wasilla.

As a neighbor of the Redingtons in Knik, Riddles hears the same

In the mid-1980s, Joe invented a training wheel that worked well at any time of year. The concept has been picked up, copied, and modified by many mushers who need to keep their dogs in shape or log training miles before a race.

type of message from Redington himself. He's not shy about praising her.

"He's always been real supportive of me," said Riddles many years after the race. "He's told me that a number of times, how important my win was. He talks me up. I talk him up. I make Joe Redington a role model."

Redington appreciates as much as anyone how Riddles' ride has been romanticized into Iditarod lore.

"All that helped," said Redington. "This blonde, the storm a-blowin'. She's out there battling to win. It made one hell of a story. Then people all over the United States knew about the Iditarod. *Sports Illustrated*. Commercials. It was a big deal. That put the word out all over the world. It was real good for the race."

Riddles never repeated her Iditarod success, and hip surgery drove her out of long-distance racing altogether. She competes in some sprint races and has been an advisor and handler on movies that used dogs. In the summer, she also conducts dogsled tours on a glacier near Juneau for cruise ship tourists in Southeast Alaska.

"Mushing in shorts is fun," she said.

In summers, Joe and Vi kept the Iditarod alive in the community's eye, entering the local Colony Days Parade with a load of puppies and an abundance of sponsorship logos.

She takes out as many as a dozen mushers at a time and a lot of the clients are senior citizens. That's when she tells people about this eighty-something guy who had a vision.

"There's not too many people who fall into the category Joe is in," said Riddles. "He's always on top of the bigger picture, of the direction of the sport. He has a love of the sport and he's always thinking up ways to bring more people into the sport. He's just done so many amazing things. He's always had a great imagination. That spirit."

Redington always did have a famous, lopsided grin, Riddles said. When she thinks of all that he's done with the race and with mushing, she views it as an all-purpose expression.

"That grin is like nobody else's," said Riddles. "That smile says, 'Ha, ha, I've just slipped out of a checkpoint ahead of you.' Or, 'Ha, ha, I've just addicted another person to the Iditarod'." Redington figures Riddles did her part to addict many, many people to the Iditarod.

"After 1985, it became the most famous race in the world," said Redington. "It came on gradually, but by 1985, it was considered the very best. Libby created a hell of a lot of interest."

While Riddles was the barrier breaker, capturing the prize Butcher so long sought and seemed so close to winning, Butcher's turn came soon enough. For a year, she was eclipsed by Riddles' monumental victory, but Butcher began an unprecedented run in 1986. She won that year in record time and followed up with championships in 1987 and 1988, too. Three in a row had never been done. She was second in 1989 and won again in 1990. Butcher's four overall titles matched Swenson at the time.

Riddles' fame came in a super nova burst. Butcher's grew gradually and spread. Even people around the country and world who didn't know her by name knew her by accomplishment. They referred to her as "That woman in Alaska who wins the Iditarod." In a blurring of achievements, eventually less knowledgeable fans simply assumed Butcher was the first woman to win the race.

"Libby and Susan both brought national attention to the race," said Redington. "Libby was a lady and Susan was a musher. Libby ain't the musher Susan is. But they both got whole families talking about the race. The women all over started falling in love with Susan."

No, it wasn't only Riddles the women identified with. Her win

Through the years, Joe has gained celebrity status in Alaska. His appearances often draw fans seeking his autograph. Here, at the 1985 Alaska State Fair in Palmer, Joe signs Iditarod posters.

symbolized something powerful for them and Butcher's wins carried the same type of torch forward. The 1970s federal Title IX legislation, providing additional opportunities for girls in high school sports and young women in college sports, was fresh, just truly gaining a foothold in American consciousness. Riddles and Butcher, too, were in the forefront of an American sports revolution.

No wonder a T-shirt screaming, "Alaska: Where Men Are Men and Women Win The Iditarod," became a bestseller. Some of the gruffer Iditarod men of a chauvinistic bent bristled at that brazen, sarcastic statement. But what could they say? A women beat them at their own game. And women kept on beating them. Four years in a row and five times in six years.

You wouldn't catch Redington sneering at the women. He had coached Butcher when she was a novice racer, and knew that no promotional scheme of his could ever approach the windfall of favorable Iditarod publicity produced by Riddles' win. Besides, he thought the T-shirts were cute.

How good was Riddles' timing? Well, when Greg Bill made the deal to reproduce the Iditarod print, he had all the race winners sign it. Then he left a blank space for the 1985 winner. Riddles. Her signature helped the sales of the print take off.

So the Iditarod had finally matured. It was now both an artistic and financial success. Sprint champion Gareth Wright questioned the staying power of long-distance mushing, but he knew things changed forever when Riddles won.

"I thought it would die out," said Wright of the Iditarod. "I said it would never last. When Libby Riddles won, it was the greatest thing in the world. It showed the men they weren't as tough as they thought they were."

Redington never flagged in his efforts to make the Iditarod world-renowned. He just didn't know how it would happen.

It is most appropriate that when Riddles thinks of Redington—fondly—she compares him to a hard-working, reliable Alaskan husky Iditarod lead dog.

"If Joe was a dog, he'd be the best dog you ever had," said Riddles. "Squared. He works harder than any dog."

As he has proven many, many times over the years, Redington is indeed dogged.

23

INTERNATIONAL FLAVOR

*—A musher only needs to know five English terms
to drive dogs: mush, gee, haw, whoa, and go on.—*

Joe continues to support young mushers who wanted to take

a stab at the Iditarod. Kevin Saiki, middle, was a handler for Knik Kennels

who ran the Iditarod in 1985 and 1989. On the left is a representative

of General Foods, the makers of Tang.

The first overseas entrant in the Iditarod was a young farmer from
Norway named Stein Havard Fejestad. Fejestad, then twenty-two, did
quite well in the 1977 race, placing twenty-second overall. He was the
first of many European and Japanese mushers attracted to the world's most
popular mushing event.

Now, when Joe Redington's phone rings he has no idea where the call
is likely originating. It literally could be from anywhere. And not just anywhere with lots of snow and a winter sports tradition.

A stop in the 1985 race gives pause for a sponsor shot and a sip of Tang.

In fact, the first foreign entry in the Iditarod whom Redington truly nursed along was from Australia. Glenn Findlay showed up at the Knik homestead months before the 1982 race. He was going to be a Redington handler, absorbing information about mushing by helping to feed the dogs, clean the dog lot, and train the huskies. "Then he decided he wanted to race," said Redington.

Always encouraging, Redington gave Findlay a team of dogs and set him up in a camp at Point McKenzie, about a half-hour's drive from Knik. Findlay had no winter wardrobe and he couldn't very well race the Iditarod in a sweater, so Redington rounded up sponsors to fund the $11,000 needed to get him on the trail. Findlay obtained some winter gear, spent the winter training, and except for a fire in his tent that nearly ruined him shortly before the start, set off for Nome. And with Redington's support, Findlay did well, finishing in twenty-third place.

When Roger Legaard of Norway appeared the next year, he made no pretense about his goal. He wanted to take part in the Iditarod. He brought his family with him, and they lived in a school bus on Redington property in the Trapper Creek area, miles from Knik. Legaard trained young Redington dogs and was going to take them to Nome. It would be good seasoning for dogs not yet at their peak, but that might some day make the main Iditarod team. These were the top minor league prospects getting a taste of the big-time in anticipation of the next year.

Redington's 1983 knee and rib injuries meant that he could not compete, so Legaard got to race better dogs and it helped him finish in tenth place and win $2,800.

It didn't matter who you were and it didn't matter how inexperienced you were, if you wanted to learn about dogs and you wanted to race in the Iditarod, you went to Joe Redington. That was true as far back as the late 1970s when Susan Butcher, Shelley Gill, and Varona Thompson gathered at their camp on Redington's land.

Redington always had an all-embracing attitude. If he met a beginning musher at a middle-distance event, he offered pointers. Indeed, that's how Eagle River musher Bob Ernisse met Redington prior to his first Iditarod in 1992. Ernisse was competing in the Knik 200. It was like getting pass pattern tips from Knute Rockne.

"I have a lot of respect for him," said Ernisse. "He put together the greatest race on earth."

Once, Ernisse was sacked out on the floor at the Skwentna checkpoint trying to get some rest, while Redington, Norman Vaughan, and Joe Delia told stories at a nearby table. Ernisse couldn't resist eavesdropping. Ernisse had his eyes closed about five feet away, but he didn't sleep.

"A lot of mushers were listening instead of getting rest," said Ernisse. "I think Joe has done for mushing what Muhammad Ali did for boxing. He put it on the map. The leaders of the race pull into a checkpoint and they always have a big entourage. But everyone wants to say hi to Joe. I strongly believe he's every young musher's mentor."

For many years, Redington really was every young musher's mentor. He did run that dog mushing school for a couple of years in the late 1980s. After five days of study, you were competent to hook up a sled, at least.

Whether it was for the whole winter or just a whole week, Redington was the man to see. Not only did he have the desire to help, he had the space on his land to put people up, and most importantly, he had what seemed to be an unlimited supply of dogs. They don't keep official records for such things, but it is generally acknowledged that at peak times, when

In 1986, Joe received a special award from the Iditarod Trail Committee: Honorary Lifetime Member.

Redington topped four hundred and even five hundred dogs on the premises, he had the largest dog lot in the world.

In 1990, in the interests of goodwill and international relations, then-Governor Steve Cowper agreed to welcome two Russian mushers to Alaska to train with Butcher. The state was going to pay their expenses. However, the Russians couldn't make it that year. They couldn't get visas. Then they surprised everyone by showing up in 1991, with their paperwork in order, but nothing else. Except it was an inconvenient time for Butcher. Iditarod race coordinator Joanne Potts took care of them for a week, but she was looking for a winter-long living arrangement.

So who stepped in? Redington, of course. Nikolai Ettyne, then twenty-seven, and Alexander Reznyuk, then forty-one, transferred to the Redingtons', who helped out the impoverished visitors.

"I said, 'We'll put them in the race'," said Joe. At a cost of $20,000, much of it out of Redington's own pocket. He wanted the newcomers from a country never before represented in the Iditarod to succeed.

The mushers lived in a cabin on Redington's land, and he bought them food. The first sponsor rounded up was the Salvation Army. Then others came on board. Of course the Russians used Redington dogs. They entered the Knik 200 and qualified for the Iditarod. Reznyuk, nicknamed Sasha, had no previous mushing experience and on his first training run with five dogs, he turned over the sled. Ettyne came from a family that had four dogs. He had experience hunting—with a spear—as well as mushing. In fact, he told Redington that he kept track of Iditarod results through radio reports virtually since it began in 1973.

Redington gave them lessons, as well as equipment and dogs. Communication, though, was frequently difficult. It involved double interpretation. Joe carefully explained things to Ettyne, who translated into Russian for Reznyuk.

"Nikolai understood enough," said Vi Redington. "Sasha didn't understand English at all."

Redington shrugged off the obstacles. He has often said a musher only needs to know five English terms to drive a team of Alaskan dogs to Nome. Once Ettyne and Reznyuk learned how to say mush, gee, haw, whoa, and go on, Redington knew they would be okay. Redington did a lot of pointing at objects. A mukluk is a mukluk is a mukluk.

Both men performed respectably in the Iditarod, Ettyne finishing thirty-sixth, and Reznyuk finishing thirty-seventh. If the goal was to further United States-Russian relations, then the diplomatic foray was even more successful. The Russians would never forget what Joe Redington did for them.

A steady stream of mushers from foreign lands has challenged the Iditarod Trail, most in the years since Riddles' victory. They came from Japan, like Kazuo Kojima and Keizo Funatsu; from England, like Max Hall; from Italy, like Armen Khatchikan; not to mention Jacques and Claire Philip, who came from France.

The explosion of interest in dog mushing led promoters in Europe to establish their own events. Although there was little terrain like Alaska's, and less consistent snowfall, the biggest of the overseas events was the Alpirod.

The Alpirod started and ended in Italy, though it crossed other nations' boundaries, cutting through France and Switzerland. The event introduced the concept of stage racing. Naturally enough, since the country is home to the Tour du France, the world's most famous bicycle race.

Mushers began each stage in the morning in a village and dash out on a course, perhaps covering forty miles. Top finishers in the stage were rewarded and overall times totaled. In each town there was a banquet. Then everyone loaded up their dogs and zoomed to the next place for the next stage. It was a newfangled type of mushing, a hybrid between sprint mushing and long-distance mushing. Each Alpirod covered hundreds of miles.

One way the Alpirod organizers sought to add credibility to their event was by inviting top Alaskan mushers to participate. Rick Swenson competed. So did DeeDee Jonrowe. In 1988, Joe Redington thought he would give it a try. Held in January, the Alpirod was advantageously placed on the calendar. A musher could handle the Alpirod and still have plenty of time to recover and sharpen dogs for a March Iditarod.

The Alpirod was new to Redington, but he reveled in mushing in a new place, a new country. This was spreading the gospel, in Italian, French, you name it. Though he did marvel at the strange pace kept between stages.

"You'd race a stage, finish, pack up, and drive like hell to the next place," said Redington, who left the actual driving to Vi.

The Redingtons piled into a van and followed lead vehicles to the next destination. The only problem was that the drivers who knew where they were going went exceptionally fast. How fast? Vi didn't really know.

"It was to the floorboard," she said. Vi tucked the van behind the lead driver and stuck close to his bumper. They couldn't afford to lose contact, or they would be lost in the countryside, trying to get directions to a place they couldn't pronounce in a language they couldn't speak.

"We didn't know where to go," said Redington. "I just shut my eyes sometimes. They don't look behind them. They only look at what's ahead. They're the goddamnest drivers I've ever seen."

The Alaskans, though, were the hottest drivers of dog teams the Europeans had ever seen. Alaskans always did well in the Alpirod. And Redington had so much fun he raced again in 1989. For the Alpirod, he was a foreigner in a foreign land. But the best part was that everyone around the race spoke dog. And anytime a group of mushers gathered to talk about the sport, Redington was sure to be in the middle of the action.

Whenever Redington had a story to tell, a hush fell over the room. Just ask Bob Ernisse.

NEAR MISSES

—I feel like an old fox being
chased by fifty young hounds.—

**Joe's 1988 dash to Cripple set a new race record of four days, nineteen hours,
twenty-four minutes, shaving twelve hours off the old record.**

■

The village fire horn blasted over and over again, signaling the arrival of a musher. Not just any musher. The lead musher in the 1988 Iditarod. Then word spread like wind-whipped fire through the community of Ruby. In first place, Joe Redington.

"Grandmothers on snowmachines and school children in minivans raced to the town hall checkpoint to welcome folk hero Joe Redington . . ." was the way the *Anchorage Daily News* reported Redington's appearance in the Yukon River town of about two hundred residents.

At age seventy-one, Redington was on the verge of the greatest race triumph of his life, a victory that might shake up the thousand-mile event as dramatically as Libby Riddles' 1985 triumph. Beauty before age, yes, but wouldn't this make the Iditarod the most egalitarian race of them all? A woman and now a septuagenarian as champs.

It was quite the scene in Ruby, home of 1975 champion Emmitt Peters, who for this race was acting as checker and collected Redington's signature on the sign-in sheet. Hundreds of people gathered around to fete and applaud Redington in a place where only hundreds of people live.

This was Redington's answer to anyone who felt he was over the hill. Ha. Make that over the next hill, heading far away.

It was after noon, and the sun baked the dogs and parka-clad musher with forty-five-degree temperatures. Redington paused to rest after a twenty-one-hour run from Cripple. Out there on the trail, hours behind him, trailed the rest of the pack of contenders, wondering how this tough old bird got the drop on them, wondering if they could close the gap.

Could it be? Could Redington make the impossible a reality? Who would have imagined such a thing? An athlete in his seventies racing head-to-head with others thirty or forty years his junior. The excitement was palpable. In Ruby and elsewhere. The founder of the Iditarod in the lead! What an amazing development.

"I think everybody's pulling for Joe," said Annie Honea in Ruby. "Nobody expected him to be so far ahead."

On the Iditarod's northern route, the village of Cripple is designated as the halfway point to Nome, even though at five hundred and thirty-four miles from the start, it is really closer to Anchorage. Still, Redington collected the halfway prize of a trophy and $3,000 in silver. Redington is very proud of this achievement. His time for the run into Cripple established a new race record of four days, nineteen hours, twenty-four minutes, breaking the old record by twelve hours.

Since Redington's accomplishment, the award, sponsored by an Alaskan telephone company, has been changed to honor the memory of Iditarod "Mother" Dorothy Page. It is a perpetual trophy made of Alaskan birch and marble, decorated with a photograph of Page and is kept at Iditarod headquarters in Wasilla.

Old friend Herbie Nayokpuk was among the pack following Joe into Ruby in 1988. For a while, cheering spectators wondered if Joe, at seventy-one, would win the race he founded.

JEFF SCHULTZ/ALASKA STOCK

Redington received a major reward when he arrived in Ruby, as well. The First Musher to the Yukon Award brings with it $3,500 in cash and a special, seven-course feast provided by an Anchorage hotel.

After living on freeze-dried for a week, the idea of a delicious dinner to a grubby, in-need-of-a-shower lead musher is so mouth-watering how can you not take the time to dine in comfort? Even if every forkful being shoveled into your mouth is recorded for a wide audience by photographers and television cameras.

"It was wonderful," said Redington, grinning with the memory of the tasty offerings. "I had about fifty people watching me eat." He didn't care. Fish, including shrimp and trout, meat, including veal, luscious desserts. Redington sampled some of everything laid out on the table.

Redington was still ahead, but he was being stalked by the best mushers of two generations. Susan Butcher, Rick Swenson, Martin Buser, Joe Garnie, and Herbie Nayokpuk lurked.

Joe contends with a storm along the Bering Sea in the 1988 Iditarod.

After his game of "fox and hounds," he would finish in fifth place.

Redington knew he had a great dog team and was determined to do well.

In 1985, falling on his ax handle cost him a finish. In 1986, he scratched again. That time, going out of Shaktoolik, Redington mushed onto glare ice and into the teeth of a fifty-mph wind. His lead dog, Bonnie, cut her foot badly and seemed terribly uncomfortable on the ice. He called it quits. Dissatisfied with the way things were going in general, when he got to Nome that year, Redington decided to sell off his whole team and start over with newly trained dogs in 1987. His asking price was $20,000. Redington thought Butcher might be interested, but she didn't buy and Redington ended up selling the team to Dick Mackey.

"I just wanted to go to a fresh group of dogs," said Redington.

Even before the Iditarod, Redington had a troubled 1986 race season. He entered the John Beargrease Sled Dog Marathon in Duluth, Minnesota, in January, but on the way south his dog truck burst into flames three times. It was reminiscent of some of his fateful airplane adventures. Although neither Redington nor his dogs were harmed, it was not a good omen. Redington intended to win the four-hundred-mile race, but did not contend.

In 1987, neither Mackey, with his recently purchased Redington dogs in the mix, nor Redington himself, with his young, inexperienced team, did well. Mackey placed thirty-second and Redington thirty-third. Redington said he knows he could have beat Mackey that year, but didn't think it was appropriate, especially since no prize money was at stake.

"I felt I shouldn't pass Dick up after he bought a $20,000 dog team," said Redington.

So once again in 1988 Redington was seeking vindication for poor past performances, an illustrative race that would prove he was still some-one to reckon with regardless of age.

One unusual, early-season dry-land training method he adopted produced chuckles when visitors came by. He invented a dog wheel that looked like a Ferris wheel turned on its side. He could hook up as many as thirty dogs at a time and watch them run in circles, sort of like gerbils. The dogs trotted at ten or twelve miles an hour around and around a loop of a hundred and fifty-five feet.

"You could sit there and watch television and put forty miles on the dogs," said Redington, who admitted he did just that a few times.

In the race, Redington first grabbed the lead in Rohn, less than three hundred miles from Anchorage, and even as he continuously glanced over his shoulder looking for headlamps approaching in the night, he held onto it. Nayokpuk stuck with him for a while and they took their mandatory twenty-four-hour layovers. Others passed, planning to rest later, but Redington's strategy proved prescient when the mushers who went on bogged down in fresh snow and wore down their teams. It was a good break for Redington and Nayokpuk.

When Redington reached McGrath, just over four hundred miles into the race, he declared, "I feel like an old fox being chased by fifty young hounds."

There were plenty of hounds pursuing, of the human and dog persuasion both. From a distance, fans cannot tell who is running strong, whose dogs are in tip-top shape. They can only judge progress by miles covered. All around Alaska, observers marveled at Redington's strength, stamina, and position.

"He's the image of the race to a lot of people," said long-time Iditarod race manager Jack Niggemyer. "The race has certainly gotten high-tech over the years, but Joe went out and gave them a run for their money. It was real interesting to see how many people cared."

That was certainly true. Redington was the one who gave the public the race. Without Joe, there was no Iditarod. For him to win it, too? Frosting on the cake.

"People who follow this race form a unique bond with him," said Stan Hooley, the current Iditarod executive director. "They fantasize about spending time sitting around a barrel stove, having coffee, hearing what Alaska was like."

Redington is the one they credit with bringing that "real" Alaska into their lives once a year.

Even in the midst of the party-like atmosphere at Ruby, though, there were signs Redington might find it hard to hang on to the lead. Of the eighteen dogs he started with, he had already dropped eight. Also, the going from Cripple frustrated him.

"I outran the trailbreakers in Cripple," said Redington. "They didn't expect me until the next day." That meant he had to break his own trail or stay still while his pursuers sliced his lead. He believes he lost the equivalent of five hours' worth of time.

At Kaltag, nearly eight hundred miles into the race, Redington was hanging tough. He had nine dogs remaining and a two-hour lead, though by then the other lead mushers had him in their crosshairs, pushing hard to the Bering Sea Coast and Unalakleet.

Soon enough they made up the difference and from a one-musher race it became a six-musher race. Leaving Kaltag, Redington lost the trail. Tourists were all over, crisscrossing the territory with snowmachine tracks.

"They went everywhere," said Redington. "It made it impossible to find the trail."

Redington took a nap, and when he woke he was snared by Susan Butcher and Martin Buser. He snacked his dogs at the Old Woman cabin on the trail between Kaltag and Unalakleet, and mushed into his old stomping grounds to visit with Leonard and Mary Brown, not singly, as he might have hoped, but as part of a group. The others were moving much faster, and it was apparent that Redington's lead had not only evaporated, but was unlikely to be regained.

"That would have been my best chance to win it," sighed Redington much later. "If I had to do over I would win it. I would have put on snow-shoes and taken the dogs to find the trail at Cripple. That would have saved me being in a storm later."

Redington has always been wistful, philosophical, but never devastated in describing his near misses on the trail. Maybe, he said, he just didn't have the killer instinct necessary. Three-time champion Buser wonders if perhaps Redington did not hunger to win so desperately because of all his other achievements.

"In his book of life there has been enough accomplishments, so maybe winning at his age was not a dominating factor," said Buser. "Maybe from his way of thinking, it was 'I've done a lot, I've seen a lot. I really don't need to win the race'."

It was no longer in his hands. After Unalakleet, Redington just tried to stay near the front, perhaps record his highest finish. He ended up in the company of his old traveling companion Nayokpuk. Over the last segment of the race they mushed almost in tandem.

"I tried to let him win that year," joked Nayokpuk. They mushed through one of the famous wind-driven, swirling snowstorms in the Topkok Hills between White Mountain and the final Safety checkpoint, twenty-two miles shy of Nome. When they stopped in the night to wait out the worst of the weather in a shelter cabin, they sat around chatting. They tried to light a fire. The wind was so strong, though, it blew the fire out in the stove.

"We could not build a fire in the cabin," said Redington. "The wind blew down the chimney. It was roaring just like a freight train."

It was the only time in his life that Redington experienced wind velocity that could snuff out a fire indoors. He and Nayokpuk sat out the storm, just trying to warm up any way they could. They didn't budge for four hours.

"When we came out, our dogs were under three feet of snow," said Redington. Only the tops of his sled handlebars peeked out from under the fresh blanket of white stuff.

Joe took an along-the-coast route. Herbie went inland. They agreed if they got to Safety at about the same time, they would mush in together or race for what was shaping up as fifth place, a familiar-enough spot for Redington.

Crossing the beach, mushing around driftwood, Redington mushed into Safety first. He waited a half-hour, and here came Herbie. Butcher was in Nome, the winner, with Swenson second. Buser and Garnie took places three and four. No personal record-placing was available for Joe. But with television crews waiting at the finish line waiting to record the end of the race for two of the Iditarod's most famous and revered contestants, they decided to race all out.

"Around me Herbie goes," said Redington. "Then I passed him. Around me he'd go again."

They worked hard at it, giving all they had. Then three miles from the finish line Joe pulled away, sailing down Front Street ahead of his old friend. Fifth again.

The next day Nayokpuk suffered a heart attack. Joe felt terrible. For a time he blamed himself for forcing Herbie to race so hard. The guilt lingered, even after a doctor assured him that the exertion had nothing to do with Nayokpuk's illness.

Nayokpuk's attack took some of the pleasure out of what had been a great race, but Redington couldn't help but feel satisfaction about the way he set the pace, won the mid-race awards, and finished in the top five. The old guy showed them he still had the right stuff.

Besides, he joked, "It wouldn't have looked good if a woman won it and then an old man."

25
STAYING THE COURSE

—Observers felt the dogs were in better shape than the mushers when they reached the end of the trail.—

As a dog lover and believer in quality dog care, Joe insisted on the same high standards for all mushers and dogs involved with the Iditarod. When Joe felt no amount of explaining would help the situation, he thumbed his nose at the Humane Society of the United States.

The sky was unbelievable. Against a backdrop of black night, it shimmered yellow, green, and red. Joe Redington mushed his panting dogs along the Yukon River in the bitter, numbing cold and kept his eyes on the sky, not the trail.

The winter of 1989 froze everything in Alaska. Car engines would not turn over. Small planes could not fly. Machinery of all types ground to a halt. When the mercury dropped to fifty below zero in Knik, the pipes

263

burst at Redington's homestead. It was even too cold for Iditarod dogs to do their normal training runs in some places. Mushers who lived in the far northern reaches of the state found themselves staring at temperature readings of seventy below zero. They spent all of their time trying to keep things working. Finally, some of those mushers packed the dogs in their trucks and drove south, where mushing friends took them in for a week or more. Of course, south meant Willow or Wasilla. Where it was only thirty below.

Race start in Anchorage brought no break in the weather. Some Iditarods are defined by the storms that blow in snow by the foot. This Iditarod was characterized by the type of raw cold that is almost unfathomable. Earlier in the season it was eighty degrees below zero at McGrath. That's about as low as thermometers go. It was not quite that bad when Redington reached the community, but it was a very cold race.

Yet the race went on and mushing along the frozen Yukon, the powerful river that runs from Canada to the Bering Sea, was one of the most glorious runs of Redington's life. For a man with thousands upon thousands of mushing miles under his belt, that said something.

Alaskans always feel a little thrill when they view the northern lights, or the *aurora borealis*. Opportunities for clear sightings in most populated parts of the state are rare, perhaps five times a winter. Sometimes the viewing is brief and the wiggling lights are small. Other times they hang in the sky like a painting, visible for an hour. Rarest of all, though, are opportunities to gaze upon the northern lights when the sky is bright and the lights not only stick around for a while, but show many colors.

This was a memorable occasion for Redington, a man who had been everywhere possible by dog team and who had seen everything there was to see in Alaska. He thought. For hours during the 1989 race, mushing along with Joe Garnie from Anvik, to Grayling, to Eagle Island, to Kaltag on the river ice, the northern lights shone brightly. All night long he inhaled a spectacular nature show.

"It was cold, it was bright, it was almost daylight at times," said Redington, grinning at the memory.

A red aurora. Redington saw something that impressed him. He said he could almost hear the lights crackling. Off the Yukon, in Unalakleet, the northern lights still held. Now he could turn his gaze upward without wondering if his dogs would leave the trail. These lights were the best he had ever seen.

A year after he led the race for days, Redington was still a top musher, racing in reach of the leaders most of the time. This year Joe Runyan of Nenana upset the odds by upsetting Butcher. He won the title, she placed second. Swenson was right there, running third.

Redington was not to be taken for granted. He finished ninth. Not bad for someone who celebrated his seventy-second birthday a month before the start. Fellow dog drivers voted Redington the race's Most Inspirational Musher Award.

"Because of my age, probably," said Redington. Rather than anything special he did, he meant.

About eight months after the 1989 Iditarod, Dorothy Page died. Page had joined forces with Redington to produce the short version of an Iditarod race in 1967 and in later years worked tirelessly to help boost the long race when it became reality. She was sixty-eight when she died in November of that year, and an active member of the Iditarod Trail Committee and treasurer of the organization at the time. She previously had been mayor of Wasilla.

Page was born in Michigan and was living in New Mexico with husband Von when they decided to move to Alaska in 1960. She saw her first mushing event that year in Dillingham and grew to admire the hard-working breed of dog driver who put in so much time training the animals with little hope of financial remuneration. Redington, she said, was the first musher to see the possibilities in the race she talked up.

"Everyone thought it was a good idea, but no one wanted to do the work," Page told an *Anchorage Times* reporter in 1977. "But without a musher interested in the race I could talk on forever."

She found that willing accomplice in Redington, who expanded on the premise and adopted Iditarod development as his life's commitment.

Redington was getting craggier, but if anything, he was getting craftier. He was old only on the calendar. The man still possessed almost inhuman stamina. If he grew weary from the pace of being on the trail around-the-clock, he napped on the back of the sled runners. Some trick that was. Once in a while he bashed himself on a tree branch the dogs ran under without leaving enough clearance, but for the most part at least it was safer than nodding off while driving a car. Vi Redington didn't think there was anything strange about Joe's sleeping habits—or lack of them.

"He lives just like he does on the race," she said. "So I can't see much difference."

Was it possible to mush forever? Well, Redington certainly intended to try.

In the stormy 1990 race, a year of another Butcher victory, Redington fell farther back in the pack. He finished out of the money. But this year he was awarded the Iditarod's Sportsmanship Award. The award was created in 1977 by the Alaska Native Brotherhood to honor Ken Chase. For several years the award was named for Redington's old friend. Then the Iditarod Trail Committee picked up sponsorship and finally when Redington collected it, Carrs and Eagle Quality Centers, the statewide grocery chain, began paying out the five-hundred-dollar prize.

Mushing with Bob Chlupach roughly three-quarters of the way through the race, a storm hit. The men mushed on, and Redington reached a cabin between the villages of Elim and Koyuk. It was dark, and the snow was falling hard. Hours passed and Chlupach still did not appear at the shelter cabin.

"I was worried about him because he camped out on the trail," said Redington.

Instead of continuing his own race, Redington alerted race officials that Chlupach could be in peril. Race volunteers were dispatched to find him and check on him. Again, rather than pushing on with his own race, Redington waited for a report on how Chlupach was doing. Only when he learned the other musher was all right, did he continue. Redington finished twenty-fifth and Chlupach twenty-ninth.

Iditarod timing is everything, especially on the Bering Sea Coast. In a storm like this one, the leaders can be free and clear, already in Nome and standing in the shower. The back-of-the-packers can be resting in their own camp in comfort. But the middle-of-the-pack guys may be getting clobbered by the weather.

"Sometimes it makes a hell of a lot of difference where you are," said Redington. "Ground storms can be very localized."

Redington slowed down a little bit more during the 1991 race. When a musher gets separated from his dog team in the wild, it can be a life-threatening experience. Even in the Iditarod, if the weather is harsh, or the temperature is extreme, walking with only the clothes on your back is risky, no matter how thick and trusty they are. A storm can close in and trap you before another musher, a snowmachiner, or a pilot comes along, or the dogs can be retrieved. All of your supplies, food, water, and fire igniting materials, are likely in your sled bag—gone with the dogs. But if a musher mushes long enough, no doubt this unhappy moment will arrive.

Redington was mushing about seven miles shy of the Rainy Pass checkpoint during the early stages of the race when things went awry. The snow hook popped out, spun around and lodged in the sled brake. The dogs took off and left him. Nobody else was around. Just Joe and the snow. He walked for an hour before he found the dogs. Given the comparative speed between beast and man, he was lucky to catch up at all. The sled had overturned, the hook caught, and the dogs got stuck. Redington righted the sled, climbed back on and resumed mushing.

"Or else I'd have to walk into Rainy Pass," he said. Typical Redington stoical behavior, said musher Bob Ernisse. Got a problem? Grit your teeth and solve it.

"What thirty-year-old would walk as far as Joe Redington if he lost his team?" said Ernisse. "He'd wait for a ride. Not Joe. For him it was, 'I lost my team, I'll go get it'."

Redington got his dog team back, but he finished thirty-first in the race. Maybe he was slipping.

By the early 1990s, the Iditarod Trail Sled Dog Race was on firm footing. It was the best-known mushing event in the world, had built followings in all parts of the nation and Europe, and national sponsors made it possible to fund its richest purses. The winner still collected $50,000, but the pay-offs down to twentieth were higher than ever. In 1993, when Kate Persons of Noatak placed twentieth, she took home $9,500. That was more than Jerry Riley made for winning in 1976, and just about as much as Swenson got paid for his 1977 championship.

Not only that, but a new race record was set nearly every year, creating a how-fast-can-they-go buzz. Once, the Iditarod was a three-week adven-

Joe erected a metal igloo near Petersville subdivision in the Mat-Su Valley
as a semi-permanent shelter for his travels with the dogs.

ture. By the late 1980s, it was run in eleven days plus. As the 1990s wore
on, gradually the record time was lowered to ten days plus, then with a
rules modification, to nine days plus. Mushers were breeding, feeding, and
training faster and faster dogs.

In the midst of this time of prosperity, Redington conjured up the idea
of individual mushing cards to provide even more publicity. He showed
them to Iditarod veteran Lavon Barve, a printer by trade, and he printed
some, too. They were the first two mushers to have personalized cards.

People loved them. Redington passed them out wherever he went,
with his autograph. Redington, who has made up many different cards since,
went with a photo of himself mushing down Fourth Avenue in Anchorage
for his debut. On the back it read, "First dog-mushing collector card."

Redington found a company in New Jersey willing to do the printing
and made up a thousand cards at a cost of $106. Then he had some made
for Nikolai Ettyne and Sasha Reznyuk, the first Russians in the Iditarod.

Other mushers printed up their own cards—Barve printed many—and the Iditarod made a deal with a contractor to produce a whole set.

Things could hardly be going better for the race Redington loved. Until the Humane Society of the United States decided that things were going too well. The Washington, D.C.-based body with a membership of 1.8 million put the Iditarod on its hit list, targeting the race for being inherently cruel to dogs. Once the group began campaigning against the Iditarod in 1991, with the long-term goal of putting it out of business, the matter became a national controversy. Caught off-guard, the Iditarod Trail Committee, its executives, and its executive board, chose to be accommodating to the organization, giving dog-yard tours to a representative and inviting an official to participate on its dog-care committee. This tenuous relationship lasted three years—three years too long for Redington's taste.

Redington has a lifetime seat on the Iditarod board of directors. His instant gut reaction was to tell the Humane Society to get lost. However, the Iditarod Trail Committee chose to write a polite letter to the HSUS thanking it for its interest and for taking the trouble to travel along the trail.

"They wanted to 'work' with us," said a disgusted Redington years later. "They got inside. We invited them in."

Redington was hardly the only Alaskan who thought this amounted to suicide, and he used his board pulpit to fight the HSUS's influence and to argue against large-scale cooperation with an organization determined to ruin the Iditarod. He did not care if such a stand alienated national sponsors. In his mind, the Iditarod was first and foremost an Alaskan race, and Alaskans damned well did not need Outsiders telling them what to do.

Redington's stance strained relations with fellow board members. He and executive director Stan Hooley were on opposite sides of the issue.

"We disagreed for a period of time on how you deal with a group like the HSUS while not giving up the financial lifeline," is how Hooley looks back on the tension. Characterizing Redington's generally subdued participation in board meetings, Hooley said, "Joe hasn't been one of the more vocal members, but when he has something to say, people listen. People respect the history."

That's what Redington counted on when he spoke up during Humane

Society debates. Race manager Jack Niggemyer said Redington might have a minority viewpoint on an issue but the public looks at him as the voice of wisdom. He has clout on Iditarod matters.

"He's a powerful guy," said Niggemyer. "Anything he says, people listen. If he has an opinion on something, people pay attention to it."

At the height of the intense feelings splitting the board, Redington took out his own ad in the local newspaper calling for the Iditarod board to break off relations with the Humane Society. That generated a storm as furious as any blowing in off the Bering Sea. It produced a temporary schism between Redington and long-time friend Leo Rasmussen, a former Iditarod Trail Committee president, mayor of Nome, and for roughly two decades, the most dedicated checker in Nome.

"He went to the news when he should have been quiet," said Rasmussen, years after the controversy subsided. "He wasn't the politician some of us were. He almost destroyed the race. He's done it right, too, over the years. On animal rights he did an admirable job."

Animal rights in this case meaning dog care. In fact, in 1977, before the HSUS came gunning for the Iditarod, Joe and Vi Redington were the recipients of a special award from the Alaska Society for Prevention of Cruelty to Animals, for just that reason: ensuring top-notch care for the dogs in the race.

In a speech made when the plaque was presented, it was noted that SPCA observers in Nome felt the dogs were in better shape than the mushers when they reached the end of the trail.

Redington disagrees with Rasmussen's assessment of his actions, of course, and race coordinator Joanne Potts feels Redington was proven correct on the Humane Society representative.

"He constantly beat the drum," she said. " 'We don't need him,' he said. 'Let's go without him.' And he was right."

Initially, the majority of Iditarod officials overruled Redington and plunged ahead with what many mushing fans felt was a misguided policy of appeasement. The controversy was extremely heated and became entangled deeply in financial considerations when some sponsors threatened to withdraw support if the Iditarod didn't cooperate with the powerful lobbying group.

No matter how far the Iditarod bent over to work with the Humane Society, additional demands were made to alter the integrity of the race and national sponsors withdrew anyway. In the end, to Redington's satisfaction, the Iditarod severed all ties with the HSUS and has thrived ever since, even as the organization's official who was most intensely involved in Alaska became embroiled in legal entanglements.

The final straw for Iditarod officials occurred in early 1994 when the Humane Society condemned the race and urged sponsors to withdraw if it was not slowed down. When a national outdoor clothing manufacturer that had been the Iditarod's main sponsor backed that position, Iditarod officials were infuriated.

"You're fussing with our heritage here," musher DeeDee Jonrowe, then a member of the board, said at the critical April meeting. "We have to stand up and say, 'This is our event. If you don't like it, I don't care'."

Redington was as pleased as any man on earth when the Iditarod pulled the plug on the HSUS connection with the race.

"Tell 'em to go to hell," said Redington at the board meeting that divorced the HSUS from the Iditarod permanently.

Since the brouhaha died down, the Iditarod has retrenched and is now basically supported by Alaska businesses.

The Humane Society war meant that once again Redington was more preoccupied with race administrative matters than training. Nonetheless Redington entered the 1992 Iditarod with his usual enthusiasm and sense of optimism. However, this Iditarod turned out to be one of his most frustrating. Twice Redington was separated from his team. Twice he had to hike the trail.

"I had a brand-new dog team," said Redington. "They were real fast, but I had no control over them. I had a hell of a time."

The first incident occurred three days into the race at Finger Lake, just shy of two hundred miles from Anchorage. His frisky pups bounded into a spruce forest, plowed over a snowdrift and crashed the sled into a tree. Redington was thrown clear, into the snow, and barely dodged the flying, sharp snow hook.

Redington yelled, as much out of anger, as any hope of convincing the dogs to halt. The dogs kept on running. They disappeared and he began walking in the minus-thirty icebox conditions. His hopes rose when through the spreading darkness he saw a sled. Only it wasn't his. Remarkably, Joe Garnie also had been heaved from his sled not far down the trail. Redington saw Garnie's tracks in the snow and spots where the snow hook dragged. Garnie eventually was reunited with his team.

Redington marched on, working up a sweat in his heavy clothes, a dangerous sweat in such extreme temperatures. He was courting hypothermia, but was well aware of it. For that reason he feared stopping. So when musher Mike Williams came along and offered a ride as a faster way to chase down his dogs, Redington refused. He would get them himself. On foot. Williams did mush up on Redington's team and tied them to a tree along the trail. It took Redington hours, but he caught up.

"I was wringing wet with sweat," said Redington. "I climbed in the sleeping bag and pulled out about ten handwarmers. The vapors were floating up."

It took Redington more than four hours to thaw out. And he worried. He knew he should build a fire for warmth, but he didn't like the terrain. Just lying in the bag using the handwarmers as a heat generator seemed a wise enough alternative course. It worked. He renewed himself by spending an uncomfortable night on the trail. He renewed his determination, too: "I'm going to take these bastards to Nome even if I have to walk."

Reporter Tim Murray was covering the race for the *Anchorage Daily News* and was at the Rainy Pass Lodge when he got wind of Redington's difficulties. Murray got his pilot to fly him along the trail until they found Redington and he recounted his tale of woe. They landed the plane on a frozen lake and waited for Redington to mush up to them. Murray later said it was the most memorable time he ever spent with Redington.

"He looked so cold and frail," said Murray. "He looked like he had had a miserable night, which he did. He looked like a tired, old man. I think if it had happened to anyone else, they would have been sorely tempted to scratch. I was impressed with how courageous he was. He was in good humor when he stopped to talk to us. He didn't pull any punches. He realized it was his mistake. He had an excellent attitude. I was standing out there shivering."

Incredibly, the next day Redington had to trek again. Approaching

Rainy Pass, Redington was searching for the best way across a creek when the dogs bolted and dumped him off the sled headfirst.

"I was laying upside down in the water," said Redington. "I was in bad shape."

It was a slow, cold, two-mile hike into the Rainy Pass checkpoint. The dogs were waiting for him there. Once again Redington had to warm up, and this time, dry out. He spent eight hours at the checkpoint.

By the time Redington recuperated, got his dogs' heads on straight, and reached McGrath, a couple of hundred miles down the trail, he was in a discouraging sixty-fourth place. Then, when his young leaders actually began to pay attention to his commands, he started moving. Redington flew down the trail the second half of the race—he recorded the fourth fastest time between White Mountain and Nome—and gained twenty-three positions to finish forty-first overall.

Not that he was happy. Joe Redington in forty-first? For the first time he wondered if racing the Iditarod was the proper pastime for a guy in his mid-seventies.

"I wasn't doing any good," he said.

Redington stepped back from the race, at least temporarily. He would have more time to spend with his twelve grandchildren and great-grandchildren. And he would also have more time to spend on an idea that had been percolating for a while.

Many people were clamoring to mush to Nome who didn't actually want to race in the Iditarod. They seemed to be potential customers ripe and willing to pay for the right guide to lead them there. Maybe it would appeal to them to hire a very well known tour leader, like the guy who founded the Iditarod.

26
TOURISTS ON THE TRAIL

—The time was right to provide mushing wannabes
with Iditarod-like experience.—

Joe took a break from mushing competitively when he started his
new "Iditarod Challenge," a winter-camping trip for citizen-adventurers
who wanted to experience the Iditarod Trail by dogsled.

Joe Redington has always been one checkpoint ahead of the curve. When
hardly anyone thought it made sense to hold a thousand-mile dog sled
race between Anchorage and Nome, he gave them the Iditarod Trail Sled
Dog Race, anyway.

When hardly anyone thought citizen adventurers would want to mush a
thousand miles for fun instead of racing, he gave them an Iditarod Trail tour.

In 1992, discouraged by his recent failings in the race he loved,
Redington decided to test the marketplace with a plan to lead inexperienced, one-time mushers over the Iditarod Trail, following the same route

as the race. His timing was impeccable. Redington introduced his tour business—his Iditarod Challenge, as he called it—just as more and more Americans with disposable income became curious about more daring, creative and unique vacations.

Those with an adventurous bent were no longer interested in spending entire vacations lying on the beach working on a tan. Too dull. The late Ray Genet made Mount McKinley accessible to the masses. By the 1990s, those type of well-off adventurers had graduated to climbs of Mount Everest.

So why not take tourists along the Iditarod Trail?

Redington, who routinely fielded mushing inquiries from all over the world, sensed that the interest was present and the time was right to provide mushing wannabes with an Iditarod-like experience, minus the tension of competition and with the tender loving care of a guide.

Redington thought things through carefully, and in April of 1992 he went public, announcing that for $15,000 a head, the next year he planned to lead a group of mushers to Nome instead of racing to Nome himself.

There were some howls. Fifteen thousand bucks seemed like a lot of money. Was Old Joe gouging people? Was it a rip-off? Clearly, mushing the Iditarod trail in mid-March—just after the Iditarod got underway— was not a vacation for everybody. And just as clearly, not everybody could afford the price tag. But at that time it cost about $20,000 for a guided trip to Antarctica, and it cost far more than that to travel to Nepal and proceed on an Everest climb. And besides, a musher training for the Iditarod spent at least as much, and probably more, to compete. No, Redington had his gig priced just right.

"I knew there were a lot of people who wanted to go," said Redington. And, he added, much later, after conducting a few of the tours, "I've never had anybody kick on the price."

He was correct. There were plenty of people with the wherewithal and the will to mush to Nome, and they were attracted by the idea of making the trip with the guy who founded the race. Of course, there were differences between mushing the trail as a serious racer and mushing the trail for vacation. Despite the officials, Iditarod air force pilots, and volunteers, the racers were essentially on their own, chasing prize

JEFF SCHULTZ/ALASKA STOCK

At home, the Redingtons kept everything within reach and joked that "it looks like a museum in there!"

money, prestige, and in the case of simple finishers, a coveted belt buckle symbolizing their journey. The tourists stuck together, camped together, had snowmachiners break trail for them, and not to be underestimated, also had a guardian angel of a guide in Redington.

You can't mush a thousand miles of the Iditarod Trail, though, without roughing it. You are still at the mercy of the weather, still at the mercy of the dogs' speed and desire. However, for the most part, it seemed you should be able to avoid the type of calamities which beset Redington in the 1992 race when he lost his dog team twice. Not guaranteed, however. There was no law that said you couldn't lose your team.

Before the first tour began Redington analyzed another key distinction between touring and racing. "It's gonna be a lot different than the race," he said. "If we hit a bad bit of trail, we can wait."

In other words, there was no hurry.

When touring time rolled around in March 1993, Redington had seven eager clients leaving Knik two days behind the Iditarod. Sure enough they were citizen-adventurers, many of whom had tried everything else and were after a new thrill. Redington provided dogs, sleds, sleeping bags, boots, and axes for the Iditarod Challenge. They provided the enthusiasm.

A great believer in the adage that if you have the proper clothing you will never get cold, Redington made himself an expert on arctic footwear. In 1986, he went to Minnesota and had a bootmaker create a special model of footwear just for him.

"I drew up what I wanted and they were just right," said Redington. Warm, lightweight, and with good traction. "They're good on the ice, too," he said.

Later, Redington switched to a Colorado manufacturer. He has worn the surprisingly durable boots for years at a time in weather as cold as fifty degrees below zero and can vouch for them.

"I've never had clients complain," he said. Good thing. While many of the mushing clients are from Alaska—people who always wanted to try the Iditarod, but for one reason or another couldn't—many others are from warm-weather climates.

One woman on the first trip, Joan Chitiea of Santa Fe Springs, California, had been birding in the Pribilof Islands and had paddled a river in the Brooks Range. But she raved about the Iditarod Trail.

"On a scale of one to ten, this is a ten," she said. "I don't think there's anything that could top it."

Max Hall, an Englishman, one of the original seven, found a way, though. He came back and raced the Iditarod.

But Hall is an exception. Redington signed up seven people hungering for adventure, but for the most part with little mushing experience, and nursed them to Nome. This was a one-time, not-so-cheap thrill for them. An Anchorage tourist, Brian Davies, said he felt he better sign up and give it a try right away just in case there never was a second trip.

"We're all guinea pigs," said Davies, who postponed his plan of buying a new car to afford the trip. "When I first heard about this, I said, "I'm not sure this will be tried again. If I'm going to do this, I better do it now.'"

By any description or analysis, the trip was an adventure, though Davies need not have worried, since the trip was repeated.

Redington crashed his sled and broke a rib, which certainly proved that anything can happen to anybody on the trail, even when not moving at race pace. Chitiea was bashed in the head, but muddled through and Harry Turner, a sixty-eight-year-old musher, who fell in love with the Iditarod when he watched the finish the year before, fell off his sled and hurt his arm.

The clients ate well. Joe always preferred steaks on the trail, so steak was part of the menu. Cake and stew, too.

Old pal Joe Delia was curious how this experiment would turn out, but was pleased when Redington and his bunch stopped in Skwentna for a long layover to jaw. Actually, said Delia, while the tourists chowed down on the fancy food, Redington slipped over to his house and ate leftovers.

That typified the Joe he knew. No pretense, comfortable anywhere, making everyone else feel good.

"His crew and clients were eating steaks," said Delia. "Joe came over to us and ate spaghetti."

Even if they weren't going all out, steering sleds with little know-how was plenty enough challenge. Nine ready-to-run huskies make for a heap of dog power, even for a musher with some background. Since there was no time limit or real percentage in going fast, the group had the advantage over real Iditarod mushers in being able to stop whenever necessary. The first tour group also lucked out because it didn't get belted by any true Iditarod storms, something that might have endangered a novice on the trail. And they didn't have any of the extreme cold that a long run on the trail almost invariably produces. They spent twenty-three days mushing from Knik to Nome without the mercury dipping below zero. Along the way, Redington entertained his customers with stories. After more than forty years of mushing on the trail, he had plenty of them.

To Redington, it felt like the earliest days of the Iditarod, when everyone camped overnight and built fires. His adventurers developed an affinity for their dogs and loved being away from ringing telephones. If at times it seemed they were on the trail forever, they began to miss the trail as soon as they reached Nome. Just like real racers, who say they can't wait for the race to end, and as soon as they get a good night's sleep and a hot meal, say they can't wait for the next one to begin.

The inaugural tourist mush on the trail ended with a champagne and orange juice celebration on Nome's Front Street, under the burled arch where the racers finish. Everyone who started made it, and so did all of the dogs.

The first tour was rated a big success. The clients had the time of their lives. Redington was pleased and said the tour would become an annual event. Word of mouth spread the news about the event and there was no shortage of clients anxious to sign up and pay the fee.

Of course, once in a while the weather didn't cooperate, and storms blasted the citizen-mushers. That was inevitable. But they mushed on.

One 1995 participant in the Iditarod Challenge got hooked on the mush because of what she read in her grandfather's diaries. Jeanne Ashcraft of Placerville, California, was moved to sign up because of what she read about his experiences overcoming frostbite and wilderness isolation and deprivation in the Yukon while searching for gold. The closest modern-day approximation she could think of was mushing the Iditarod Trail.

It was apparent almost immediately that again Redington touched a nerve. Iditarod contender DeeDee Jonrowe said Redington clearly knew what he was doing with the tourists.

"There is such a perfect niche for that," she said. "They really don't want to race, but they want the experience. They have no business in the race, but they want to get to Nome."

Not only was it a savvy business decision for Redington, taking clients on the trail was naturally consistent with his desire to publicize the Iditarod, the Iditarod Trail and mushing.

Before, he brought mushers to the Iditarod. In a way, this was merely bringing the Iditarod to mushers.

OLYMPIC TRIALS

—Redington was considered by many to be the best-known dog musher in the world . . . a living legend.—

Knik Kennels has always had an open-door policy,
and over the years, Joe's celebrity has created many impromptu
autograph-signing parties, especially for tourists who wander
down his way from the nearby Iditarod Headquarters.

One day in the fall of 1993, Redington opened a letter from overseas. Even though he knew people in Norway, he wasn't expecting anything and there was no clue about the contents. The letter posed a question: Are you interested in being in the Olympics?

The 1994 Winter Olympics in Lillehammer, Norway, included a long-distance dog mushing exhibition race. They knew Joe and they knew Joe knew dogs. So he was an invited participant.

The Olympics? Redington was immediately enthusiastic. He didn't care if they were awarding official gold, silver and bronze medals, or not. He was always game to try something new, and this sounded as if it would be great for the sport.

Once before, in 1932, dog mushing was an Olympic exhibition sport in Lake Placid, New York. One of the entrants in that event, amazingly enough, was Norman Vaughan. Long before he came to Alaska, Vaughan was a peppy young dog musher from Hamilton, Massachusetts. While a Harvard University student, he talked his way onto Admiral Richard Byrd's 1928 expedition to Antarctica. The publicity from that exploration helped make Vaughan a well-known musher and a natural choice for the Olympics.

On the Antarctic journey, Bryd named a 10,000-foot peak Mount Vaughan. Decades later, after he became a fan-favorite Iditarod musher, Vaughan climbed it. He was in his eighties and the achievement thrilled the state.

More than sixty years after Lake Placid, Redington joined Vaughan as an Olympic dog musher for a three-hundred-mile race that wound through the mountains of Norway, to Sweden, back around a huge lake in Norway, and on to a small-town finish line.

Unlike the Alpirod race, for which mushers from the United States brought their best dogs, racers in the exhibition sponsored by the Lille-hammer Games Olympic Arts Committee were prohibited by quarantine rules from bringing their own animals. Under the law in Norway and Sweden, dogs brought from the United States had to stay in quarantine for six months before they could be unleashed.

Redington and his handler, an Anchorage friend named Nan Elliot, traveled to Kiruna, Sweden, one hundred and twenty miles above the Arctic Circle, where he obtained a team to use from another old friend. Taisto Thorneus had once come to Alaska with the goal of running the Iditarod, but was sidetracked by food poisoning. Although there were sixty-three teams involved, Redington was one of only eight entrants in the Olympic contest allowed to start where the Olympic medals were awarded, and the only one from North America.

Joe had most of a week to familiarize himself with the dozen dogs on loan from Thorneus. For anyone who thinks a dog is a dog is a dog and a musher is a musher is a musher, there was one major point of confusion. Redington spoke English and the dogs listened in Swedish. When Redington barked orders, the dogs merely barked.

Redington has always been able to talk dog, but speaking Swedish was a whole different challenge. Thorneus sent advance word to Knik that Redington's biggest problem would be communication and Redington joked at the time that he was sure he could say "gee" and "haw," left and right, in Swedish. As it turned out, issuing those simple commands with the right accent and inflection proved as difficult as memorizing the Gettysburg Address. The training course out of Thorneus's property was a challenge, as well. Just exiting the drive was a slippery, steep exercise because of a drastic downhill and an immediate sharp curve.

Yet as always, Redington was undaunted and figured things would work out. And they pretty much did.

It was twenty degrees below zero when Redington, then seventy-seven, lined up his sled in the No. 3 starting position beneath the Olympic flame on February 15, 1994. Mushers from Italy, Norway, Sweden, and others surrounded him. Roger Legaard, the Norwegian musher who placed tenth in the 1983 Iditarod with Redington dogs when Redington had to scratch because of his moose-induced injuries, was nearby.

When the event started, Redington's dozen dogs bolted from the line at full speed. It was hang-on-and-steer the best he could, especially since sharp curves appeared on the course within just thirty yards.

"It was a better than ninety-degree turn right out of the stadium," said Redington. "It was set up by someone who didn't know dog mushing, but I had no problem on the turn."

While other mushers hunkered down on the backs of their sleds for balance, Redington mushed away standing straight. What stunned him was the lack of crowd and automobile control as what began as a ceremonial start turned into a life-and-death dash through city streets. Legaard was right in front of him and Redington's dogs bounded along, following him.

"The traffic was terrible," said Redington.

Alaskans are used to mushing in front of big crowds, either at the start or finish of the Iditarod, or in the Fur Rendezvous. But they are not used to dodging cars. If a dog team must swerve to avoid a vehicle, it means something's wrong.

Legaard was supposed to make a left turn on the route, which led out of town, but he mistakenly kept going directly into the heart of downtown traffic. Redington was on his heels. Legaard was out of control, and Redington felt he was about to be, but his hurtling dogs crashed into each other, got their lines tangled, and then angrily began fighting. Suddenly, he had a gang war on his hands.

"I had one heck of a dog fight," said Redington. "They were going to kill each other."

With the help of a young spectator, Redington got the dogs calmed down. At least the dogs were no longer sprinting through traffic.

Redington removed the three worst fighters from the team. The dog rumble probably saved his life, Redington said at the time. But it also forced him to scratch from the event, a gloomy development after all the travel, training, and excitement.

Then he luckily and thankfully received a reprieve. A shorter, one-hundred-and-eight-mile companion race was being conducted in Tyrsil, and Redington was not only invited to join that race, he was given the honorary No. 1 start position in the field of sixteen mushers. Redington got off to a great start and was in second place in the early going. The route took the mushers through picturesque snow-covered villages in rural Norway and Sweden.

"Once we got out of the city, it was the best trail I've ever seen," said Redington. "Good, wide trails, like a ski trail. It was a wonderful place to mush dogs."

The race went smoothly for Redington until he reached the Norwegian community of Solenstua, where his dogs sat down and refused to run. He was shocked. He dropped two dogs, and then was able to continue. In the cold, dark night, after a snack of reindeer soup and peanut butter (a perpetual Redington energy treat), he mushed the final miles into Roros, where a cheering crowd greeted him in third place. The solid finish was gratifying.

"It would have been terrible if I had to scratch in that race, too," Redington told his handler, Elliot.

Redington was considered by many to be the best-known dog musher in the world, and his appearance at the Olympics seemed to confirm that. Elliot, who wrote a story for the *Anchorage Daily News* recounting Redington's Olympic adventure, quoted Swedish musher Erik Sundin as calling Redington "a living legend."

Thorneus echoed the same sentiment, saying that mushers throughout Scandinavia knew of Redington and were impressed that a man as old as he was still competed. Elliot made the case that only Norwegian polar explorer Roald Amundsen, of the early twentieth century, and Leonhard Seppala, were as renowned as Redington.

The victor in the official Olympic exhibition race was Sven Engholm, regarded as Sweden's top long-distance musher. Redington predicted that when they were able, the best Scandinavian mushers would perform admirably in the Iditarod. Engholm soon became an Iditarod competitor and immediately began claiming top-twenty money. Redington always could judge mushing skill.

Redington enjoyed every minute of his Olympic sojourn. He hopes some day dog mushing will become a regular part of the Olympic program, but he doesn't think it likely.

"I kind of doubt it," said Redington. "I hope I'm wrong. I think the people would enjoy it."

Even if dog mushing gains Olympic acceptance, though, Redington thinks races will more resemble the Fur Rendezvous than the Iditarod.

"If they have it," said Redington, "I'm sure that sprints, with heats, is what it will be."

Between the citizen-musher tours and mushing in the Olympics, Redington was out of the Iditarod, but he had miles to go with a dog team. The wheels never stopped turning in his head, and the sled runners never stopped churning on the trail. The year 1995 was the seventieth anniversary of the famed serum run to Nome, and Redington felt something special should mark the occasion.

Why not do it again? Or at least something like it. Redington organized a Commemorative Serum Run Relay from Nenana to Nome, following the tracks of the original diphtheria serum run. The Redington event, beginning January 27, 1995, was more a mush than a race, designed

From Joe's dog lot, you can see the Knik Arm of Cook Inlet. At its peak, Knik Kennels had well past five hundred dogs in residence.

to boost Alaska Native involvement on the trail and to publicize a statewide immunization program against childhood diseases. The state issued a proclamation declaring it Serum Run Day.

Once, the great Eskimo and Athabascan mushers of the Alaskan Interior were key players and contenders in the Iditarod. George Attla, Emmitt Peters, and others, were among the race stars, but over time, Native participation diminished. Partially because the costs of doing the race had escalated into the tens of thousands of dollars, and partially because it was hard to find sponsors in small communities.

Originally four teams were scheduled to mush from Nenana to Nome, but while the new serum run called for a breakdown of fourteen legs, only a couple of teams were constants. Much like the original mushers seeking to provide life-saving medicine to combat the epidemic, the mushers passed through the small villages of Tolovana, Old Minto, Manley, Tanana, Ruby, Galena, Nulato, Kaltag, Unalakleet, Shaktoolik, Koyuk, Elim, White Mountain, and Nome. By Ruby, of course, the mushers were following the route of the Iditarod Trail Sled Dog Race.

Mushers like 1989 Iditarod champ Joe Runyan and perennial contender Bill Cotter, mushed legs once the serum relay got underway. Getting going, though, was tricky because the day of the scheduled start it was a paralyzing sixty-four degrees below zero in Nenana.

"I took a thermometer out in the street," said Redington, as if to prove the number to himself. It was hard to stop staring at the reading. "It was so damned cold."

Many of the mushers couldn't get their dog trucks started, and those are vehicles used to revving up in the most extreme cold.

If Redington was complaining, you knew it had to be cold. Many mushers retreated to a nearby home to warm up. But Dick Mackey put in a trail and after some delay, the relay began.

It did not go as well as Redington hoped. Villagers offered warm greetings, but there were fewer participants than expected. However, nurses and doctors did fly in to give shots.

"The only thing that was done successfully was the vaccinations," said Redington. "We couldn't get enough support along the way. It interfered with some of the local racers."

Redington flew the trail to supervise and gleaned his greatest satisfaction meeting young people in the villages from families whose previous generations were involved in the original serum run.

"A lot of the kids we met along the way would say, 'That was my grandfather who was in it'," said Redington.

The spirit of the Serum Run was alive, after all.

28

STILL RACING AT EIGHTY

—I went out number one,
which was quite an honor.—

Some of the old gang of 1973 showed up for the twenty-fifth running
of the Iditarod. Pictured with Joe in this 1997 photo at Nome are, from left,
Terry Adkins, Herbie Nayokpuk, Dan Seavey, and Howard Farley.

Joe Redington stood on the back of his sled, waiting for the countdown that would send him mushing to Nome once more. Spectators lining Fourth Avenue applauded and shouted support as the public address announcer recited a list of Joe's accomplishments. The cheers grew.

In March 1997, Redington came back to the Iditarod for the race's twenty-fifth anniversary competition. He hadn't raced since 1992, but there was no way he could miss this. So what if he was eighty years old? The Iditarod was throwing the biggest party in its existence, and Redington aimed to be part of it.

The race was a milestone for an event that had become an institution on The Last Frontier. It was all grown up, respected as a great adventure challenge and the most prestigious dog sled event in the world. Retired mushers who gave up the sport years earlier came back for one more run, less with thoughts of trying for first place or top-twenty money than simply to be part of the festivities.

For this race, many of Joe's recent Iditarod Challenge clients contributed a thousand dollars each to help sponsor him. And in recognition of Redington's contributions and his return, Iditarod officials permitted Redington to be the first musher out on the trail.

"I went out number one, which was quite an honor," said Redington. "I had a good little team."

While Redington found it easy to maintain a slender, wiry build, and he never succumbed to a sedentary lifestyle, he did not feel physically sharp. While others trained with intense focus and improved their speed, he'd been away from competitive mushing for years, so he wondered if he'd lost his edge. Besides, even before the race start, Redington was exhausted.

Few Iditarod mushers get enough sleep in the days leading up to the sleep-deprivation event and he was no exception. Not only did he have what seemed like thousands of things to do, a sled to pack, dogs to examine, and plans to make, Redington was besieged by requests for interviews. It was a big deal that the founder of the Iditarod was back in the race after half a decade away. What better observer to pontificate on the meaning of it all, to tell tales about the growing pains, the crises of the past, and to reflect on the changes the race had undergone?

Newspaper reporters and television crews made the pilgrimage from Anchorage to Knik to soak up the get-ready atmosphere at the homestead. Not only did Redington feel obliged to give everyone some time— still promoting his race—but he enjoyed it. He charmed all comers, hiding his weariness. Yes, Redington had that legendary stamina, but he was getting older, and even the strongest individuals are affected by age. Not that Redington would admit it flat out.

"I don't feel eighty," he said before the race.

Well, maybe for a few minutes during the hectic pace of the race's first day, he did. Only later did he concede that when he started his nineteenth Iditarod race, he already suffered from a rest deficit.

As Redington had so many times, though, when confronted with a daunting wilderness challenge, he simply inhaled a deeper breath and kept going. His dogs ran well early, and he was the eighth musher into Skwentna, a hundred and fifty miles into the race, where Joe Delia manned the checkpoint. Couldn't complain about that position.

Delia took one look at Redington's lined and haggard face, though, and said he'd never seen his pal look wearier at this stage. Redington made camp and after being warmly received by onlookers and talking with Delia, he ate a hot meal and rolled himself into his sleeping bag on the nearby frozen river. It wasn't hard to sleep soundly.

It was a clear night, and Redington slept under a small, but noticeable vision of northern lights and even the passing comet Hale-Bopp. That was a new one for natural trail phenomena. Stars, moon, the aurora borealis, and a comet.

Anchorage Daily News reporter Frank Gerjevic and photographer Bob Hallinen accompanied Redington the length of the trail for a series about his return to the race. Redington did not look good in Skwentna, said Gerjevic.

"I was really beginning to wonder, 'Is this guy going to make it all the way down the trail'?" Gerjevic said much later. "He was obviously weary. At one point he said, 'I'm so stressed out, I don't know who I am'." As Redington performed his chores, Gerjevic turned to Hallinen and said softly, "That was painful to watch."

The sound of a passing snowmachine provoked a fight between two Redington dogs, and their scuffle woke Redington from his slumber by the Skwentna River. Then his son, Raymie, mushed in and they talked. Raymie made camp, then pushed out. Joe lingered an additional two hours, mushing back onto the trail in minus-seventeen-degree weather.

For several hundred miles in the heart of the race, with the front pack sorted out, Redington drifted to the rear of the Iditarod. In every village enthusiastic fans greeted him, and he stopped to talk, shake hands, pose for pictures, and make friends for the race. And whenever there was time—there seemed to be more time than usual since he wasn't contending—Redington told stories, in essence talking in chapters about some of

JEFF SCHULTZ/ALASKA STOCK

Those in attendance at the 1997 Nome Awards Banquet roared when the Father of the Iditarod stepped to the podium. Joe couldn't run the race in 1973, but he had in 1997, at close to eighty years old.

the great adventures of his life. Ray Genet and the McKinley mush came up. He told how the Iditarod began and stayed alive, and he said old Herbie Nayokpuk was the best trail partner a musher could find.

Inescapably, the race took on overtones of a farewell tour, a twilight appearance on the trail.

In Nikolai, one of Redington's old sponsors shipped a box of a half-dozen Alaska silk pies. Joe always did like pie on the trail. He shared slices with anyone who wanted some. He brought steaks with him, too. Only the best meats on the trail. Despite the goodies that seemed to offer many of the comforts of home, though, Redington did not eat well. He had trouble swallowing and digesting, and didn't finish his portions. But while he just didn't feel right much of the time, he never let on to others.

Gerjevic thought Redington seemed renewed, particularly after his twenty-four-hour layover. "He was in really good spirits," said Gerjevic. "He was in a really good mood."

An Iditarod rookie, James Ritchie, approached Redington as he walked towards his dog team, and said what so many younger generation mushers thought: "I'd like to shake your hand, sir," Gerjevic quoted Ritchie as saying. "I think about you every time I drag my sorry ass down a hillside. You're an inspiration, sir."

Redington would have preferred being called "that old SOB" by an irate musher as he zoomed past to steal a higher top-twenty place in the race, but "Sir" seemed an acceptable alternative. Use of the appellation did tend to remind you that you were older than everyone else, though.

Race manager Jack Niggemyer, whose job it is to monitor the field and trail conditions, said he heard some observers ask if Redington belonged in the race at his age. Norman Vaughan had to be rescued once, went the thinking; maybe Redington will be in the same situation.

"I said, 'Hell no, I'm not worried about Joe'," said Niggemyer to the insult posed to a man who had survived and conquered just about every life-threatening circumstance Alaska could muster. " 'He's an old man, but he knows what he's doing. I'm more worried about him getting in the top twenty'."

That answer reminded questioners it was best to button their lips.

People in the villages kept Redington going. Everywhere it was as if a local hero had come home for the holidays.

"He is one of those people who invites everyone to come along on the adventure," said Gerjevic. "The time he takes to sign an autograph, to say hello. He always seemed to have time for a smile, even if he was under pressure. He may be the most recognized guy in the state."

Redington was fatigued and moved slowly along the trail. Actually, it wasn't so slowly compared to early Iditarods, only in relation to the speed at the front of a transformed race. Where once completing the course in under three weeks might get you the championship, now completing the course in two weeks might get you the red lantern.

Things turned sour for Redington again on the trail into McGrath when a dog named Nip died. A necropsy was performed, and not only was no blame placed on Redington, but no explanation could be found for the dog's demise. That depressed Redington mightily, though, and for miles he seemed to be merely going through the motions on the trail. He took longer and longer unscheduled layovers in village checkpoints, hanging out for as many as seventeen hours at a time. It wasn't until he reached

Unalakleet, less than three hundred miles from the finish, that Redington seemed to break out of his funk. Maybe it was Mary Brown's cooking.

Nowhere was there a bigger reception for Redington on the trail during the twenty-fifth Iditarod than at Unalakleet. Mary Brown cooked him a steak at Brown's Lodge and got her picture in the newspaper doing it. Everyone wanted a piece of Joe there. He could have moved into the lodge for days and still people would have hung on every one of his trail tales.

"Old home ground," said Redington.

He was in forty-second place, far behind the hard-core racers. He definitely didn't want to drop out, and he didn't want to finish last, either. Only two mushers trailed Redington when he left Unalakleet. His back hurt, he was bummed out by the dog death, and he was using a sled that was ill suited for him, until he got a replacement. Then he got a second wind. The Joe Redington everyone knew was back in business. He was no longer touring, but racing. When he said "gee" and "haw," he said it with gusto.

Redington picked up speed and began picking off mushers. A finish was no longer in doubt, just how high and how fast. In the end, the mush down Front Street was a triumphant one. Hordes of fans, his wife Vi, son Raymie, who finished in twenty-fifth place, and other relatives, came out to greet the Father of the Iditarod. Winner Martin Buser stepped under the burled arch to shake Redington's hand. Veteran musher Bill Cotter made sure he was there. Former Governor Wally Hickel offered congratulations.

"I was told it was a bigger crowd than the winner had," said Redington. "That makes you feel pretty good."

Redington's finish time of thirteen days, four hours, eighteen minutes, wasn't bad at all. It was actually the third fastest of all his races. The fact that he was so far back meant only that the race sped up. He was tired, but the aches, pains and weariness probably weren't so different than mushers forty years younger felt.

Sure, Redington wanted to go faster. But he got where he wanted to go and he was pleased about that. He wasn't even certain this would be his last race trip down the trail. Everyone was talking about how the race to celebrate the new century in the year 2000 would be pretty special. Just maybe Joe Redington had another thousand-mile race in his old bones. After all, he would only be eighty-three then.

29

DOING BATTLE

—I decided I'd hate to die and leave Vi
with all this mess we're got.—

News that cancer had invaded his esophagus hit Joe hard, but he was
sidelined only briefly. The same indomitable spirit that helped him through
so many trials in life also helped him get through the surgery and recovery.

■

After the tests at Anchorage's Providence Alaska Medical Center, the
doctor looked into Joe Redington's eyes and told him he had cancer.
Cancer of the esophagus, a form of the disease that frequently is fatal.

Attached to the tube through which food passes to the stomach was a tumor that the doctor described as large and inoperable. It was late November 1997, just before Thanksgiving, he was eighty years old, and suddenly Redington was measuring the rest of his life in months. Cancer. The word struck fear in him in a way that none of his other perilous adventures did. Plane crashes he shrugged off. Blizzards he ignored. But cancer couldn't be denied.

Although there have been quantum medical advancements in treating different types of cancer over the years, Redington not only thought he'd just been issued a death sentence, his first reaction was to believe it could not be commuted.

He said, "Well, I've lived eighty good years. I'm not going to complain."

He was fatalistic, almost defeatist, and both the doctor and Vi got angry with this uncharacteristic Joe outlook.

The doctor immediately told him he had a poor attitude. *You've got to be a fighter,* he was told. Vi Redington was taken aback by Joe's gloomy assessment. She also urged him gently, but firmly, that he must perk up and refuse to give in.

To some extent, Redington was in denial for months before he finally sought medical attention. Tracing the evidence back, Redington was sure the first signs of cancer appeared while he was on the trail during the 1997 Iditarod.

"I couldn't eat meat," he said. "It just didn't want to go down. I had the most beautiful steaks, and I couldn't eat them. I thought I had stomach problems. High acid. I lived on Tums."

Many times over the years Redington had suffered from acid stomach and was tested for ulcers. Always the tests came back negative. So he had thought this was just more of the same, not anything more serious.

Once he received the cancer diagnosis, Redington recounted the race mile by mile in his mind. In retrospect he thought his need for those excessively long checkpoint rests, the fifteen- and seventeen-hour stays, might be related. Just maybe his fatigue was caused by illness, not overwork, by the cancer, not intense race preparation and racing.

"I just didn't feel like going," he said.

After the race, back home, between March and November his stomach distress continued. He suffered periodic flare-ups, then felt fine for a time.

"I put up with it all summer," said Redington.

But gradually, the problem worsened. Some days when he tried to swallow, he'd choke his food right up. Visits to restaurants were cut back, then finally cut out.

"It got to where it was embarrassing," said Redington. "I wouldn't go anymore."

And still he didn't consult a doctor. The urgency of the problem was finally brought home to him while eating a meal at one of his favorite places, the Country Kitchen in Wasilla. Not only could he not eat the meat he ordered, but he couldn't even swallow a glass of water. For the next twelve hours Redington tried to drink water and could not. He was perplexed because he had no pain, but he just could not swallow. He thought he was experiencing an extreme case of indigestion. Never did he imagine his health problem involved cancer.

This time he went to the doctor. *We need to take a closer look at this.* Then to another doctor. *I think you need some hospital tests.* And another. He went to Providence for tests and various outpatient examinations. *Cancer.*

Although the original prognosis sounded hopeless to him—especially when the doctors told him the tumor could not be cut out—there was an alternative. Intensive chemotherapy might shrink the tumor blocking the esophagus to manageable size, and then follow-up surgery might be arranged.

After the initial shock and depression, Redington regained his typical resolve. From distressed, he became determined. He was no longer scared. And he decided he wasn't done yet.

That's what Vi wanted to see. She always believed in Joe's will, and he had always beaten the odds and overcome every obstacle, hadn't he? Why couldn't he do it now?

"I never doubted he would lick it because he's licked everything else," she said. "I'm not a worrier. I never was. He never panicked and he never let the kids and I panic."

Word leaked out that Redington was sick and Iditarod fans and friends did worry about him. They also wrote get-well notes and cards by the thousands. Entire schools wrote letters of support. They came by the box load and they boosted his spirits.

Iditarod officials did not say anything of the kind publicly, but they feared Redington was going to die. Joanne Potts braced for the worst.

"I didn't think he would ever be the same again," she said.

Vi was the only one who saw the Joe whose early confidence wavered. By the time others heard about his condition, or heard how he was coping, Redington was deeply engaged in the fight for his life. Redington was a pretty tough guy, one who always took care of himself. He also never smoked or drank. He had otherwise basically always been healthy.

"I never remember my dad going to a doctor," said Joee.

The first chemotherapy treatments were administered in December 1997 before Christmas. Joe traveled to Anchorage. The four treatments lasted most of each day and made him sick. The discomfort of the treatment was significant.

"There were times it was so goddamn miserable I wondered if it was worth it," said Redington. "You're eighty years old, and you're fighting for another year or two. I decided I'd hate to die and leave Vi with all this mess we've got."

The so-called mess was the homestead with all the dogs and a half-century's worth of souvenirs piled in boxes. That was the wry Joe talking that everyone knew.

After the initial sessions, Redington took a break to recuperate. After Christmas, another four days of chemotherapy treatment followed. Joe and Vi were under an incredible strain. This was literally a battle for life. Joe began to lose his hair, but he never again lost his spirit.

One way that the Redingtons coped was through the generosity of neighbor Joyce Garrison, an inactive home health nurse. Garrison lives a mile or so away in Knik. Her daughter, Melissa, used Redington dogs to compete in four Junior Iditarod events, and the families had been friendly during the five years she lived there. Joyce and her husband Roy mushed in the 1995 Commemorative Serum Run.

But it just so happened that around the time when Redington got sick, she had little contact with him. It had been perhaps six months since

Many decades ago, Joe's father James built this cabin on his homestead adjacent to Joe's. It still stands, although a tree recently fell across its roof.

JEFF SCHULTZ/ALASKA STOCK

she saw him when she learned he had cancer. She was watching television one day when a report came on the air detailing Redington's woes.

"I was in shock," said Garrison.

Garrison swiftly contacted the Redingtons and volunteered to work with Joe. This was her specialty, and she felt she could help his recovery with constant attention.

"I told him if he would try I would stick with him all the way," said Garrison.

Right away, Garrison began advising Redington and helping to monitor his recovery program.

"She's been a real big help, a wonderful friend," said Redington.

After the second round of chemo treatments, Redington was informed the tumor had shrunk by 20 percent. That meant an operation was now an option. Vi said doctors were hesitant to perform the operation on someone of Joe's age, but she tried to tell them they were underestimating this guy. He was hardly an average eighty-year-old. After all, only months before he had raced a thousand miles on the Iditarod Trail.

Joe entered the hospital and underwent five hours of surgery on January 19, 1998. The doctors cut into Redington's chest from front to back and while rummaging through his organs, they took out a rib, and discarded his gall bladder. And they got the tumor.

However, after Redington was closed up, the incision began to leak. The doctors had to open him up again.

"That really set me back," said Redington.

He was in the hospital for ten days and was not the Redington of old. He was more of an old Redington: weak, frail, sick.

"In the hospital, he couldn't even move," said Raymie Redington. "He had no choice but to get the operation. But he always took care of himself. And he always thinks positive."

Between the end of January and mid-April, Redington underwent two more four-day chemotherapy bombardments. And for two weeks in February he wore a pump that injected medicine into his veins night and day. February 1 was not the best birthday Redington ever had—though he had to be happy to even have one.

By this time he was bald and weak, but he was also in a fighting mood, and visitors who came by to talk were impressed by his attitude. They didn't know he had given up even for that brief moment after receiving the scary news.

"What a resilient guy," said Iditarod executive director Stan Hooley. "It was almost as if it was barely a bump in the road of his daily life. All I saw was Joe Redington with his head up. He and Vi had this wonderful confidence."

The Redington image—the toughest man in Alaska, remember?—was so ingrained in the public's mind that no one who knew him doubted he would battle disease the same way he tenaciously dug in against blizzards or enemies of the Iditarod.

However, it was sobering to hear statistics about the incidence of recovery from cancer of the esophagus. The most recent information available from the American Cancer Society indicated that five years after diagnosis only 12 percent of those afflicted could be expected to survive. Frightening figures. Redington, his friends and relatives, just knew he was going to be in the 12 percent.

When he had the time and energy to think about it, Redington got frustrated because he wasn't mushing. It was winter. He was supposed to be out on the trail, taking advantage of good snow, mushing his dogs over the Iditarod Trail. No mushing for Joe in December, January, February, or March, though.

The twenty-sixth Iditarod began in Anchorage in early March, a year after he had returned for the special anniversary race. Only Redington was at home instead of at the starting line. When he was able, he sipped his meals through a straw and rocked in a comfortable chair in the living room.

At the end of the twenty-fifth race, Redington had collected one more award to crowd his memorabilia shelf—Most Inspirational Musher. If the rules didn't state that award winners actually had to be in the event itself, it may have been more appropriate to present the honor to him in 1998.

By Iditarod time, Redington was down about twenty pounds from his normal one hundred and fifty. The operation, the illness, the lack of food, took a toll. Not even food supplements seemed to rebuild his energy. Not yet. For one thing, more chemotherapy was on the agenda.

Once again, though, Redington made mention of racing the Iditarod in the year 2000. Always got to have a goal. People wondered if Joe was going to live and he wondered which dogs would be ready for his next racing team.

After the final round of chemo in April, he gained strength. The hair on his head, reduced to stubble, began growing, sprouting in small patches. Most of the time he wore a baseball cap. Oh yes, and that lopsided grin was back in place.

In May, Redington had a CT scan, a routine procedure for a cancer patient, and the most important measurement in gauging how much the disease has spread or receded. When Joe walked out of the hospital that time, the doctors said, "Go have a good summer. You're okay."

No cancer. None. He was cancer free.

He said thank you and went home to the rest of his life, eager to rebuild muscle and energy. Garrison was right there with him. Initially, she was his nurse. Now she became his coach. If the dogs had to train to run the long miles of the Iditarod, so did the musher. Redington began a vigorous workout program, though occasionally he suffered a setback. He made the mistake of journeying to Seward for an Iditarod advisory board meeting, but after only an hour of participation nearly collapsed in exhaustion.

"I think I'm in bad shape," Redington told Vi.

He went back to his hotel and went home early. For the next week he was worn out from the exertion. It was too much, too soon.

Finally, in mid-June, Redington felt ready to start walking. Garrison supervised his workout program, though it wasn't much at first. Just walking back and forth from the house to the mailbox at the end of his driveway, about a hundred yards each way, was all the effort he could sustain. That was the beginning, and for a week that was the maximum. Soon enough, though, the yardage became mileage. From mailbox walks, Redington graduated to longer laps around the property. Then he began walking back and forth to his little cabin, a mile each way.

After another week or so of just walking, Redington began working out on an exercise machine that required simultaneous hand and leg movement against resistance. At one time, it was nothing for Redington to do a hundred pushups. He wasn't ready for that yet. But his stamina increased.

By early fall, he was walking four miles a day at a pretty good clip, amazing his son.

"That's good for anybody even thirty or forty years old," said Raymie.

Joe was itching to mush. Even on dirt. In June he took dogs out on a four-wheeler, but that was a bad idea. The jolting hurt. Better wait, he thought. It was hard to hold back, though. He hadn't been on snow since November of 1997. That was an eternity for Joe Redington. Being patient was tough, but smart. Later in the summer he and Garrison began training dogs in earnest, using four-wheelers, the normal no-snow mode of travel for the dogs. This time he had the strength. He was on the path back to real mushing, but he couldn't wait for it to snow.

Redington started thinking about leading another tour group to

Nome. And 2000 didn't seem so far away, or so far-fetched anymore. One more Iditarod.

"It's the start of a new century," said Redington. "It will show I'm back in the saddle, back on the runners."

There were other ways to show he was back. Each summer, the Iditarod sets up a booth at the Alaska State Fair to sell souvenirs and publicize the race. Frequently, well-known mushers appear for an afternoon or evening. One day in late August, Redington manned the booth. He was mobbed by fans of the race and fans of Joe.

"People just flock to him," said Joanne Potts, who was present. "It was the first time many people had seen him since he got sick. He acted like he knew them all. He treated them all like long lost friends."

Everyone told Redington how great he looked, how they'd been pulling for him and praying for him. He told them how great he felt.

Now, darn it, if it would only snow.

FATHER OF THE IDITAROD

—He didn't do it for money reasons.
He did it for his interest in dogs.—

**Sorry to see winter go, Joe sorts through a pile of
harnesses at Knik Kennels in the spring 1999.**

Father of the Iditarod. In the beginning, when the nickname came up,
Joe Redington blushed. *Aw go on,* he'd say.

But the appendage stuck. And he got used to it. Now no newspaper story is written without mentioning it. Now no television interview is conducted without mentioning it. Father of the Iditarod. There are worse things to be known for, worse things to be remembered for. He'll take it.

"At first I thought it wasn't necessary," said Redington. "It used to embarrass me. Then it got to the point that when I looked back, I realized the Iditarod probably wouldn't have kept going without me plugging away."

It is hard to argue that. And it is hard to argue that the nickname isn't a perfect fit. Certainly Redington is the proud parent. But he was also the parent present for the nurturing, for the midnight feedings when there were screams in the night.

The nickname is catchy and does seem to give Redington all credit for the Iditarod's stressful 1973 birthing. Redington himself always praises the contributions of Tom Johnson and Gleo Huyck. But they acknowledge he is the one who has longevity.

Should it be three men and a baby? Or is Father of the Iditarod just fine?

"We don't mind that," said Huyck. "We love Joe."

Redington has come to value the description of Father of the Iditarod, perhaps more so in the months when he became ill. Anyone who follows the race, in Alaska or elsewhere, knows Redington's connection. He is as famous as any of the champions. Sometimes visitors from the Lower 48 or overseas don't realize he is still alive and active. They either believe the Iditarod is so old that he must be dead through the normal passage of time, or they think his highly publicized bout with cancer resulted in his death in 1997 or 1998.

Which makes the sudden appearance of strangers on his doorstep all the more delicious. For the past few summers, Raymie, who lives just a mile down the street, has worked at Iditarod headquarters giving dog rides to tourists. On wheels, of course. It's a booming business satisfying the curiosity of the Outsiders. For five dollars, riders zip along on a quarter-mile loop. Plus they can get their picture taken. It's an exhausting pace of eight hours a day, seven days a week. One day Raymie gave more than a hundred rides. One summer he gave more than two thousand.

But it's the Q and A that leads people to Joe's homestead. Raymie tells the patrons he is an Iditarod veteran and that his father created the race. *Why don't you go visit him?* he says. Those who come with groups by bus aren't able to, but families with kids in their campers like the idea of meeting an Alaskan icon.

Joe accommodates them if he is home. He has met people from Germany and Switzerland that way.

"A lot of them claim I'm pretty well known in Europe," said Redington. "I wouldn't think so, but they claim it."

Another woman who homesteaded down the street in Knik forty-five years earlier showed up. She hadn't stayed in touch, but soon she was chatting as if they'd been pen pals all those years. Redington shows the visitors his dogs, poses for pictures, and signs autographs, sometimes including the words "Father of the Iditarod."

"I give them my mushing card and they leave happy," said Redington.

Got to make sure of that. That way they'll remember the Iditarod fondly.

Increased fame and exposure for the race and himself has turned Redington into a practiced celebrity. Everyone feels they know him, but after fifty years of life in Alaska it's not easy to recall every face. Rather than offend anyone, Redington just assumes he's met them along the way.

"I practically have got to say hello to everyone I meet," he said.

What is satisfying is being recognized for establishing something that became an Alaska institution. Joe had the right idea all along and lived to see his dream grow to fruition. Redington sought to ensure that Alaskan sled dog travel and Alaskan dogs would not die out. He sought to ensure that the Iditarod Trail retained its gold rush-era glory. And he poured his heart into the event that could make both things a reality.

"He put a lot of time into it," said Joee Redington. "He didn't do it for money reasons. He did it for his interest in dogs. I think he deserves a lot of credit."

Redington fought every battle he felt needed fighting to preserve the Iditarod and protect it from attacks, misguided or innocent that might ruin it or detract from its stature.

Calling him Father of the Iditarod implies an elder statesman status, and even if Redington has rarely viewed himself as an elder anything despite his years, it is an appropriate and earned status. Redington flexes his muscles on the Iditarod Trail Committee's board of directors when he believes it necessary.

Among the vehicles and buildings on the Knik homestead in 1999 is this familiar shed
with an invitation to go mushing.

That was evident when it meant taking a firm stand against the
Humane Society of the United States, and it was evident when a proposal
was considered to split the Iditarod into professional and amateur classes.
Slower, less experienced mushers would be relegated to another class,
leaving a day behind the speedsters.

"Nothing remains the same," said Redington, "but damned few things
change for the better."

The Iditarod has been so successful because it retains a complex
image. It seems both intensely challenging and yet completely accessible.
It may intimidate the poorly prepared, but woo anyone, man or woman,
equipped with woodsman's skills and a sense of adventure.

The public cheers first place and last place with almost equal vigor.
Favorites may not always be champions, but someone with an offbeat
background, or someone who has conquered the odds to reach Nome.
Winning a belt buckle emblematic of an official finish may be as coveted
as winning big prize money. That's why Redington was horrified when the
threat of separating mushers into an elite class and a so-called amateur tier
was floated. Such an idea would tamper with the dreams of the average

Two generations of Redingtons gather for a family portrait. Standing, from left, Raymie, Joee, and Tim join Vi and Joe. Not shown is Joe's daughter, Shelia, and Vi's son, Tommy.

fan, who may never race the Iditarod, but who wanted to imagine that someday he could. Redington recognized immediately that plan would sour many supporters. In the debate, Redington was a fierce advocate of the status quo, the representative of Everyman.

"I always gripe when TV or radio stops covering the race after five racers come in, like they were the only ones running the race," said Redington. "The racers in back are going along at a good pace and enjoying themselves. I think it really helps the race. They were the types who were enjoying it and doing it more like they did in the old days."

Redington blamed the Iditarod's near-capitulation to this plan on animal rights activists. Howard Farley, whose race involvement dated back to the inaugural event, was just as vehement, blaming front-runners.

"I've worked my entire life to promote this race as one where everyone who finishes is a hero," said Farley. "You've got to watch them. They forget from whence they came."

Redington won that battle. No suggestion to divide the Iditarod has been heard in several years. Other rules changes, though, have altered the character of the race. The "corralling" rule means mushers may no longer spend the night as guests in the homes of villagers, but must camp in a common area. Redington considers this terrible. The idea behind the Iditarod was to unite the state, he said, not separate people. Mushers and villagers shared the race more intimately the old way.

That type of sharing was a cross-cultural exchange, the way Libby Riddles remembers it, and she is in Redington's corner.

"The Iditarod just isn't the same without it," she said. "You can't even go to someone's house for a cup of tea without the permission of three race marshals."

Yet Martin Buser, the Big Lake champion who pushed for the change, argued that corralling represents a more level playing field, that the best-known mushers are always welcome in homes and treated like royalty, but lesser-known mushers trying to work their way up can't count on the same treatment.

"It's more equitable," said Buser. "It's exciting when the top group comes through, but after ten or fourteen days having people come knock on your door at any time of the day or night gets old. There are three hundred and sixty-four other days when mushers are free to go to anyone else's house they want. They aren't your friends if that's the only day of the year you see them."

The Iditarod has also sped up so much that it seems mushers and their teams barely pause for breath the entire race. It took Dick Wilmarth twenty days to win in 1973, but in the 1990s champions like Doug Swingley of Montana, who became the first musher from outside of Alaska to win the Iditarod in 1995, and multiple champs Jeff King and Buser, finish in nine days-plus. No time is spent lollygagging around the campfire chewing the fat.

"I do think the competition is so keen," said King, of Denali Park, "we have taken all the sabbaticals out of the race. There's no padding left. I think to win it now takes a tremendous amount of focus and desire and instinct."

Too much for Redington. He understands that the best mushers have the killer instinct he may lack, and that to become the best at something means you must pour yourself into it.

"Martin Buser was a terrible loser," said Redington. "I think that's what it takes to be a good winner. That's probably why I never won the Iditarod."

When it came to racing, Redington was never truly hard-core. He was more pioneer than competitor. Someone once compared him to Chuck Yeager. Not for breaking the sound barrier with super speed, but more for being a generic barrier breaker by imagining a major-league Iditarod. The early Iditarod mushers more resembled Redington as a group in outlook.

Rick Swenson, to the point as usual, said it's still possible to hang around the campfire during the race. "You can still do it if you want to finish in the back of the pack," he said.

It's all where you're coming from. Artist Jon Van Zyle, whose two inspirational Iditarods in the 1970s were slow races, said to him racing the Iditarod meant you could be out in the wilderness for awhile.

"If I were king, it would be a twenty-day race like it was in the old days," said Van Zyle.

Of course, there has been evolution in all sports. Football players get stronger, basketball players get taller. Huskies get faster.

"That's why they call it racing," said Tim Redington. "The Indianapolis 500 has gone from 65 miles an hour to 217 miles an hour. Dog racing itself is better now."

It has been Joe Redington's gift to identify with both the front-runners and the back-of-the-pack mushers. He was always rock-solid and consistently motivated to keep the doors open to all who want to come in, and to make them feel equally welcome as part of the Iditarod.

"A lot of the mushers who enter year after year know they're not going to win the race," said Redington. "They must love the race. Some get their belt buckles, but they keep coming back."

There is no doubt that when Redington discusses Iditarod issues, he commands an audience. So it is no wonder that Stan Hooley, whose office is about a dozen miles down the road from Redington's homestead, said top Iditarod officials listen carefully when Redington speaks.

"He certainly believed in his vision," said Hooley. "And he has the ability to make others feel it. It's a special thing to drive down Knik-Goose Bay Road and make a pilgrimage to Joe and Vi's place."

Added Jack Niggemyer, who has not always agreed with Redington on board matters, "We still look west on Knik Road once in a while for guidance."

Redington hustled to make his dream reality. He sacrificed. He did indeed have a vision, and the capability of articulating it. Some people were skeptics, but became believers. Gareth Wright, the great sprint mushing champion, tips his fur hat to Redington.

"The Iditarod is the only race now. Period," said Wright. "If you haven't raced the Iditarod, you haven't raced. It's owed to Joe. He put up his money, his time, his homestead. The man is an unbelievable person."

Few could imagine that the Iditarod would become as big as it is today, followed each March worldwide. The Iditarod was once an obscure regional event. More and more, though, results are carried in large newspapers throughout the Lower 48, even in the Sun Belt. Schoolteachers receive instructional packets by the thousand to educate elementary school pupils on Alaskan geography as the race unfolds. Thousands of adults surf the Internet for updates.

And every year perhaps ten wide-eyed rookie mushers set out on the Iditarod Trail for the first time. They have invested uncounted hours and ever-so-closely counted dollars—often $20,000 or more—to take a gamble. No matter how fast they go, they know it will always be a special trip. Every Iditarod Trail journey remains an adventure.

"It's a huge adventure," said Buser. "An extreme test of perseverance. I think it's that extreme that attracts people. It is a true event, not just for those people in Tallahassee, Florida, following it, but for those of us racing."

Redington was once seen as a crackpot, but now is thoroughly appreciated. In 1995, Redington was honored as the Alaskan of the Year. He had been nominated several times, but the Commemorative Serum Run that year added to his stature.

In the 1970s, the Iditarod sought recognition as a special event. In the 1980s, the Iditarod sought to establish sound financial footing. In the early 1990s, the Iditarod fought off the attacks of the Humane Society. But by the late 1990s, the Iditarod seemed more secure than ever.

"I wouldn't know now what could mess it up," said Redington. "The only thing that could stop the Iditarod is the mushers themselves."

The Father of the Iditarod remained as vigilant as ever. If you want to mess with the Iditarod, you still have to go through Joe Redington.

BACK ON THE RUNNERS

—Joe was an impatient patient.
Now he had to be a patient musher.—

The proud grandma, Vi poses with Ryan Redington, Raymie's son
and winner of the Junior Iditarod in 1999. Ryan's win earned him the right
to ceremonially represent the 1999 Iditarod Honorary Mushers and
leave the starting chute of the full-length Iditarod in the No. 1 position.
Honorary mushers for 1999 were the late George Rae, a well-respected
harness maker, along with Ryan's own grandmother, Vi Redington.

As October approached, he became a calendar watcher. Nearly a year
had passed since Joe Redington was on snow, since cancer sidelined him.
The dogs were ready to switch from cart training. The ground was not.
Frozen ridges of mud pockmarked the trail leading from his homestead to
the Iditarod Trail.

Mid-October passed. No snow. The calendar flipped to November. *No snow*. Now it really was a full year. Nineteen ninety-eight was ending, 1999 looming. The delay drove Redington batty.

Joyce Garrison was now his mushing partner. Logical extension of the workout program.

"He was always saying, 'I wish the creek would freeze'," she said.

Vi said Joe was antsy, edgy, even depressed when days and days passed without snow. He was renewed, re-energized after the illness, and he wanted to prove it. He worked on his harnesses and tug lines for hours. It was busy work. The equipment was as ready to go as he was.

Finally, some flurries. Then some flakes. A few inches. Something to measure. Joe seized upon it. With Joyce as a companion on another sled, they hooked up teams and mushed out of Knik.

On to Fish Creek. The old ritual. Three miles, that's all he wanted. Good. The creek was frozen.

"I was the first one to Fish Creek," said Redington.

The second visit surprised him. The creek was slick with overflow, water seeping through surface cracks. Redington and Garrison found themselves in water up to their knees.

"If anybody had asked, 'Is there any problem with Fish Creek?' I would have said no," said Redington.

He didn't care. They had fun. It felt great to be out. But the trail was not ready for serious mushing. The little bit of snow was pounded into the turf by too many dog teams. Pretty soon, twigs and leaves poked through the snow cover. Not good.

Joe was an impatient patient. Now he had to be a patient musher. When a few more inches of snow fell, Redington improvised. He and Garrison loaded up the truck and drove to Point McKenzie, a half-mile away, for a training mission. From there it was clear mushing to Flat Horn Lake. This was the old route Redington followed decades earlier between Knik and his other homestead. They spent the night on the trail, his first time truly back on snow. He will remember that trip. It was December 1.

However, the next run out of Point McKenzie two days later was almost as memorable. Redington got more snow than he was after. They mushed their sleds to Flat Horn, but when it was time to return, the snow was falling wet and thick and the wind was blowing. Blizzard. Visibility reminded him of the Bering Sea Coast.

"It was so hard we couldn't see," said Redington. "I hadn't been on that route in thirty years. I had a little trouble finding the way back."

It was new to Garrison. She has mushed, but is not a veteran. Her headlamp went out and that added fresh intrigue to the adventure. "It was something," she said.

In the near future another snowstorm followed. Then another.

"Getting on snow means quite a bit to him," said Vi. "He's different." Different, as in livelier, because he was back in his element.

You would think a three-snowstorm dump would be enough to mush directly to Nome. But there was so much traffic on the trail, the covering was quickly beaten down. The sled rode smoothly only if it was not heavily loaded. Redington didn't want any riders in the sled basket. He was afraid someone would break a vertebra being jounced around.

Now his days had rhythm, though. Before he and Garrison hooked up seven-dog teams for sixteen-mile runs, there were chores to do. In late December, the sun does not rise over the horizon in Knik until ten A.M. On this particular day, the sky was gray—snow was promised again by weather forecasters.

Redington wore a black hat with earflaps, an olive green jacket, dark green wool pants, and black boots. He stepped out the front door into the dog yard where the huskies reclined until they saw him coming. As soon as they noticed Redington's approach, they yelped, stood, and strained against the chains attached to the fifty-five gallon drums that were turned on their sides to serve as doghouses.

Entering a stone storage building, Redington loaded square, white plastic buckets with the dogs' breakfast. He had ten pups segregated in a corner of the yard. They were five months old, getting bigger. He ladled giant scoops of the dried, nutritious food mixed with water into food dishes made of large cans. Redington moved from dog to dog, providing the young dogs with their chow. They got fed twice a day until they were six months old.

As they aged, feeding once a day was sufficient, unless they were racing long-distance. At the time, one hundred and thirty grown dogs lived in the vast, open yard. They only barked when they got excited about feeding time or running time. About a hundred yards across the main yard, in the birch trees, Redington housed a new mother with her four four-week-old puppies. The little dogs, two black-coated, two brown-coated, were tiny. So dainty, so cuddly, they resembled the otherworldly Ewoks of the *Star Wars* movies.

Lugging their food between the barrelhouses of the other dogs, Redington laughed. The hair on his head was now thicker than the dogs' coats. Gray, dense and wavy, his hair came all the way back after the chemotherapy, and he was happy about it.

"I hate to even get a haircut," he said.

When Redington poured food into flat dishes, the puppies sprang for it, lapping it up with the slurping noise like a person draining a milkshake through a straw. A few weeks later, Garrison would take the puppies to her home and begin the process of socializing them by taking them for walks. Only later would they move into a regular home in the dog lot and begin training for running.

One of the dogs stationed closest to the house was Galena, named after the community that is an Iditarod checkpoint. Galena was an entertaining dog. A four-year-old brown dog with big eyes, he pined for affection and developed a trick to obtain it. When Galena was sure neither Redington nor Garrison was looking, he purposely tucked his right rear leg between his body and his chain, so it appeared he was tangled. It seemed to be a sure-fire way to get petted. Only the humans eventually figured out he was just faking his problem.

When Redington came close, Galena reared up on hind legs and threw himself forward for a hug.

"You're a character, kid," said Garrison.

Training with Redington made Garrison think of the first time she met him. He took her for a sled ride. He hooked up fourteen dogs, but as soon as they started, a tug line broke and ten of the dogs ran away.

After the morning chores, they adjourned to the kitchen. Vi made coffee and Joe snacked on small, sugarcoated doughnut bites and his usual peanut butter. Ever since the surgery he'd been unable to eat large quantities at once. Digestion was a slow adjustment.

Riding the runners is second nature for Joe Redington.
The years may age him, but inside he'll always be that

little boy from Oklahoma reading Jack London novels

and dreaming about snow.

Later, as he pulled on a camouflage sweatsuit before training, Redington reflected on the passage of time.

"A year ago, I was in bad shape," he said.

A year ago. Now he was a musher again.

It was almost noon as old Joe tromped through his dog yard, choosing seven dogs for a run over the slick trails in his neighborhood. Light snow fell as Redington stretched the tug line out straight. He plucked Billy from the crowd and placed the dog in single lead. Then came Trigger and Kaltag, Rusty and Rudy, and finally, Skwentna, and playful Galena as wheel dogs.

The sled bag was blue, decorated with the words "Eagle Pack Premium Pet Food," a sponsor. There was a yellow handy bag in the rear, right where Redington stood on the sled when he mushed. It was a place to stash quickly needed utensils within reach. Made by the late harness maker George Rae, Redington won the bag as a prize at the Kuskokwim 300 in 1980 for being the first musher to reach Aniak.

"It's made out of the stuff they make bulletproof vests," said Redington of the durable, canvas-like material.

Once the dogs were harnessed, the sled vibrated as they pulled. Good thing the sled was anchored by a snow hook and a line clipped to a hook attached to a sturdy pole. The dogs' power seemed capable of uprooting the pole at any time. Without such an anchor the sled might imitate a lightweight plane in a windstorm and be lifted away.

When Redington pulled the snow hook, the sled rocked, still holding firm. He climbed on the sled runners. When he unclipped the line, the dogs broke from a standing position as if they were horses erupting from the starting gate at the Kentucky Derby. In no time, they dashed through the wide path in the dog yard, headed for the trees and the trail.

On the back of the sled where he belonged, Joe Redington balanced on the runners. As the dogs quickly sprinted to a pace of fifteen miles an hour, and the runners whooshed along the snow, he raised one gloved hand from the handlebars and waved.

He waved, but he never looked back.

SO LONG FOR NOW, JOE SR.

**Alaska mourned the passing of a great
pioneer with flags lowered to half-mast.**

W hile this book was in production during the spring of 1999, cancer returned and eventually claimed Joe Redington, Sr.'s life. He died at his Knik home on June 24, 1999, surrounded by his family. He was 82.

Two days later, Redington was buried in a private ceremony and, at his request, in a dogsled. Afterward, about seven hundred people attended the memorial service conducted on the lawn in front of the Iditarod Trial Sled Dog Race headquarters in Wasilla. For three hours, friends of Joe Redington told stories about way the Father of the Iditarod had touched their lives, provoking laughter and tears.

Alaska Governor Tony Knowles ordered flags throughout the state to be flown at half-mast. Family members announced plans for the creation of a Joe Redington Museum.

A

All-Alaska Sweepstakes, 46, 233–236
Allan, Scotty, 46
Alpirod, 251–252
Arch, burled, 176
Attla, George, 81, 86, 100

B

Bill, Greg, 174, 238
Brown, Leonard and Mary, 161–162
Butcher, Susan, 181–192, 196–208, 230, 245–246
Butler, Jake, 45, 63, 86
Byrd, Richard, 281

C

Call of the Wild, The, 20
Carter, Jimmy, 214
Carter, May, 37–38
Collins, Stanley, 46–48, 53, 57
Cripple, 254

D

Delia, Joe, 57, 103, 225
Devine, Bill, 142–145

E

Egan, Bill, 99, 109
Ellexson, Lee, 42–43, 45–46
Elmendorf Air Force Base, 65
Ettyne, Nikolai, 250–251

F

Farley, Howard, 77, 109–111, 117, 132–133
Flat Horn Lake, 37, 56–63
Fleckenstein, Sharon, 48–50
Fur Rendezvous, 46, 79

G

Garrison, Joyce, 13–16, 296–297, 300, 311–313
Genet, Ray, 193–208
Gill, Shelley, 183–184
Good Friday Earthquake, 76–77
Grapes of Wrath, The, 25
Gravel, Mike, 210–214

H

Humane Society of the United States, 152, 162, 269–271
Huntington, Carl, 140–141, 155
Huyck, Gleo, 106–107, 142

I

Iditarod Trail, 43, 57, 92–95, 100, 102–103, 121, 138, 209–215
Iditaski, 215
Inaugural Parade, 216–221

J

Johnson, Iron Man, 46, 234
Johnson, Tom, 106–107, 142
Jonrowe, DeeDee, 149–150, 271

K

Kaasen, Gunnar, 120–121
Kendall, Bruce, 114–115
King, Jeff, 224–226
Knik, 37–38
Knik Museum and Dog Mushers Hall of Fame, 41, 95

L

Lear, Cliff, 27, 30
Legaard, Roger, 248–249, 282–283
Lombard, Roland, 81, 86
London, Jack, 20

M

Machetanz, Fred, 174–175
Mackey, Dick, 84, 95, 108, 159, 165–168, 179–180
Marston, Marvin (Muktuk), 111–114
Mount McKinley, 194–208
Murkowski, Frank, 114

N

Nayokpuk, Herbie, 96–99, 216–221, 228, 234–235, 261–262
Norman, John, 171–175
Norris, Earl, 46

Northern lights, 264–265

O, P

Page, Dorothy, 92–93, 265
Pourchot, Pat, 210–212

Q, R

Reagan, Ronald, 216
Redington Family: Cathy, 30–32, 43; James Wesley, 21–27, 37; Joee, 30–32, 86–88, 139; Keith, 78; Mary Eizabeth, 22; Ray, 21–27, 29–30, 43–44; Raymie, 31–32, 86–87, 141, 303; Shelia, 32, 43, 192; Tim, 44, 61–62, 86–87; Vi, 29–32, 43–44
Red Lantern, 130
Riddles, Libby, 239–246
Reznyuk, Alexander, 250–251

S

Seppala, Leonhard, 20, 46, 99, 120
Serum Run, 20, 120
Sled Dogs: Balto, 120–121; Co-Pilot, 190; Dodger, 33; Granite, 190; Nugget, 150; Polar, 71; Tennessee, 150; Togo, 120
Stapleton, Rob, 196–208
Steinbeck, John, 25
Swenson, Rick, 146–148, 150, 177, 179–180, 184, 234–235

T

Tellman, Clem, 46, 53, 86

U, V

Van Zyle, Jon, 175–176
Vaughan, Norman, 84–85, 216–221, 281

W

Wilmarth, Dick, 131
Winter Olympics, 280–284
Wright, Gareth, 80–81, 85, 120

STEVEN L. NELSON/ALASKA STOCK

Lew Freedman is writer and journalist with two professional careers. In Anchorage, he is well known as the award-winning sports editor and columnist for the *Anchorage Daily News.*

Throughout the U.S., Freedman also has become one of Alaska's most popular and prolific authors, having written a dozen books about the northern state and its people, including three other books about the Iditarod Trail Sled Dog Race®. His bestseller is *Iditarod Classics: Tales of the Trail from the Men and Women Who Race Across Alaska.* A graduate of Boston University, he has a master's degree from Alaska Pacific University. He makes his home in Anchorage with his wife Donna and daughter Abby.